Other Books by Dennis V. Damp

The Book of U.S. Government Jobs - 7th edition
Post Office Jobs: How To Get A Job With The U.S. Postal Service - 2nd edition
Take Charge of Your Federal Career

— REVIEWS —

The Book of U.S. Government Jobs

"Presents realistic job search strategies and viable options to landing a job with the U.S. government and guides job seekers through the maze of the federal hiring process..."
— JOURNAL OF ECONOMIC LITERATURE

"...Includes updated statistics, added electronic tools, a discussion of new application forms, revised federal job outlook, and some expanded sections. Provides a good overview of qualifications, pay, and benefits; requirements for civil service exams; veterans preference considerations; opportunities for disabled; and interviewing tips. The text is visually enhanced with a good use of bold topic headings, boxes, margin comments, and tables. Recommended for academic and public library career collections. (April 2000)
— LIBRARY JOURNAL

Post Office Jobs

" Anyone applying for a postal service job could use this book to good advantage. In fact the level of competition for jobs suggests its use is a must."
— CAREER OPPORTUNITIES NEWS

"Like the Postal Service, Damp delivers. His research shows."
— Jim Pawlak
"Career Moves" Columnist

"This book aims to help applicants identify job openings, match their skills to job classifications, provide information on when and where to take qualifying exams, and deal with applications, resumes, and interviews. A large portion of the book is devoted to how to take qualifying exams, with sample questions and answers. Recommended for public libraries." (April 2000)
—LIBRARY JOURNAL

HEALTH CARE
JOB
EXPLOSION!

High Growth Health Care Careers and Job Locator

Third Edition, Completely Revised

Dennis V. Damp

Bookhaven Press LLC
Moon Township, PA

Health Care Job Explosion!
High Growth Health Care Careers and JOB LOCATOR

by Dennis V. Damp

Copyright © 2001 by Dennis V. Damp

First Printing 1996   Second Printing 1998 **(Revised)**   Third Printing 2001 **(Revised)**

For quantity discounts and permissions, contact the publisher:
Bookhaven Press LLC, P.O. Box 1243, Moon Township, PA 15108
http://members.aol.com/bookhaven, E-mail: Bookhaven@aol.com

Distributed to bookstores by:
Midpoint Trade Books, 27 West 20th St., NY, NY 10011
212-727-0190, E-Mail midpointny@aol.com

Disclaimer of All Warranties and Liabilities

The author and publisher make no warranties, either expressed or implied, with respect to the information contained herein. The information about periodicals, web sites, and job services reported in this book is based on facts conveyed by their publishers and operators either in writing , through Internet E-mail or by telephone interview. The author and publisher shall not be liable for any incidental or consequential damages in connection with, or arising out of, the use of material in this book.

Library of Congress Catalog-in Publication Data
Damp, Dennis V.
   Health care job explosion! : high growth health careers and job locator / Dennis V. Damp. -- 3rd ed.
      P.   cm.
   Includes bibliographical references and index.
   ISBN 0-943641-20-9
   1. Medicine--Vocational guidance. 2. Allied health personnel --Vocational guidance. 3. Medical personnel--Employment--Directories. 4. Health facilities--Employees - -Supply and demand--Directories. 5. Job hunting --Information services--Directories. 6. Employment Forecasting.   I. Title.
   R690.D36 2001
   610.69--dc21   2001020215

Table of Contents

Preface

This completely revised third edition steers readers to high growth health care occupations and provides occupational exploration information. This new edition covers all major occupations and includes a comprehensive chapter on home health care, updated resources, two new sections on medical billing and scholarships, expanded sections, and interviews with health care workers. Many Associations and employers now have web sites (listed in this edition) that provide abundant career information including job vacancies. The Department of Labor projects that jobs in health care will grow by 26 percent (**OVER 2,800,000 NEW JOBS**) by 2008.

A special thanks must go to Erin McMichael Taylor and Walter Pickett. Ms Taylor, our editor and researcher for this project, and Mr. Pickett, associate editor, completed an exhaustive search to update this edition's resources. Thanks to their diligence and foresight, they have significantly contributed to this update. The Bureau of Labor Statistics is quoted throughout this work and without their extensive employment statistics this book could not have been written. I also must thank Suzan Hvizdash. She contributed the section on medical billing to this new edition.

Many others contributed to this revision. Several interviews were updated and literally hundreds of associations and health care providers were interviewed. A special thanks also goes to all of the health care workers that we interviewed for this work.

Finally, I must thank the millions of dedicated health care workers who provide competent health care services to all of us. We literally could not survive without their dedication and commitment to quality health care services.

Dennis V. Damp

Chapter

1

THE HEALTH CARE EXPLOSION!

Health care careers are still the rising stars of the employment outlook! The Department of Labor projects a 15% increase in the number of jobs by the year 2008. However, replacing workers who retire or leave for other reasons may double the number of job openings.

Job opportunities are escalating in the health care field and related industries. Before the year 2008, the U.S. will require millions of additional medical workers, including: 567,000 home health aides, 59,000 physical therapists, 208,000 medical assistants, 36,000 occupational therapists, 131,000 dental assistants, 93,000 laboratory technicians and technologists, 62,000 medical secretaries, 794,000 registered nurses, and 515,000 nursing aides, orderlies and attendants.[1]

Many of the fastest growing occupations are concentrated in the health services field, which is expected to increase more than twice as fast as other sectors of the economy. Contributing factors include the aging population, which will require more services, and the increased use of innovative medical technology for intensive diagnosis and treatment.[2] The number of older Americans will grow from three to eight million over the next 30 years.[3] In addition to the increased health care needs of elderly patients, retirement of baby boomers is expected to cause worker shortages. In some areas, nuclear medicine technologists are offered signing bonuses of up to $5000 and registered nurses are offered up to

$10,000. Students in fields with the greatest shortages may receive financial support and guaranteed a job upon graduation.[4]

WHERE THE JOBS *REALLY* ARE!

The majority (75% or more) of job vacancies never make it to the classified ads. Therefore, individuals must identify viable employment opportunities through associations, newsletters, Internet sites, directories, job fairs, personal contacts, job hotlines, corporations, and other published listings. Alternative hiring resources offer a wide variety of career possibilities.

Health Care Job Explosion offers a distinct advantage over other books of this type. It is two books in one - a comprehensive CAREER GUIDE plus a dynamic JOB FINDER. First, it provides a detailed description of each of the major health care career fields. Second, comprehensive resources are listed for job announcements (publications with job ads, job hotlines, and job fairs), placement services, directories, and general information (associations, and job related books).

This dual format permits comparisons between specialties and offers insight into qualifications, cross training potential, and pay. You may locate occupations with similar skills and required training.

Later chapters explore the following occupation groups:

- **Health Technologists**
- **Health Technicians**
- **Dietetics, Pharmacy, & Therapy**
- **Nursing**
- **Health and Social Services**
- **Health Diagnosing & Assistants**
- **Home Health Care & Computers**

The job descriptions offer the most up-to-date information available from the Bureau of Labor Statistics' 2000-2001 Occupational Outlook Handbook interspersed with succinct input provided from many health care professionals and organizations. Each occupational listing covers the nature of the work, working conditions, employment statistics, training, other qualifications, advancement, job outlook, earnings, and related occupations. Following each job description is a compendium of career and job resources.

VARIETY AND GROWTH CHARACTERIZE THE FIELD

The opportunities aren't limited to traditional health care occupations. Health care institutions will need thousands of additional accountants, auditors, personnel specialists, directors of personnel, attorneys, buyers, computer programmers, computer support specialists, chemists, engineers, drafters, computer operators, photographers, file clerks, secretaries, purchasing clerks, and food service helpers. Furthermore, employment growth is not limited to the traditional full-time job. Part time employment is on the increase as well.

The increased demand for health care services, fed by the growing proportion of elderly in the population is expected to continue for a full 50 years![5] It is not just traditional medical jobs that are growing. According to the Bureau of Labor Statistics, eight of the twenty occupations with the fastest employment growth are in computers, an industry with increasing importance in medicine.

2.8 MILLION NEW JOBS

America's demographics are changing medical care delivery. According to the Administration on Aging, the number of persons age 65 and over was 35 million in 1999, and will reach 40 million by the year 2010, and 53 million in 2020. People at age 65 can be expected to live an additional 17.7 years.[6] As the baby-boomers approach their 50s they require increased medical care and services. Additional sources of new jobs will be in the rehabilitation field, health and fitness, wellness, imaging technologies, home health care, nutrition, new diagnostic services, and prevention.

Twelve of the 30 occupations with the fastest projected growth rate are health-related. (See Table 1-1.) The Bureau of Labor Statistics predicts that while the private hospital industry is expected to grow slowly, employment in offices of health practitioners and in nursing and personal care facilities is expected to grow faster than in most other industries.[7] Health care manpower shortages are now commonplace and many health care providers take months to locate qualified personnel. An American Hospital Association survey found that 70% of the surveyed hospitals reported a lack of qualified candidates.

Table 1-1
Health Care Projected Employment Increases
1998 - 2008

OCCUPATION	Growth	Growth plus net replacement
Clinical lab technicians & technologists	53,000	93,000
Dental assistants	97,000	131,000
Dental hygienists	58,000	90,000
EMTs and paramedics	47,000	84,000
Home health aides and personal care	433,000	567,000
Medical assistants	146,000	208,000
Medical records technicians	41,000	63,000
Nursing aides, orderlies & attendants	325,000	515,000
Occupational therapists	25,000	36,000
Physical therapists	41,000	59,000
Physical therapy assistants and aides	36,000	56,000
Physician assistants	32,000	43,000
Registered nurses	451,000	794,000
Respiratory therapists	37,000	50,000
Social and human service assistants	141,000	211,000
Speech-language pathologists	40,000	56,000
Surgical technologists	23,000	36,000

Source: BLS, Occupational employment projections to 2008, *Monthly Labor Review*, Nov., 1999, revised May 2000

THE IMPACT OF NEW TECHNOLOGY AND COMPUTERS

New technologies are creating a wealth of employment opportunities in diverse fields such as radiology's MRI (magnetic resonance imaging), nuclear medicine, laser surgery, ultrasound, and diagnostic testing.

Biotechnology will have a profound impact on the health care industry. The market for therapeutic biotechnology products is projected to reach $24 billion by the year 2006, creating thousands of new jobs.[8]

Computer technology is having a huge impact on the U.S. economy as a whole, with predicted increases of over 100% in jobs for computer engineers and computer support specialists by the year 2008. As medical facilities computerize information storage and delivery systems, computer specialists with health care backgrounds will be in demand. One personnel office manager at a major West Coast hospital said the jobs he had the most difficulty filling with qualified employees were in computer support services.

WAGE SURVEYS

Hourly earnings range from $7.70 for nursing aides performing simple personal care housekeeping tasks, to $10.59 for dental assistants, and $18.84 for registered nurses. Median yearly income of a first year physician assistant is $54,000 while experienced physicians average $164,000.[9] *Health Care Job Explosion* reports the range of earnings with each listed health care career description.

Individuals often fail to negotiate a salary that reflects their intrinsic value and qualifications for the job. This holds true in the health care field where employers must be highly competitive to attract applicants. Knowing the normal salary range in your profession and in your location can be important in deciding which job offer to accept. Salary surveys are provided for all occupations listed in this book.

EDUCATIONAL REQUIREMENTS

The level of education required for health care occupations varies depending on the field entered. The Bureau of Labor Statistics states that 24 percent of workers in hospitals have a high school diploma or less. Some hospitals and nursing facilities provide training or tuition assistance. Each occupational description listed in the following chapters describes the required education and/or on-the-job training. Table 1-2 outlines the level of education required per specialty.

TABLE 1-2
EDUCATIONAL REQUIREMENTS

Group 1 - Occupations that generally require high school graduation or less education or on the job training:

Human service worker	Ophthalmic laboratory technicians
Home health aides	Personal and home care aides
EKG technicians	Psychiatric aides
Dental Assistants	Ambulance drivers and attendants

Group 2 - Occupations that generally require some post secondary training or training below a bachelor's degree:

Radiologic technologists	Nuclear medicine technologists
Radiologic technicians	Physical therapy assistants/aides
Respiratory therapists	Medical records technicians
Surgical technicians	Licensed practical nurses
Medical assistants	Medical secretaries
Dental hygienists	EMTs and paramedics

Group 3 - Occupations that generally require a bachelor's degree or more education:

Physical therapists	Occupational therapists
Psychologists	Chiropractors
Dieticians and nutritionists	Speech-language pathologists
Optometrists	Physician assistants

PREPARING FOR SUCCESS

Individual job seekers are also competing with each other. To give yourself the edge, make sure your resume looks professional and your interview skills are well rehearsed. Chapter two of this book has numerous recommendations to help you with both.

Follow our recommended job hunting process to expose hundreds of job sources for you to explore. It is advisable to investigate as many career alternatives as possible. It's necessary to explore related fields to uncover a large pool of job options and to identify a career with the greatest potential and most desirable salary range.

EASING THE CHALLENGE OF FINDING A JOB

The *Health Care Job Explosion's* resources can help you find hundreds of jobs that are not advertised in your local newspaper. Resources include professional associations, Internet sites, employment advertising, directories, and job related books. Job opening resources are comprised of publications with job ads, web sites with job ads, job hotlines, placement services, and job fairs. Associations frequently have career information and advice on education. Some web sites feature employment ads and directories as well as career information. Your search through the chapters' resource sections will be guided by the icons defined at the start of each resource section.

CORPORATE LISTINGS

Corporate contacts offer an additional avenue of opportunity for the health care worker. Thousands of companies manufacture products or provide services to the medical profession. The major manufacturers have large research and development budgets and several operate health care facilities. Research facilities must be staffed by medical professionals, technicians, assistants, and scientists. Other positions include sales representatives who demonstrate complex systems and equipment.

Large corporations like Merck, Medtronic, Bergen Brunswig, and Baxter International realize billions in sales yearly. Baxter employs approximately 42,000 people in 100 countries, markets thousands of health care products, and operates outpatient health care centers. Baxter's web site allows you to link your résumé on their system for up to ten job openings. (**http://www.baxter.com**).

Appendix A provides information on directories, both on-line and print, listing major health care corporations. It's advisable to read the *Value Line Survey* sheet or *Standard & Poor's Index* for detailed information including product lines, gross sales, number of employees, names of the company officers, and other helpful data. These references are available at many libraries or copies may be obtained from full service stock brokers or on the Internet. Companies often have informative web sites and many job search web sites have company profiles.

ADDITIONAL INFORMATION

Uncle Sam employs over 100,000 health care workers. There are 173 Veterans Administration hospitals (**http://www.va.gov**), 233 outpatient clinics, and 120 nursing homes located throughout the United States.

To explore health care jobs with the federal government visit **http://federaljobs.net** and obtain a copy of the author's *Book of U.S. Government Jobs* - 7th edition, available at book stores or direct from the publisher (800-782-7424).

If you are uncertain about which career to enter or even if health care is really for you, *Health Care Job Explosion* is a good place to start. Books such as *Joyce Lain Kennedy's Career Book, What Color is Your Parachute?*, and *Tips for Finding the Right Job* - a free Department of Labor pamphlet,[10] can be used in conjunction with *Health Care Job Explosion* to determine your job skills, develop comprehensive resumes, and to help you prepare for job interviews. Many universities have career centers to help you–often posting advice on their web sites.

BIBLIOGRAPHY

[1] Douglas Braddock, "Occupational employment projections to 2008," *Monthly Labor Review*, Nov., 1999, revised May 2000.

[2] Allison Thomson, "Industry output and employment projections to 2008," *Monthly Labor Review*, Nov., 1999, revised Mar., 2000.

[3] Maurice Nelson, "Health Care Panelists Want to Improve Labor Force," *The Chicago Flame*, http://www.chicagoflame.com, Sept. 25, 2000.

[4] Dave Carpenter, "Help Wanted," *AHA Health Forum*, http://www.healthforum.com/hfpubs, Sept., 2000.

[5] Mary N. Haan, et.al., Journal of the American Geriatrics Society, Vol. 45, pp776-674, 1997.

[6] "Older Population by Age: 1900-2050" *Administration on Aging,* http://www.aoa.gov/aoa/stats/agepop2050/ , Oct. 1, 1999.

[7] Allison Thomson, 1999.

[8] *The U.S. Biotechnology Industry*, Office of Technology Policy, U.S. Department of Commerce, Jul., 1997.

[9] *Occupational Outlook Handbook 2000-2001*, Bureau of Labor Statistics, U.S. Department of Labor, Jan., 2000

[10] *Tips for Finding the Right Job*, Consumer Information Center of the U.S. General Services Administration, 28 pp, 1996. The text is also available online at http://www.pueblo.gsa.gov/.

Chapter

2

THE NEXUS
MAKING A CONNECTION

I vividly recall taking a school entrance exam when I was nine years old. The examiner held up pictures and asked me what was wrong with each one. I only remember the one I missed; a frontiersman was standing in a forest and firing his musket at several bandits 10 paces away. Three paces to the frontiersman's left was another attacker with weapon raised.

When I first viewed the picture, I couldn't find anything wrong with it. The examiner asked me to look a second time. I asked if all three bandits were the enemy and he nodded yes. I still found nothing wrong with the picture. We spent 25 minutes discussing this singular event.

My perception of the event did not meet with his expectations. He wanted me to say that the frontiersman should be taking care of urgent business — the attacker three paces away. What he didn't realize was that I felt this person was out of the frontiersman's field of view and that he wasn't aware of the imminent danger approaching from his left.

> **Excellent job opportunities are
> often just three paces away,
> hidden from our field of view.**

This reminds me of one of my favorite stories as told by Earl Nightingale in his taped Insight series. Earl tells of an African farmer who dreamed about finding a diamond mine. Bound and determined to do what ever was necessary to realize his dream, he sold his farm, and headed for the coast. After many years of fruitless searching he returned to his home to discover that one of the most valuable diamond mines in Africa's history was discovered on the property he had abandoned.

THE JOB NEXT DOOR

Like the African farmer, job hunters are often unaware of valuable employment options within their reach. Most are programmed to respond to local classifieds or to rely on employment agencies. A small percentage of all jobs, less than 25%, are actually advertised in classifieds. To locate the remaining 75%, start knocking on doors.

Networking is the process of opening doors — employment opportunities — through the development of relationships that are mutually beneficial to both parties. The end result is to provide you with contacts that will assist you with your employment and career goals. Networking provides mutual benefits for both parties and offers direct access to people who often know in advance when jobs will become available.

Most health care occupations described in this book have their own association. Contact them for membership information and seriously consider joining the one that will best represent you. These resources often provide job source listings and networking contacts. Directories, discussed in Chapter Three, provide additional contact sources.

NETWORKING PRINCIPLES

Many would have you believe that networking requires complex planning strategies and toastmaster capabilities. Most, including myself, prefer the informal approach. Remember, networking is natural - it's something you do all the time. How? Every time you meet people in your profession on the job or in a social situation and start talking about work, you are networking.

The essential components of a viable networking plan are personal commitment, the ability to identify resources (such as *Health Care Job Explosion*) and above all else, following through with action.

Personal contact is the key!

Motivated job seekers should make every effort to meet face-to-face with key officials long before they submit their resume. The ability of an interviewer to match a face or telephone conversation to an application prior to the actual job interview can be invaluable. Informational interviews are one of the best ways to set up these meetings.

The importance of professional associations in networking cannot be over-emphasized. If one of the organizations for your profession has a local chapter, attend the meetings and keep in touch with the members by phone or e-mail.

Networking books are available at your public library. These valuable books offer proven networking techniques, introduction letter samples, and formats that you can use to expand your personal network.

Don't forget to search the Internet for networking opportunities and advice. Many sites have articles on networking and/or information on e-mail discussion groups, chat rooms and message boards for professional. These are especially useful if you are relocating.

IMPROVING YOUR CHANCES

Too often job seekers pin all of their hopes on one effort. Health career jobs are plentiful but they are still highly competitive. The more contacts you make the better your chances are to find the job you want.

Another sidebar to networking is the ability to retain your initial contacts and use them - and they use you - for career advancement and growth opportunities after you get hired.

Note your contact's name (correct spelling is important), address, phone number, and a brief summary of the discussion in a journal or binder. It's perplexing when you forget who you talked with and the content of the discussion. It is also appropriate to send a short thank you note. These contacts will appreciate it and remember your name down the road when it counts.

Begin by using the resources this book offers and build on each contact. Look through your local telephone directory for additional contacts. Do something everyday to expand your network. It's important to define your employment goals, then develop a basic action plan to achieve what you set out to do.

I've been on many selection panels. Interviewers naturally have an opinion of who the best candidate is from reviewing resumes and employment applications. They are also highly influenced by anyone who has had personal contact with any of the job applicants. I can't stress enough just how important a face-to-face informational interview is and how dramatically it can influence a selection panel!

Those most technically or professionally qualified may not be hired. Officials look at a wide range of criteria; special skills, education, motivation, personality, ability to present one's views orally and in writing, organizational knowledge, and the ability to get along with others. Through networking, job seekers impart a positive image to the organization long before the interview. Supervisors want motivated employees who can work independently, have the basic skills and training and, most importantly, can get along with co-workers and patients. As long as you have the basics, don't be over concerned about others having more experience or training. If you demonstrate that you are really eager to learn, you may have the advantage over someone who gives the impression that they are a "know-it-all." With the constant technological advances in health care, many supervisors know that employees who enjoy learning new skills will be long-term assets.

Selections are often based more on personality, positive attitude, and motivational characteristics than you can imagine. Organizations prefer to spend funds to educate someone technically marginal than to hire a problem child who may disrupt the work environment. I've personally counseled many applicants who weren't selected because of these intrinsic characteristics. These individuals knew they were highly qualified and couldn't understand why they weren't selected.

It is a true statement that supervisors deserve the employees they have. Once a supervisor observes unacceptable behavior or performance, it's his or her responsibility to counsel the employee immediately to correct the deficiency. The primary goal of the supervisor is to improve the employees' performance or behavior. It's unfortunate that many supervisors go to great lengths to avoid constructive confrontation and often ignore behavior and/or performance problems until they get out of control. This is a disservice to the employee and to the organization.

TURN DISAPPOINTMENT INTO A POSITIVE EXPERIENCE

Many selecting officials will counsel candidates who were not selected. Ask if you can spend 15 minutes discussing what you could do to improve your chances. This is very important information. Even if the company doesn't plan to hire in the near future, the information you obtain from this counseling session will help you with future interviews and resumes. And it may be a big boost to your self-esteem! Maybe the interviewer thought you were wonderful, and the only reason you weren't hired is that there were several other equally good candidates.

Find out how to improve your chances for future positions. Do you need to improve your proficiency, complete additional training, or improve interpersonal skills? Ask the selecting official for a candid counseling session and handle it professionally. The job has already been filled, so find out what you need to do to be considered next time. Be courteous and thank the supervisor for his/her time and assistance.

I often hear recent graduates talking about how scarce jobs are. While talking with these individuals, I find many are doing very little to locate job openings. They tend to focus their search on traditional classified ads and placement services. Health care is an excellent field for networking and locating jobs that aren't listed in the classifieds. If you're motivated, willing to write a letter of introduction, and make a few phone calls, jobs are available. Most towns have medical facilities and large cities have thousands of health care providers, including nursing homes, hospitals, rehabilitation centers, veterans hospitals, and private care physicians.

The Secret to Success Is That The Harder You Work, The Luckier You Get.

INFORMATIONAL INTERVIEWS

Call or write potential employers and ask to talk with a personnel specialist or a specific specialty supervisor, ie; radiologist, registered nurse, etc.. Briefly explain what you are interested in and ask if he/she would be willing to talk with you in person about career opportunities. If you're uncertain whether or not specific job skills are needed by a local health care organization, ask for the Personnel or Human Resources Department and query them concerning available positions.

For your informational interview have a copy of your resume and a cover letter describing your desires and qualifications. Your resume and cover letter must have correct spelling and grammar. If you don't have a computer, pay a service to give it a professional appearance. These job hunting tools are essential.

The informational interview will help you investigate familiar and diverse employment opportunities. It's best not to limit your informational interviews strictly to supervisors or personnel specialists. Any employee can provide important information. The outcome of these interviews will help you make an objective career decision and hopefully develop a company contact to help you land a job.

Many supervisors and employees are willing to talk about their job even when no vacancies exist. These interviews often provide insight into secondary careers and upcoming openings that can be more attractive than what you were originally pursuing.

When contacting people to request interviews, add that you will only take 15 minutes of their time. Time is a critical resource that most of us must use sparingly. If the supervisor's schedule is tight, you might suggest meeting in the hospital cafeteria during lunch. Some health care workers need this rest period for themselves, but others use it as a social hour and may even introduce you to co-workers who walk by.

For interviews, be prepared to ask *specific* questions to get the information you need. Write them down and take them with you. Amend the following interview questions to suit your individual needs:

Visit **http://healthcarejobs.org** for up dated information and helpful networking links.

INFORMATIONAL INTERVIEW QUESTIONS

EXPERIENCE AND BACKGROUND

1. What training and skill is needed for this type of work?
2. How did you personally prepare for this career?
3. What experience/training is absolutely essential?
4. What do you find most and least enjoyable with this work?
5. How does my background compare?

CREDENTIALS

Of the items listed below which do you consider most important?

1. Education
2. Special skills
3. Former work experience
4. Personality
5. Organizational knowledge
6. Other

GENERAL QUESTIONS

1. What advice would you give to someone interested in this field?
2. How do I find out more about jobs and how are they   advertised?
3. Does this company hire from this office or do they hire through a centralized personnel office?
4. Is there career advancement potential?
5. Is travel involved?
6. Are you required to work shifts?
7. What type of additional training would be helpful?

REFERRAL

1.   Are there others I should talk to?

2.   May I use your name when I contact them?

If an interview is not granted ask permission to send a cover letter and resume for their prospective employee file. **When going for the interview dress appropriately for the position applied for**. You can expect numerous rejections while pursuing these methods. Don't get discouraged. A good manager is always on the lookout for needed talent. If you present yourself professionally and have the necessary background, you will make a connection. Persistence pays when networking. Many promising candidates give up prematurely before giving their efforts a chance to work.

INTERVIEW PREPARATION

It isn't uncommon for prospective employers to open up a dialogue with you to discover your suitability for various positions within the company. Be prepared and visit your local library or bookstore to pick up a book on interviewing techniques such as *101 Dynamite Answers to Interview Questions: Sell Your Strength!* , by Caryl & Ronald Krannich, Ph.Ds. If you can't find this book, a librarian can find you another title on the topic. Don't overlook publications such as *Career Magazine*.

Most interviewers will ask you to tell the group about yourself. They purposely leave the question open to your interpretation. Many applicants I interview limit their response to work experience and education. It's important to some degree but remember, they already read your application and resume and know your background. Give them a brief overview of your education and experience and then expand on your personal life and outside activities. This lets the interviewers see you as a person and not simply a robot that has punched all of the technical buttons to get to where you are. Tell them about your outside interests; make it interesting and personable.

Many organizations are now involved with QWL, Quality of Worklife, and they need people-oriented workers to improve productivity and to use their creative talents for the betterment of the organization and the people in it. "Participative" management is becoming pervasive within many organizations, including government.

Another leading question is: What did you like and dislike most about your present or past employer? Remember that no matter how you actually feel, be diplomatic. Interviewers are looking for divisive behavior, attitude problems, overconfidence, and cooperative intent with this question. If you truly hate your current employer or company, soften the answer with tact. Employers are looking for employees who will support their organization, not bring it down. For instance, this answer to "What did you like least about your current job?" was very creative and, I believe, sincere, "I enjoy my work and I voluntarily take a considerable amount of work home. This tends to take time away from the family. I resolved the conflict by devoting one day off each week entirely to family activities. Actually, this has helped me at work also. I'm more energized because of the one day break each week." This creative response indicated that the individual was highly motivated to take work home voluntarily. Secondly, he was able to overcome the negative aspects affecting his family.

I'm surprised by how many people are totally candid with this question. One individual I interviewed bad-mouthed his boss for thirty minutes. His negative attitude over-shadowed the rest of the interview. Needless to say he didn't get the job. It's acceptable to talk about difficulties with a supervisor but it must be done tactfully.

INTERVIEW FOLLOW-UP

After you've had your first interview, sit down for a few minutes to collect your thoughts and add items to your action plan. Take your plan and start penciling in your changes. Remember that a plan is simply a starting point and it evolves as you progress through it.

If the person you interviewed indicated that additional training would be helpful, look at what you need to do to get it. Many positions require computer skills so if you have them, put this on your resume and consider bringing it up in the interview. Even if the job you are applying for doesn't directly require it, many companies find it helpful.

How about communications skills? If you need to improve your ability to talk to groups, contact a local chapter of Toastmasters International and join one of their clubs. They have an excellent program developed to improve all facets of oral presentations. The cost is minimal and you will expand your network simply by joining a club.

I was a manager participating in a local Toastmasters Club I helped to set up in the late 70's. I became a competent Toastmaster in my group and met a diverse cross section of managers and specialists. One member was anticipating a layoff. She had specific experience that we needed in my organization. I referred her for an interview and she was hired for an engineering position. She has since been promoted several times and now holds an upper management position.

Don't forget to put your activities such as Toastmaster membership, computer users group participation, volunteer work, Little League Management, etc. on your resume. This proves that you are self motivated. This is a highly desirable attribute. I always look at extracurricular activities when I am hiring. Many managers participate in volunteering or clubs such as Toastmasters. If two people are equally qualified, this is often the determining factor in my selections.

THE NEXT STEP

The remaining chapters provide detailed occupational descriptions with extensive job source listings. Before going on to specific occupations, read Chapter Three to locate general job or information sources for most occupational groups.

Good luck with your job search. Remember, it isn't as much a matter of luck as persistence. Follow the guidance in this and other stated references and you can't help but make a connection.

http://healthcarejobs.org
http://federaljobs.net

Chapter

3

JOB SOURCES FOR EVERYONE

This chapter presents job resources that are useful for many health care occupations. Associations or publications that focus on a narrow range of professions or on a single specialty are placed with the discussion of the specific profession in the following chapters. After reviewing these resources refer to the Table of Contents and Index to locate more job sources for your specific vocation.

A number of periodicals and directories in this chapter are available at libraries. Many publishers will send complimentary review copies of their publications upon request. Others, like *USA Today*, are available at most news stands. Many are available on the Internet. Professional journal advertising practices are changing. In order to provide faster service, some are posting job openings on the Internet, rather than in their print publications. It would be wise to check current advertising volume before subscribing if jobs are your only interest.

Several excellent books, such as the author's *The Book of U.S. Government Jobs* and *Post Office Jobs,* target federal government employ-ment and are valuable resources for those seeking jobs with Uncle Sam. These titles are available at your local library or bookstore or you can call 1-800-782-7424 to order copies.

HOW THE RESOURCES ARE ORGANIZED

Each occupation's resource section will offer one or more of the following, with icons to help you find exactly the services you want.

📖 JOB-RELATED BOOKS

Recommended books that provide career advice or that offer general job search guidance.

📑 JOB ADVERTISING SOURCES

Newspapers - Start with the classified and display ads in your local newspaper. Include national newspapers such as the New York Times and USA Today. Many have web sites.

Special purpose periodicals - These listings provide classifieds for specific careers or occupational segments. Job ads number from a dozen to thousands per issue.

Professional association publications - A number of associations' newsletters, journals, Internet sites and other publications list classifieds and provide networking contacts.

Internet - The Internet has changed the way job seekers access classified advertising. Many professional associations have employment ads on their web sites. Many web sites focus solely on employment ads and advice. Some specialize in health care such as http://healthcarejobs.org. Internet service providers and search engines often have career sections on their home pages.

🔥 JOB HOTLINES and E-MAIL JOB NOTIFICATION

Job Hotlines - A number of health care facilities, businesses, and government organizations offer job hotlines. The charge for this service varies, but many are free. To find job hotlines, call the employment (human resources) of hospitals or local government agencies. Alternately, use an Internet search engine by entering the name of your state, county or city and the key words "job hotline."

E-mail job notification - Many of the Internet sites listed in chapter three have services using e-mail to notify you of jobs that fit your specifications. Most are free, but to access some you must be a member of the sponsoring professional organization or alumni association.

⮞ JOB FAIRS

Job Fairs - Organizations occasionally conduct jobs fairs throughout the country. They provide direct contact with potential employers and offer a wide array of career literature and job listings. "Mini-job fairs" are often held at annual professional conventions. Ask your professional association(s) if recruiters will be present at meetings.

✍ RESUME MATCHING SERVICES

Resume Matching Services (Placement Services) - Trade, professional, and government organizations operate placement services, often referred to as resume matching services. Resumes are matched to vacant positions. Computers are often used to analyze resumes and match them to job vacancies.

State government services are free, while others charge the applicant and employers often pay a fee to use the service. Many states, professional associations and private recruiters have their job placement services on web sites. Many professional associations and web job sites will allow you to post your resume free.

⚕ ASSOCIATIONS

Associations. Health care associations provide a wealth of valuable information, career guidance, and services to members and, often, to students. They may advertise job vacancies in their publications and web sites, sponsor annual job fairs, and offer placement services. Position wanted ads may also be accepted. Services and member benefits can be extensive. The AAPA (American Academy of Physician Assistants) is an excellent example. They offer a directory of accredited programs, career guides, resume assistance, publications, internet job listings, CME credit logging service, and insurance. They also have 57 local chapters to facilitate networking. Hundreds of organizations provide similar services.

Membership cost varies. Students can join many professional associations at reduced rates. Nonmembers can often purchase subscriptions and publications or receive free career information.

Some publications of associations may be listed in the Resource sections under the publisher's name, if the publisher provides a special service, such as Lippincott's *Nursing Center* on the web.

Write for a sample newsletters and association membership information. Many publications and directories are available at university medical libraries or you may be able to read a copy at your local medical center. Also, your local public library may be able to obtain some materials through inter-library loans.

    DIRECTORIES

Directories - Directories provide detailed listings of association members, companies, medical practices, allied health providers, homes for the aging, laboratories, specialists, research facilities, special care facilities, and much more. They offer abundant resources for the job hunter.

It's best to research the companies that interest you. The more information you have concerning a potential employer the better. This information can help you select companies with the best benefits, comprehensive retirement packages, and working conditions. Individual contacts can steer you to personnel directors, under-staffed offices, and provide inside information on the working environment. Some of the employment Internet sites provide employer profiles.

Directories are available from thousands of organizations. Prices range from free to several thousand dollars for extensive packages. Many directories are now published on CD ROM in a database format for computer users. Computers offer key word sorting and fast access to any one of thousands of retrieval formats. A diligent search of the Internet may turn up the directory you want online at no charge. Libraries have many directories; ask for them at the reference desk.

ElderConnect, a web site provided by Extended Care Information Network, Inc., has a searchable directory of over 75,000 acute rehabilitation providers, retirement communities, long-term nursing care facilities, and home health agencies. (**http://www.elderconnect.com**).

⌐Ⓤ INTERNET SITES

The Internet - Information Capitol of the 21st Century - The Internet is an important source for employment opportunities, career information and networking. If you do not have a computer, many public and college libraries can provide Internet access. Most of the above resources can be found on web sites. Many commercial web sites are devoted entirely to job ads. The larger Internet service providers frequently provide their members with employment ads or links to employment web sites.

Networking on the web can be accomplished through message boards, chat rooms or e-mail lists. The e-mail list process allows you to send messages to a central server and then it sends out your message to every subscriber on the "list." In that way, members of a specific profession can join with others in discussing topics through a centralized e-mail exchange. Some Internet sites provide message centers or chat rooms where students or professionals can "discuss" their careers.

This edition of *Health Care Job Explosion* provides URLs, (Internet site addresses,) for numerous professional organizations and job ad sites. Listings also include sites with links to medical centers and hospitals that may have employment offices (human resource centers) to contact. E-mail lists can be located by search engines or through professional associations, while message boards may be accessed through your Internet provider's interface menus or association web sites.

The Internet is a rapidly evolving information source, so expect some of the URLs (addresses) to have changed by the time you begin your job search. Visit **http://healthcarejobs.org** for updated book resource listings. Conducting a search of the web on your own is more effective if you follow a few simple guidelines. (If you are unfamiliar with the Internet, ask a librarian to show you how to get started.) First, read the Internet search tips section of your search engine. Second, there are many web search engines available in addition to the one your Internet service lists on its main menu. Some search engines, such as Yahoo, are set up with directories (categories) so they offer easy access to job listings and other information.

One final word on Internet searches. Expect a search to locate about 40% of the web sites that fit your search criteria. Therefore, if you don't find your target on the first try, refine your technique using the search engine's help section, and then try another search engine. Each engine uses a different method of indexing web sites, which may produce very different results. Why are we emphasizing search engines when we are listing hundreds of web sites for you? *New sites pop up daily and web addresses change, so an hour or so invested in learning how to "surf the net" will pay off by saving many hours—and much frustration—later!*

The Internet is an important source for employment opportunities, career information and networking. The resource section begins with a few sites that teach you how to use the Internet. The Web is a rapidly evolving information source, so expect some of the URLs (addresses) to have changed by the time you begin your job search. If the site is still available, but at a different "address," you can phone the sponsoring organization or use one of the search engines listed below to find it. If you do not have a computer, many public and college libraries can provide Internet access.

Appendix A provides a comprehensive guide to locating health care companies that may also offer job opportunities. Also included are web sites that list medical companies. Contact their employment offices for job possibilities.

One resource that we can't list specifically is your local college or university. Many have career descriptions available at a central information office, in individual departments, or on their web sites. Most do not require you to be a student to access information.

RESOURCE GUIDE

Resources are listed alphabetically by association or title. <u>The larger resources are underlined</u>. The icons below will guide you.

SURFING LESSONS:
HOW TO USE THE INTERNET EFFECTIVELY

🖱 **New to the Net (http://home.netscape.com/index.html)** Netscape provides this very informative page for those who need to learn how to use Internet browsers.

🖱 **Search Engine Watch (http://www.searchenginewatch.com)** This site keeps you informed on the best search engines. Like everything else on the web, search engines are constantly undergoing changes. Check the "Webmaster's Guide to Search Engines" area for information on how search engines work.

Spider's Apprentice (http://www.monash.com/spidap.html) This site teaches you how to use the web and evaluates the major search engines. Service provided by Monash Information Services and conceived by Linda Barlo. Even advanced surfers can benefit from this.

NETWORKING SUPERSOURCE:
LISTSERVs (MAILING LISTS or E-MAIL GROUPS)

Liszt (http://www.liszt.com) Health/Medicine is a catalog of public Internet mailing lists (also called Listservs). If you are looking for a group to discuss your profession with via e-mail, Liszt can help you find it. Great source for networking.

Yahoo! Groups (http://groups.yahoo.com) This site makes it easy to find people to chat with or set up your own list and exchange mail with your fellow students or professionals.

Some search engines provide direct access to mailing lists in their directories. You can use the words "newsgroup," "mailing list" or "Listserv" with a topic keyword in any search engine. Not all lists are public. Private groups can be found by contacting your professional association.

SEARCH ENGINES

Many search engines have employment or classified sections; most that are organized by categories could be considered a type of directory.

About.com - (http://careerplanning.about.com) One of the most extensive career advice and job search sites. Hundreds of informative articles and links to job sites.

C|Net: Search.com - (http://www.search.com) or use their alternate URL at **(http://www.cnet.com)**. Choose a category, such as Jobs or use the metasearch capabilities. *PC Magazine* selected this as one of their 100 best sites.

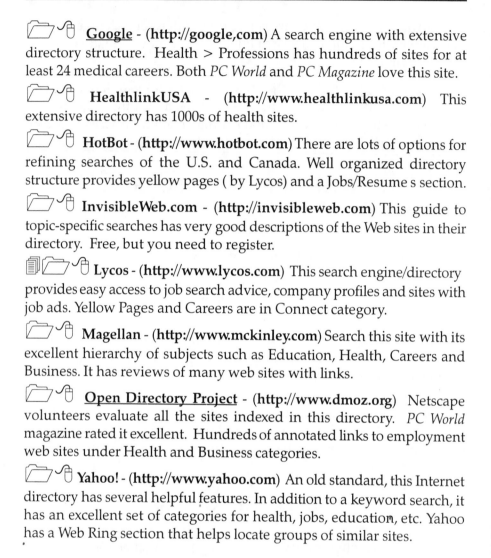

Google - (http://google,com) A search engine with extensive directory structure. Health > Professions has hundreds of sites for at least 24 medical careers. Both *PC World* and *PC Magazine* love this site.

HealthlinkUSA - (http://www.healthlinkusa.com) This extensive directory has 1000s of health sites.

HotBot - (http://www.hotbot.com) There are lots of options for refining searches of the U.S. and Canada. Well organized directory structure provides yellow pages (by Lycos) and a Jobs/Resume s section.

InvisibleWeb.com - (http://invisibleweb.com) This guide to topic-specific searches has very good descriptions of the Web sites in their directory. Free, but you need to register.

Lycos - (http://www.lycos.com) This search engine/directory provides easy access to job search advice, company profiles and sites with job ads. Yellow Pages and Careers are in Connect category.

Magellan - (http://www.mckinley.com) Search this site with its excellent hierarchy of subjects such as Education, Health, Careers and Business. It has reviews of many web sites with links.

Open Directory Project - (http://www.dmoz.org) Netscape volunteers evaluate all the sites indexed in this directory. *PC World* magazine rated it excellent. Hundreds of annotated links to employment web sites under Health and Business categories.

Yahoo! - (http://www.yahoo.com) An old standard, this Internet directory has several helpful features. In addition to a keyword search, it has an excellent set of categories for health, jobs, education, etc. Yahoo has a Web Ring section that helps locate groups of similar sites.

EDUCATION RESOURCES

Many of the search engines above and resources below include advice or directories of school among their other services.

Accrediting Bureau of Health Education Schools - 803 West Broad St., Suite 730, Falls Church, VA 22046. (http://www.abhes.org) This association has a list of ABHES-accredited educational programs.

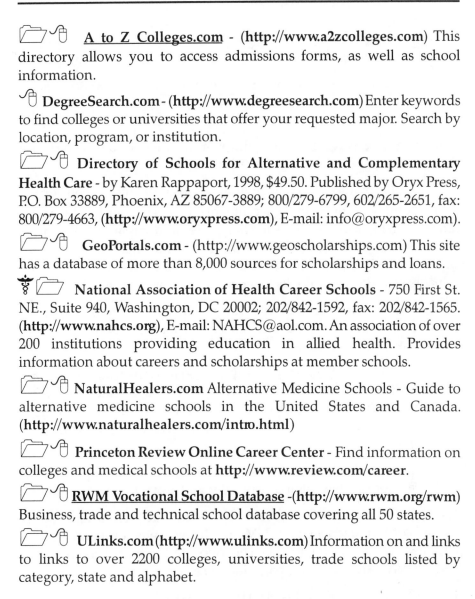

A to Z Colleges.com - (http://www.a2zcolleges.com) This directory allows you to access admissions forms, as well as school information.

DegreeSearch.com - (http://www.degreesearch.com) Enter keywords to find colleges or universities that offer your requested major. Search by location, program, or institution.

Directory of Schools for Alternative and Complementary Health Care - by Karen Rappaport, 1998, $49.50. Published by Oryx Press, P.O. Box 33889, Phoenix, AZ 85067-3889; 800/279-6799, 602/265-2651, fax: 800/279-4663, (http://www.oryxpress.com), E-mail: info@oryxpress.com).

GeoPortals.com - (http://www.geoscholarships.com) This site has a database of more than 8,000 sources for scholarships and loans.

National Association of Health Career Schools - 750 First St. NE., Suite 940, Washington, DC 20002; 202/842-1592, fax: 202/842-1565. (http://www.nahcs.org), E-mail: NAHCS@aol.com. An association of over 200 institutions providing education in allied health. Provides information about careers and scholarships at member schools.

NaturalHealers.com Alternative Medicine Schools - Guide to alternative medicine schools in the United States and Canada. (http://www.naturalhealers.com/intro.html)

Princeton Review Online Career Center - Find information on colleges and medical schools at **http://www.review.com/career**.

RWM Vocational School Database -(http://www.rwm.org/rwm) Business, trade and technical school database covering all 50 states.

ULinks.com (http://www.ulinks.com) Information on and links to links to over 2200 colleges, universities, trade schools listed by category, state and alphabet.

CAREER RESOURCES

This chapter presents job and career information resources that are useful for many health care occupations. For directories of health care-related corporations, check below and in Appendix A.

 **Health Care Careers and Jobs** (http://healthcarejobs.org) The Health Care Job Explosion Web site. Check here for updates.

 **Federal Jobs Net** (http://federaljobs.net) This is a companion site to the above. The federal government employees over 100,000 health care professionals. Use this site to explore all occupations. Extensive information includes job openings, pay scales, information for veterans and the disabled, and job search techniques and resources, including valuable web site links. Books to aid your job search are available.

 **100 Hot Jobs & Careers** (http://www.100hot.com) Directory listing the 100 most visited web sites, with job sites under Business, updated regularly. Produced by Go2Net.

 **Absolutely Health Care** - (www.healthjobsusa.com) This award-winning site lets you search by state and job category for full time, part-time or traveling jobs. Employers directory links to the facility or recruiter Web site. Post your resume and receive E-mail job notices. Don't miss this one!

 **Allied Health Jobs** (http://www.alliedhealthjobs.com) Search job ads by categories, view company profiles and apply for jobs online.

 **American College of Sports Medicine** (Membership information contact dsanchez@ACSM.org, **http://www.acsm.org**). Offers placement service to members. The Web site has a Careers in Sports Medicine & Exercise Science page and job ads.

 **American Industrial Hygiene Association** - 2700 Prosperity Avenue, Suite 250, Fairfax, VA 22031; 703/849-8888, fax: 703/207-3561. (**http://www.aiha.org**, E-Mail: infonet@aiha.org). Resume matching service and job ads on the Internet site for industrial hygienists and health and safety positions. Well-organized site.

 **American Medical Association (AMA)** - 515 N. State St., Chicago, IL 60610; 312/464-5000. (**http://www.ama-assn.org**) Membership consists of physicians and medical societies. Web site information for

Patients area has Doctor Finder and Hospital Finder. *Health Professions E-Letter* newsletter covers educational and career-related issues for over 50 professions .

✍️🗒 **American Mobile Health Care** - 12235 El Camino Real, Suite 200, San Diego, CA 92130; 800/282-0300, fax: 800/282-0328. (E-Mail: contact@americanmobile.com, **http://amn.travelnurse.com**). Staffing company offers 8 to 26 week assignments to professionals in nursing and allied health willing to travel.

⚕️📖✍️🗒 **American Public Health Association** - 800 1 St. N.W., Washington, DC 20001; 202/777-APHA, fax: 202/777-2534. (E-mail: comments@apha.org, **http://www.apha.org**) Membership includes a diverse cross section of the medical community. Offers a number of services to members including a job placement service, research, training, and education. Publishes a newsletter and informative guides. Web site includes job listings and information on continuing education.

⚕️📖🗒 **American School Health Association** - P.O. Box 708, Kent, OH 44240-0708; 330/678-1601, fax: 330/678-4526. (**http://www.ashaweb.org**, E-mail: asha@ashaweb.org). Targets all medical specialties that are utilized in school systems including dental hygienists. *Journal of School Health*, monthly publication free to members, nonmembers $70/year.

⚕️📁🗒 **American Sleep Disorders Association** - 1610 14th Street NW, Ste. 300, Rochester, MN 55901; 507/287-6006. This Web site at **http://www.asda.org** lists accredited member centers and laboratories by state. Student membership ($35) includes member directory.

📁🗒 **America's Career Infonet** - (**http://www.acinet.org**) One of the best career planning sites, ACINET has an excellent assortment of annotated links to help you find a career that fits your personality, get information on financial aid, check employment trends, find counseling, plan a job search and locate job openings. State profiles have extensive resources: links to educational institutions, city web sites, employment needs for specific careers and links to state job banks. Don't miss it!

📖🗒 **America's Job Bank**   A product of the Public Employment Service, this site at **http://www.ajb.dni.us** allows searching for a job using a menu of occupations, keywords, or various occupational codes. There are over one million jobs–excellent site design. Contains links to the state public employment services, to employers' web sites and private placement agencies' sites. (E-mail: skrcomm@ajb.dni.us)

Association for Gerontology in Higher Education - For Information about job opportunities in a variety of fields try http://www.aghe.org. Articles cover finding the right career in gerontology. The site has a few jobs and good links to job ad sites.

BestJobsUSA.com - (http://www.bestjobsusa.com) This Web site is both a job bank and recruitment center. Post your resume for free and search for career fairs. Sign up for free e-mail newsletter.

Billian Publishing - 2100 Powers Ferry Road., Suite 300, Atlanta, GA 30339; 770/955-5656, sales: 800/533-8484, fax:770/952-0669. (http://www.billian.com). Current publications, which may be in your library, include *Nursing Home Industry Directory*, *Managed Healthcare Organizations* (HMO, PPO and POS facilities) and *Hospital Blue Book*.

Black Collegiate Services - 909 Poydras Street, 36th Floor , New Orleans, LA 70112; 504/821-5694. (http://www.black-collegian.com). *The Black Collegian*, $4 for students, has two annual career issues. Web site has "Search Jobs" section and has won awards. Free resume database service. Their **Minorities' Job Bank**, at http://www.minorities-jb.com is a subsidiary of Black Collegiate Ser-vices, and operates similarly.

The Book of U.S. Government Jobs - Where They Are, What's Available, & How to Get One by Dennis V. Damp, 256 pages, $18.95 plus $4.50 shipping. Available with check or money order direct from Bookhaven Press, P.O. Box 1243, Moon Township, PA 15108, or with all major credit cards at 800/782-7424.

CareerBuilder.com - (www.careerbuilder.com/index.html) It provides resume advice, counseling and Personal Search Agents to e-mail you the results of your job searches. There is plenty of advice on job issues.

CareerCity (http://www.careercity.com) This Web site has articles on careers and job hunting with links to online job fairs. Click on Health Care/Medical category and limit your search to a single state.

Career Magazine Good for resume writing information. Published by National Career Search. Their Internet site is located at http://www.careermag.com. Career Magazine has job openings, employers, resume listing service, resume writing tips, a recruiter directory and you can create an e-mail job agent.

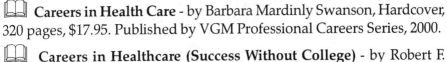 Careers in Health Care - by Barbara Mardinly Swanson, Hardcover, 320 pages, $17.95. Published by VGM Professional Careers Series, 2000.

📖 **Careers in Healthcare (Success Without College)** - by Robert F. Wilson, Paperback, 184 pages, $8.95. Published by Barrons Educational Series, 1999

📖 **Careers Inside the World of Health Care** - by Beth Wilkinson, Hardcover, $17.95. Published by Rosen Publishing Group, 1999.

CareerWeb (http://www.careerweb.com) This service has several affiliated job sites for job advice and ads. You can search by city. Resources include "post a resume," "career bookstore," and a free e-newsletter. They also will e-mail you job notices.

College Grad Job Hunter - Collegegrad.com, Inc., 1629 Summit, Suite 200, Cedarburg, WI 53012, Phone: 262/376-1000; Fax: 262/376-1030. **http://www.collegegrad.com**. This award winning site has several categories allowing you to search for entry level job opportunities, internships, hiring companies, or employer web sites. There are 500 pages of job search strategies and thousands of employer profiles. You can read articles from the Job Hunter E-zine or ask questions about job hunting. (E-Mail: webmaster@collegegrad.com).

Consumer Information Center (http://www.pueblo.gsa.gov, Pueblo, CO 81009. E-mail: catalog.pueblo@gsa.gov).This service is provided by the U.S. General Services Administration. Employment section has lots of good links to career info. Many employment information or small business pamphlets can be downloaded free or ordered for a small fee.

The Continuing Care Accreditation Commission (CCAC) - 901 E Street NW, Suite 500, Washington, DC 20004-2037;.202/783-7286. (**http://www.ccaconline.org**). CCAC site lists Accredited Continuing Care Retirement Communities across the country, organized by state and including addresses and phone numbers, with links to facility Web sites when available.

DiversityConnection.org - Institute for Diversity in Health Management, One North Franklin Street, Chicago, IL 60606, (800) 233-0996.(**http://www.diversityconnection.org/default.htm**)This organization's goal is to expand leadership opportunities for ethnic minorities in health services management. Scholarships are available. Jobs are posted and notices can be e-mailed to you. Post your resume.

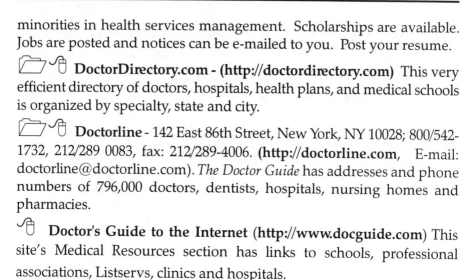 **DoctorDirectory.com - (http://doctordirectory.com)** This very efficient directory of doctors, hospitals, health plans, and medical schools is organized by specialty, state and city.

Doctorline - 142 East 86th Street, New York, NY 10028; 800/542-1732, 212/289 0083, fax: 212/289-4006. **(http://doctorline.com,** E-mail: doctorline@doctorline.com). *The Doctor Guide* has addresses and phone numbers of 796,000 doctors, dentists, hospitals, nursing homes and pharmacies.

Doctor's Guide to the Internet (http://www.docguide.com) This site's Medical Resources section has links to schools, professional associations, Listservs, clinics and hospitals.

Dorland Healthcare Information - 1500 Walnut Street, Suite 1000,Philadelphia, PA 19102; Phone: 800/784-2332; Fax: 215/735-3966. **(http://www.dorlandhealth.com,** E-mail: info@dorlandhealth.com). *Case Management Resource Guide,* published annually, is the largest directory of healthcare services in print. It contains over 110,000 entries covering 40 different categories of services and manufacturers and free searching is available on the Web site. *Directory of Physician Groups & Network,* approximately 750 pages may be available at libraries.

eBility, Inc. - (http://www.ebility.com) Job seekers with disabilities will find their Resources Career Center section helpful.

ElderCare CareGuide (http://www.eldercare.com) This site provides a nationwide directories for housing and residential care, home care, day programs, hospice and more.

ElderConnect (http://www.elderconnect.com) This database contains information on over 33,000 rehabilitation providers, retirement communities, and providers of long-term nursing care as well as home health agencies.

Emory University (http://www.cc.emory.edu) Click on "MedWeb" to find an impressive list of medical sites. Type the "employment opportunities" into the search engine for an impressive set of links. Extensive links to companies on this site.

▤⌐🖰️🖰 **Equal Opportunity Publications** - 1160 East Jerico Turnpike, Suite 200, Huntington, NY 11743; 631/421-9421. (**http://www.eop.com**, E-mail: info@eop.com). This company publishes a number of excellent target audience publications including *Equal Opportunity, Careers & The Disabled, Information Technology Career World,* and *Workforce diversity* magazines. Display ads feature national employers seeking applicants for many varied fields. Each issue offers a dozen to sixty or more display job ads. Call for subscription rates. Submit your resume for recruiters to view.

🖰 **eResumes & Resources** - (**http://www.eresumes.com**)This award winning site from Rebecca Smith is a top-notch guide to preparing electronic resumes that looks good when delivered by e-mail.

▤🖋⌐🖰 <u>**Federal Research Service**</u> - (**http://www.fedjobs.com**, E-mail: info@fedjobs.com) Visit this site to sample their services online or call them at 800.822-5027 or 703/281-0200. FRS is a private company offering information on federal job vacancies for a monthly fee. This online database of federal jobs is updated every work day. Personalized search capability helps the job seeker zero in on openings that match specific criteria. (*Federal Career Opportunities*) A 64 page biweekly publication containing 4000+ listings for federal job vacancies. (*Search & Send*) is a custom-designed service sends you e-mail notification of jobs that fit your criteria or in print for and extra fee.

▤🖰 **FedWorld Federal Jobs Search** - National Technical Information Service, U.S. Department of Commerce, Springfield, VA 22161; 703/605-6585. (**http://www.fedworld.gov/jobs/jobsearch.html**, E-mail: webmaster@fedworld.gov).   You can search this government site by keyword and limit the search to a single state. U.S. government job openings include Army and Air Force Reserve. FedWorld downloads files from the FJOB bulletin board system, see USA Jobs below. **FedWorld Information Network** homepage: **http://www.fedworld.gov**.

📖📁🖰 **Ferguson Publishing Company** - 200 West Madison St., Suite 300, Chicago, IL 60606; 800/306-9941, fax: 800/306-9942. (E-mail: fergpub@aol.com, **http://www.fergpubco.com**). *Free and Inexpensive Career Materials: A Resource Directory* is a directory listing more than 700 sources of free or inexpensive career materials (2001, $19.95). *Big Book of Minority Opportunities,* $39.95, includes information on careers and scholarships. Other titles include *Exploring Health Care Careers* (1998, $89.95) and *Resources for People with Disabilities* (print or CD version, 1998, two volumes, $89.95). Highschool and college guidance counselors and libraries frequently have these guides and many others from Ferguson.

FlipDog - (http://www.flipdog.com) PC Magazine ranked FlipDog one of their Top 100 Web Sites. Post your resume, receive e-mail job notices, find employer profiles and get help with job interview skills.

Gale Research Company - 835 Penobscot Building, 645 Griswold Street, Detroit, MI 48226; 313/961-2242, 800/877-GALE. (http://www.gale.com). Publishes *Directories In Print*, 19th edition, lists over 15,000 published directories worldwide. The *Job Hunter's Sourcebook*, 1996, 1100 pages, $99 lists thousands of placement options for 179 specialties. These publications are available at many libraries.

Government Job Finder by Daniel Lauber. (paperback, $16.95.) Published by Planning Communication. Everything you need to find a job in local, state, and the federal government. Available by phone at 1-800-782-7424.

headhunter.net - (http://www.headhunter.net) This well-organized site deserves its good reviews. It provides very flexible search facilities, e-mail job notices and allows you to post your resume and keep records about your job search progress. Over 35,000 healthcare jobs listed, including international employment, with comprehensive advice on resumes, interviews and more. Don't miss this one!

HealthCareerWeb - (http://www.healthcareerweb.com) Search job ads, post your resume, have openings e-mailed to you, and get advice on topics such as choosing a recruiter.

Health Care Recruitment Online - Lists job classifieds and national staffing companies with a section on featured employers. (http://www.healthcareers-online.com)

HealthCareSource, Inc. - (http://www.healthcaresource.com) This Internet division of Call24, Inc., a health care recruiter, has over 10,000 jobs from clerical workers to physicians. Post your resume.

Health Direction - (http://www.healthdirection.com) If you want to experience different areas of the U.S., this travel health care placement service specializes in 3-6 month positions.

HEALTHeCAREERS.com - (http://www.artofsearch.com)
This site, sponsored by associations and schools, provides job search tools by discipline, location, and organization. Post your resume.

Healthfinder (http://www.healthfinder.gov) This web site, sponsored by the U.S. Department of Health and Human Services, provides access to many types of libraries, online journals, state health departments and not-for-profit organizations.

Health World Online (http://www.healthy.net). The web site contains a searchable database of holistic practitioners and has access to local professional groups for networking and directory of associations.

Health Hippo (http://hippo.findlaw.com) This site is mainly concerned with health legislation, it does provide extensive links to job sites and career information under "Hippjobs."

hirehealth.com - (http://www.hirehealth.com) Over 150 companies post jobs here for pharmaceutical, biotechnology, medical and healthcare professionals. Create a job agent, submit resumes to companies directly from the site and view profiles of some of the companies.

hospitalhub.com - (http://www.hospitalhub.com) Extensive job database and other career information including an excellent directory of hospitals. It has a "virtual job fair," meaning it contains detailed medical facility profiles with job ads pages for each.

HospitalWeb - Massachusetts General Hospital Department of Neurology. **(http://neuro-www.mgh.harvard.edu/hospitalweb.shtml)**. This site's goal is to list links to all of the hospitals on the web. There are also links to medical companies and organizations.

HotJobs.com - (http://www.hotjobs.com) This well-organized site lets you post jobs and create an agent to e-mail you notices. Job notices are from companies, not recruiters.

IMDiversity.com   (http://www.imdiversity.com) Well-organized site has employer profiles, job ads and career advice. Post your resume and create a job notification agent.

Internet Career Connection (http://www.iccweb.com) Provided by Gonyea & Associates, Inc., this site has extensive online career and employment resources, including Help Wanted-USA, Worldwide Resume/Talent Bank, Recruiters an Placement agencies, Government Employment and much more. The Government Jobs Central area contains advice written by Dennis V. Damp. Versatile search options are provided.

JobBank USA (http://www.jobbankusa.com) Large database, free, has jobs in all fields, not just healthcare. Post your resume, use the Job Search page and/or create a job agent to e-mail job notices to you. This site provides yellow pages, e-mail list access and more.

Job Finders Online (http://jobfindersonline.com) Publishes a number of helpful books, including topics such as international jobs and job hotlines.

JobHunt (http://www.job-hunt.org) Well designed site with hundreds of links to Internet job ads and job hunting information.

JobHuntersBible - (http://www.jobhuntersbible.com) This site is a supplement to Dick Bolles' book, *What Color Is Your Parachute? A Practical Manual for Job-Hunters and Career-Changers*, published by Ten Speed Press. It has extensive information on job hunting and the "Contacts" section of this site explains how to use Listservs and newsgroups for job hunting and networking. Bookmark it!

jobscience.com - (http://www.jobscience.com) Post your resume, search job ads, create a search agent to e-mail you about jobs. Well-organized.

Joyce Lain Kennedy's Career Books - Ms. Kennedy is a noted columnist on career issues. Her books present valuable tools to help make a career selection, write resumes and search for jobs. Find out about them at **http://www.sunfeatures.com/books.htm** or you library or bookstore.

Lippincott, Williams & Wilkins (http://www.lww.com) Located at 351 West Camden Street, Baltimore, MD 21201-2436; 800/882-0483, E-mail: custserv@wwilkins.com. Williams and Wilkins is a major publisher of medical and scientific journals. All of the employment ads from their journals can be found online at **http://www.lww.com/classifieds**.

▣   MANAGED HEALTHCARE (Aster Publishing Corporation, 859 Williamette St., Eugene, OR 97440; 800/949-6525, 503/343-8841). Monthly, $59/year. Classifieds section lists around 15 job ads for administrative directors, account executives, general managers, sales directors, etc.

▣⚞✎⌖ Med Hunters (http://www.medhunters.com) Register (free) with MedHunters to allow employers access to your profile. You can also search specific categories for jobs world wide. Post your resume and set up an agent to e-mail you job notices.

▣⌖ Medical Ad Mart - (http://www.medical-admart.com) Compiles classified advertising from medical journals. The focus is Physicians, Veterinarians, Physician Assistants, Nurses, and Nurse Practitioners.

▣📁⚞↣✎⌖ MediMatch.com - (http://www.medimatch.com) Search jobs by category, including allied health and administration, post your resume and receive e-mail job notices. Their "virtual job fair" means they have detailed employer profiles with job ads, mostly in California at this time. They have a directory of health care providers and networking/chat features.

✎⌖ Med Options USA - 6542 Hypoluxo Road, Suite 294, Lake Worth, FL 33467, 800-863-8314, Fax: 800-357-8684, E-mail info@medoptions.com. Visit (http://www.medoptions.com, http://www.rehaboptions.com and http://www.nurseoptions.com) This free placement service will give your profile to prospective employers and the employer can contact you directly. Professions served include: nurse practitioner, physician assistant, PT, PTA, speech language therapist, OT, COTA, midwife, RN, nurse management, pharmacist and respiratory care practitioner.

⌖ MedWeb: Biomedical Internet Resources, see Emory University.

▣✎⌖ Monster healthcare -Monster.com won PC Magazine's Editor's Choice in 2001, and their healthcare site is loaded with information, including advice on resumes specifically for the health care field. (http://www.medsearch.com or http://healthcare.monster.com)

⚕⌖ National Health Service Corps (NHSC) -The NHSC is a federal program whose mission is to increase access to primary care services and reduce health disparities for people in areas with shortages of health professionals. (http://www.bphc.hrsa.gov/nhsc) Among other benefits, they offer student loan repayment and scholarships.

⊟🗁⌐⊖ **National Hospice and Palliative Care Organization** - 1700 Diagonal Road, Suite 300, Alexandria, VA 22314; 703/837-1500. (E-mail:info@nhpco.org, **http://www.nhpco.org**) Has a search engine to locate a hospice by state, county or city. Career center has few ads.

⊟⌐⊖ **National Institutes of Health (NIH): Job Vacancies at NIH** - NIH Human Resources Services, National Institutes of Health, Bethesda, Maryland 20892. (**http://www.nih.gov**). NIH job vacancies are posted weekly. Proof of U.S. citizenship is required for employment in most jobs.

NIH: National Center for Complementary and Alternative Medicine (NCCAM) - NCCAM Clearinghouse, PO Box 8218,Silver Spring, Maryland 20907-8218; 888/644-6226, TTY/TDY: 888/644-6226 fax: 301/495-4957. (**http://nccam.nih.gov**)

NIH: Center for Information Technology (NIH Building 12A, Room 1011, Bethesda, MD 20892; 301/496-6203. (**http://www.dcrt.nih.gov http://www.dcrt.nih.gov**)

♀⊟✍⌐⊖ **National Rural Health Association (NRHA)** - One West. Armour Blvd., Suite 301, Kansas City, MO 64111; 816/756-3140, fax: 816/756-3144. (**http://www.nrharural.org**, E-mail: mail@nrharural.org, E-mail for publications: pubs@nrharural.org). Offers a placement service. Membership consists of physicians, health planners, physician assistants, nurses, nurse midwives, state and national policy-makers, hospital and clinic administrators and others that are interested in rural health care. *The Journal of Rural Health* bimonthly newsletter, is free to members; nonmembers$45, students $35. Job ads offered in each issue. Students should check their fellowship program.

⊟✗✍⌐⊖ **NationJob Network** (601 SW 9th Street, Suites J & K, Des Moines, IA 50309; 800-292-7731, **http://www.nationjob.com**). Features a Personal Job Scout, which notifies you via email about suitable jobs.

🗁⌐⊖ **Nelson and Wallery. Ltd** (**http://www.nursinghomeinfo.com** and **http://www.assistedlivinginfo.com**) These two Web sites have databases which provides basic contact information for thousands of long-term care or assisted living facilities, including addresses, phone numbers, and maps.

⊟✗✍⌐⊖ <u>Netscape</u> - (**http://home.netscape.com/index.html**) Search ads by category or location. Post your resume, have job opportunities mailed to you and browse extensive career advice.

▤☞✖✁Online Career Center(http://www.occ.com) Search for both jobs and company profiles by city, state, industry (biotech, pharmaceuticals, medical/healthcare, etc), government, agencies, etc. Link to health care sites. Advice on resumes, job interviews.

▢ **Opportunities in Medical Sales Careers** by Chad Wayne Ellis. 1997. Paperback, 160 pages, $11.95. Published by VGM Career Horizons.

▤✁ **Pam Pohly's Net Guide** (http://www.pohly.com) Pam Pohly is a healthcare administrator and a recruiter who has authored an incredibly informative web site. Job ads for health care administrators with abundant resources useful for everyone else: links to health care companies and directories of medical facilities, advice on handling job interviews, and articles such as "What You Should Know About Recruiters" and "How to Handle Job Interviews Successfully."

▢☞✁ **Petersons Guides** - 202 Carnegie Circle, Princeton, NJ 08543; 800/338-3282. **http:www.petersons.com** *Peterson's Internships 2001: The Largest Source of Internships Available* ($19.96), *Job Opportunities in Health and Science* (1999, $15.96) *Peterson's Vocational and Technical Schools: West 2000 and Peterson's Vocational and Technical Schools: East 2000* are available at many libraries and bookstores.

▢ **Professional's Job Finder: 1997-2000** by Daniel Lauber, Paperback, $18.95. Published by Planning Communications, 1997. Presents over 3,000 tools for finding private sector job vacancies and getting hired. Includes extensive chapters on health care jobs. Order toll free at 1-888/366-5200. Highly recommended.

✁ **The Riley Guide** (http://www.dbm.com/jobguide) Employment Opportunities and Job Resources on the Internet, compiled by Margaret F. Dikel. This award-winning site has career and education guidance, and tips on using the Internet, with info on Usenet Newsgroups, mailing lists (Listservs), FTP: File Transfer Protocol, Telnet and Gopher.

♉▤☞✁ **Rural Recruitment and Retention Network (3R Net) - (http://www.3rnet.org)** (800) 787-2512, Fax: (608) 265-4400, E-mail: info@3rnet.org. The 5R Net provides names and addresses of those involved with rural recruitment and retention around the nation. Professions served include MD, PA, NP, CNM, Dentist, dental hygienist or pharmacist. Currently 45 states have job ads on this site.

Saludos Web (http://www.saludos.com) Supported by *Saludos Hispanos* magazine, this site promotes Hispanic careers and education. Articles about career fields and financial aid.

State job banks Every state employment service maintains a state job bank with a web site. To find it, use your search engine and type in the name of your state and "job bank" or search one of these Web sites: **http://www.edd.cahwnet.gov** or **http://www.acinet.org**.

thingamajob.com - (http://www.thingamajob.com) Lot of career advice, including transition from the military. Jobs in the U.S. and Canada, including information technology. Online resume, e-mail job alerts.

TROA: The Retired Officers Association - 201 N. Washington Street, Alexandria, VA 22314; 800/245-TROA, 703/549-2311. **(http://www.troa.org)**. Membership open to anyone who served as a commissioned officer in any branch of the service including warrants. Offers scholarship (also for members' children), loan, and other information on education and has employment services.

U.S. Administration on Aging - Department of Health and Human Services, **(http://www.aoa.dhhs.gov/aoa/webres/nursingG.htm**, E-mail: Bcraig@ban-gate.aoa.dhhs.gov). Offers a directory of Web sites on aging, as well as national and state directories. It also has information and locators for nursing homes and long-term care facilities.

USA Jobs - (http://www.usajobs.opm.gov) The US Government's official site for jobs and employment information provided by the United States Office of Personnel Management. Searchable by category or alphabetically, with online application.

Wall Street Journal - (http://www.careers.wsj.com) Excellent advice on job hunting, resumes and interviewing.

WORKsearch (http://www.worksearch.gc.ca) This Web site has some great resources for Canadian job hunters.

Chapter

4

HEALTH TECHNOLOGISTS

Robin Brandt

Robin Brandt, Radiological Technologist and manager for Airport MRI Associates in Aliquippa, Pennsylvania, was born in Pittsburgh, PA. She graduated from Hopewell High School in 1973 and completed X-ray school in 1975 at the Aliquippa Hospital's School of Radiological Technology.

After passing her state boards she moved to West Virginia for her first job with West Virginia University. "Actually, relocating to West Virginia was one of the best things I could have done. The hospital that I trained in had only four X-ray rooms. WVU had 12 X-ray rooms and their technology was more advanced." Robin found her first job through a trade journal's classified advertisement. "Basically, I've been very fortunate in that every job I've ever interviewed for I've received."

Robin takes a very personal approach to her profession. "I try to treat each patient that I scan or X-ray as if they were one of my family members. I think that gives you more compassion for people than if you just treated them as if they were some stranger off the street."

I asked Robin how she maintains such a high level of competence. She agreed that it had a lot to do with training, staying abreast of new technology and procedures and reading trade journals. Also, she replied, " I'll be honest with you; a part of it is laziness. The reason why I say this is that I try to do everything right the first time. I don't want to duplicate effort or to needlessly do something over again."

Robin worked previously at WVU, North Hills Passavant Hospital and Sewickley Hospital near Pittsburgh. She also worked in sales for two years with Fonar Corporation as a MRI sales representative.

Her interest in science and math lead her to the radiologic technologist profession. " I enjoyed science and math in high school and during my senior year I was able to take a course in nuclear science that I thoroughly enjoyed. I knew I wanted to do something in the medical field and at the time I didn't want to attend college for four years. Radiology was something that interested me, the technology behind it, the diversity."

An aptitude and interest in math through algebra 2 and science including physics and biology are prerequisites for entering the radiologic field. " It helps to be willing to relocate after graduation. Radiologic technologists are in short supply in many areas around the country. Radiology is a great field; technology is always improving and there is always something new and challenging to learn."

This chapter features health care technologists. The major occupational groups are:

Clinical Lab Technologists   Nuclear Medicine Technologists
Clinical Lab Technicians   Radiologic Technologists
Cardiovascular technicians   Surgical Technologists
Cardiovascular technologists   EEG Technologists

Each specialty is described below. Following each job description is a list of job resources: Associations, Books, Directories, Internet Sites, Job Ads, E-mail Job Notification/Job Hotlines, Job Fairs, and Resume/Placement Services with icons to guide you.

CLINICAL LABORATORY TECHNOLOGISTS & TECHNICIANS

OCCUPATIONAL TITLES:

Blood Bank Technologists   Medical Laboratory Techs
Clinical Chemistry Technologists   Medical Technologists
Microbiology Technologists   Cytotechnologists
Histology Technicians   Phlebotomists
Immunology Technologists

Nature of the Work

Clinical laboratory testing plays a crucial role in the detection, diagnosis, and treatment of disease. Clinical laboratory technologists and technicians, also known as medical technologists and technicians, perform most of these tests.

Clinical laboratory personnel examine and analyze body fluids, tissues, and cells. They look for bacteria, parasites, and other micro-organisms; analyze the chemical content of fluids; match blood for transfusions, and test for drug levels in the blood to show how a patient is responding to treatment. These technologists also prepare specimens for examination, count cells, and look for abnormal cells. They use automated equipment and instruments capable of performing a number of tests simultaneously, as well as microscopes, cell counters, and other sophisticated laboratory equipment. Then they analyze the results and relay them to physicians. With increasing automation and the use of computer technology, the work of technologists and technicians has become less hands-on and more analytical.

The complexity of tests performed, the level of judgment needed, and the amount of responsibility workers assume depend largely on the amount of education and experience they have.

Medical and clinical laboratory technologists generally have a bachelor's degree in medical technology or in one of the life sciences, or they have a combination of formal training and work experience. They perform complex chemical, biological, hematological, immunologic, microscopic, and bacteriological tests. Technologists microscopically examine blood, tissue, and other body substances. They make cultures of body fluid and tissue samples, to determine the presence of bacteria, fungi, parasites, or other microorganisms. They analyze samples for chemical content or reaction and determine blood glucose and cholesterol levels. They also type and cross match blood samples for transfusions.

Medical and clinical laboratory technologists evaluate test results, develop and modify procedures, and establish and monitor programs, to insure the accuracy of tests. Some medical and clinical laboratory technologists supervise medical and clinical laboratory technicians.

Technologists in small laboratories perform many types of tests, whereas those in large laboratories generally specialize. Technologists who prepare specimens and analyze the chemical and hormonal contents of body fluids are clinical chemistry technologists. Those who examine and identify bacteria and other microorganisms are microbiology technologists. Blood bank technologists collect, type, and prepare blood and its components for transfusions. Immunology technologists examine elements and responses of the human immune system to foreign bodies. Cytotechnologists prepare slides of body cells and microscopically examine these cells for abnormalities that may signal the beginning of a cancerous growth.

Medical and clinical laboratory technicians perform less complex tests and laboratory procedures than technologists. Technicians may prepare specimens and operate automatic analyzers, for example, or they may perform manual tests following detailed instructions. Like technologists, they may work in several areas of the clinical laboratory or specialize in just one. Histology technicians cut and stain tissue specimens for microscopic examination by pathologists, and phlebotomists collect blood samples. They usually work under the supervision of medical and clinical laboratory technologists or laboratory managers.

Working Conditions

Hours and other working conditions vary, according to the size and type of employment setting. In large hospitals or in independent laboratories that operate continuously, personnel usually work the day, evening, or night shift and may work weekends and holidays. Laboratory personnel in small facilities may work on rotating shifts, rather than on a regular shift. In some facilities, laboratory personnel are on call several nights a week or on weekends, available in case of emergency.

Clinical laboratory personnel are trained to work with infectious specimens. When proper methods of infection control and sterilization are followed, few hazards exist.

Laboratories usually are well lighted and clean; however, specimens, solutions, and reagents used in the laboratory sometimes produce odors. Laboratory workers may spend a great deal of time on their feet.

Employment

Clinical laboratory technologists and technicians held about 313,000 jobs in 1998. About half worked in hospitals. Most of the remaining jobs were found in medical laboratories or offices and clinics of physicians. A small number were in blood banks, research and testing laboratories, and in the Federal Government—at Department of Veterans Affairs hospitals and U.S. Public Health Service facilities. About 1 laboratory worker in 5 worked part time.

Training, Other Qualifications, and Advancement

The usual requirement for an entry level position as a medical or clinical laboratory technologist is a bachelor's degree with a major in medical technology or in one of the life sciences. Universities and hospitals offer medical technology programs. It is also possible to qualify through a combination of on-the-job and specialized training.

Bachelor's degree programs in medical technology include courses in chemistry, biological sciences, microbiology, mathematics, and specialized courses devoted to knowledge and skills used in the clinical laboratory. Many programs also offer or require courses in management, business, and computer applications. The Clinical Laboratory Improvement Act (CLIA) requires technologists who perform certain highly complex tests to have at least an associate's degree.

Medical and clinical laboratory technicians generally have either an associate's degree from a community or junior college or a certificate from a hospital, vocational or technical school, or from one of the Armed Forces. A few technicians learn their skills on the job.

Nationally recognized accrediting agencies in clinical laboratory science include the National Accrediting Agency for Clinical Laboratory Sciences (NAACLS), the Commission on Accreditation of Allied Health Education Programs (CAAHEP), and the Accrediting Bureau of Health Education Schools (ABHES). The NAACLS fully accredits 288 and approves 249 programs providing education for medical and clinical laboratory technologists, histologic technicians, and medical and clinical laboratory technicians. ABHES accredits training programs for medical and clinical laboratory technicians.

Some States require laboratory personnel to be licensed or registered. Information on licensure is available from State departments of health or boards of occupational licensing. Certification is a voluntary process by which a non-governmental organization, such as a professional society or certifying agency, grants recognition to an individual whose professional competence meets prescribed standards. Widely accepted by employers in the health industry, certification is a prerequisite for most jobs and often is necessary for advancement. Agencies certifying medical and clinical laboratory technologists and technicians include the Board of Registry of the American Society of Clinical Pathologists, the American Medical Technologists, and the Credentialing Commission of the International Society for Clinical Laboratory Technology. These agencies have different requirements for certification and different organizational sponsors.

Clinical laboratory personnel need good analytical judgment and the ability to work under pressure. Close attention to detail is essential, because small differences or changes in test substances or numerical readouts can be crucial for patient care. Manual dexterity and normal color vision are highly desirable. With the widespread use of automated laboratory equipment, computer skills are important. In addition, technologists in particular are expected to be good at problem solving.

Technologists may advance to supervisory positions in laboratory work or become chief medical or clinical laboratory technologists or laboratory managers in hospitals. Manufacturers of home diagnostic testing kits and laboratory equipment and supplies seek experienced technologists to work in product development, marketing, and sales. Graduate education in medical technology, one of the biological sciences, chemistry, management, or education usually speeds advancement. A doctorate is needed to become a laboratory director. However, federal regulation allows directors of moderate complexity laboratories to have either a master's degree or a bachelor's degree combined with the appropriate amount of training and experience. Technicians can become technologists through additional education and experience.

Job Outlook

Employment of clinical laboratory workers is expected to grow about as fast as the average for all occupations through the year 2008, as the volume of laboratory tests increases with population growth and the development of new types of tests. Hospitals and independent laboratories have recently undergone considerable consolidation and restructuring, to boost productivity and allow the same number of personnel to perform more tests than previously possible. Consequently, competition for jobs has increased; and individuals may now have to spend more time seeking employment than in the past.

Technological advances will continue to have two opposing effects on employment through 2008. New, increasingly powerful diagnostic tests will encourage additional testing and spur employment. However, advances in laboratory automation and simple tests, which make it possible for each worker to perform more tests, should slow growth. Research and development efforts are targeted at simplifying routine testing procedures, so non-laboratory personnel, physicians and patients, in particular, can perform tests now done in laboratories. In addition, automation may be used to prepare specimens, a job traditionally done by technologists and technicians.

Although significant, growth will not be the only source of opportunities. As in most occupations, many openings will result from the need to replace workers who transfer to other occupations, retire, or stop working for some other reason.

Earnings

Median annual earnings of clinical laboratory technologists and technicians were $32,440 in 1998. The middle 50 percent earned between $24,970 and $39,810 a year. The lowest 10 percent earned less than $19,380 and the highest 10 percent earned more than $48,290 a year.

CLINICAL LABORATORY
TECHNOLOGISTS and TECHNICIANS

Don't forget! Refer to the general resources listed in Chapter Three.

☤ Association   📖 Book   🗀 Directory   ⌁ Internet (Web) Site

📄 Job Ads   💥 E-mail/Hotline   📖 Job Fairs   ✍ Resume Service

---

☤ 🗀 **Accrediting Bureau of Health Education Schools** - 803 West Broad St., Suite 730, Falls Church, VA 22046; 703/533-2082. (**http://www.abhes.org**, Ee-mail: abhes@erols.com) This organization can help locate accredited schools.

📄⌁ **ADVANCE Newsmagazines** - 650 Park Avenue West, Box 61556, King of Prussia, PA 19406-0956; 800/355-1088. Publishes *ADVANCE for Medical Laboratory Professionals* and *ADVANCE for Administrators of the Laboratory.* Free for professionals, numerous job ads. Their URL is **http://www.merion.com/sitemap.html**.

☤📄⌁ **American Association of Blood Banks (AABB)** - 8101 Glenbrook Road, Bethesda, MD 20814-2749; 301/907-6977, fax: 301/907-6895. (**http://www.aabb.org**, E-mail: aabb@aabb.org) Web site has a directory of education programs. Sponsors workshops and accredits blood banks. *AABB News Briefs* has job ads, 11/ yr, free to members. *AABB Weekly Report*, also has job ads, $150/year for nonmembers, members free. Sample issue on web site. Jobs ads on Web site are for subscribers only.

☤📄✍⌁ **American Association for Clinical Chemistry (AACC)** - Suite 202, 2101 L Street NW, Washington, DC 20037; 800/892-1400, 202/857-0717. (**http://www.aacc.org/services**, E-mail: info@aacc.org) The AACC has a job bank in which employers can find technologists and vice versa. Web site has links to laboratories and other resources.

☤📄⌁ **American Association of Pathologists Assistants (AAPA)** - Rosewood Office Plaza, Suite 300N, 1711 W. County Rd. B, Roseville, MN, 55113; 800/532-2272, E-mail: mspindler@MN.state.net. The AAPA represents 470 anatomic pathology professionals in the in the United States and Canada. Visit **http://pathologistsassistants.org** . The web site explains the duties of these professionals.

♀📖🖱 **American Medical Technologists (AMT)** - 710 Higgins Rd., Park Ridge, IL 60068, 847/823-5169, fax; 847/823-0458, E-mail: amtmail@aol.com, **http://www.amt1.com**. The AMT has free information online on these careers: phlebotomist, medical assistant, dental assistant technicians, instructors, and technologists. The Web site has a few classified ads.

♀ **American Society for Clinical Laboratory Science** - 7910 Woodmont Ave., Suite 530, Bethesda, MD 20814. (**http://www.ascls.org**)

♀📖🖱 **American Society of Clinical Pathologists (ASCP)** - 2100 W. Harrison Street, Chicago, IL 60612-3798; 312/738-1336, fax: 312/738-0102. E-mail: info@ascp.org. Web site **http://www.ascp.org/bor** has jobs section for medical technologists. *Laboratory Medicine* has technologist and technician job ads.

♀📖🖱 **American Society for Cytotechnology (ASCT)** - 4101 Lake Boon Trail, Suite 201, Raleigh NC 27607; 919/787-5181, 800/948-3947. (**http://www.asct.com/home.html**)*ASCT NEWS*, monthly newsletter, is free with membership. Job ads and educational programs on web site.

♀📁🖱 **American Society of Cytopathology (ASC)** - 400 West 9th Street, Suite 201, Wilmington, Delaware 19801; 302/429-8802; fax: 302/429-8807. (**http://www.cytopathology.org,** E-mail: asc@cytopathology.org) One copy of the brochure, *Consider a Career in Cytopathology* is free.

📖🖱 **Acta Cytologica** - P.O. Drawer 12425, 8342 Olive Boulevard, St. Louis, MO 63132-2814; 314/991-4440, fax: 314/991-4654, (**http://www.acta-cytol.com**). The Classifieds section on the web contains ads, mostly for pathologists but a few ads for cytotechnologists.

♀✏🖱 **American Society for Microbiology** - 1752 N Street NW, Washington, DC 20036; 202/737-3600, (**http://www.asmusa.org**). ASM's resume matching service is available to nonmembers. ASM publishes a free brochure, *Your Career in Microbiology: Unlocking the Secrets of Life.*

♀📖🖱 **Clinical Laboratory Management Association (CLMA)** - 989 Old Eagle School Road, Suite 815, Wayne, PA 19087-1704; 610/995-9580, fax: 610/995-9568. (**http://www.clma.org**) Career opportunities section of the web site has jobs for management and a few technicians.

♀📖📁✏🖱 **Clinical Ligand Assay Society (CLAS)** - 3139 S. Wayne Rd., P.O. Box 67, Wayne, MI 48184; 734/722-6290. (**http://www.clas.org,**

E-mail clas@clas.org) *CLAS Newsletter* features classified ads, members only. Publishes a membership directory.

📖✒️ **CytoLink (http://www.cytology.com/home.htm)** Positions Available with many ads for cytotechnologists.

📖✒️ **CytoPathNet (http://www.cytopathnet.com/)** This web site has a student section, bookstore, chat section, continuing education, journals and classified job ads. You can post in "Positions Wanted" for $30/month. Produced by J Cyrisse Productions.

⚕️ **International Society for Clinical Laboratory Technology** - 917 Locust St., Suite 1100, St. Louis, MO 63101-1413. Career and certification information is available.

✒️ **Internet Resources for Pathology and Laboratory Medicine** **(http://www.pathology.med.umich.edu/pathresourceak_resources.html)** Sponsored by the University of Michigan, this site has a good collection of links to positions available, pathology departments' Web sites, Listserv addresses, usenet newsgroups and commercial links.

✍️✒️ **Med TechNet (http://www.medtechnet.com)** Informative site has educational presentations, conferences, files and a Listserv. Public can post resumes. Good links to other sites.

📁 **National Accrediting Agency for Clinical Laboratory Sciences,** 8410 W. Bryn Mawr Ave., Suite 670, Chicago, IL 60631. Contact about accredited and approved educational programs.

📁 **National Association of Health Career Schools,** 2301 Academy Dr., Harrisburg, PA 17112. Contact for information about a career as a medical and clinical laboratory technician and schools offering training.

⚕️📖📁✒️ **National Society for Histotechnology** - 4201 Northview Drive, Suite 502, Bowie, MD 20716-2604; 301/262-6221. Membership, $40/year, students $20. Job lists for histotechnicians and histotechnologists members. Free brochure on the profession includes a list of schools. **(http://www.nsh.org,** E-mail histo@nsh.org)

📖 **Opportunities in Medical Technology Careers** by Karen R. Karni, Hardcover, $14.95. Published by VGM Career Horizons, 1996.

CARDIOVASCULAR TECHNOLOGISTS AND TECHNICIANS

Nature of the Work

Cardiovascular technologists and technicians assist physicians in diagnosing and treating cardiac (heart) and peripheral vascular (blood vessel) ailments.

Cardiovascular technologists specializing in cardiac catheterization procedures are called cardiology technologists. They assist physicians with invasive procedures in which a small tube, or catheter, is wound through a patient's blood vessel from a spot on the patient's leg into the heart. This is done to determine if a blockage exists and for other diagnostic purposes. In balloon angioplasty, a procedure used to treat blockages of blood vessels, technologists assist physicians who insert a catheter with a balloon on the end to the point of the obstruction.

Technologists prepare patients for these procedures by first positioning them on an examining table and then shaving, cleaning, and administering anesthesia to the top of the patient's leg near the groin. During the procedures, they monitor patients' blood pressure and heart rate using electrocardiogram (EKG) equipment and notify the physician, if something appears wrong. Technologists may also prepare and monitor patients during open-heart surgery and the implantation of pacemakers.

Cardiovascular technologists and technicians may specialize in noninvasive peripheral vascular tests. Those who assist physicians in the diagnosis of disorders affecting circulation are known as vascular technologists. Vascular technologists use ultrasound instrumentation, such as doppler ultrasound, to noninvasively record vascular information, such as blood pressure, limb volume changes, oxygen saturation, cerebral circulation, peripheral circulation, and abdominal circulation. Many of these tests are performed during or immediately after surgery. Technologists and technicians who use ultrasound on the heart are referred to as echocardiographers. They use ultrasound equipment that transmits sound waves and then collects the echoes to form an image on a screen.

Cardiovascular technicians who obtain electrocardiograms are known as electrocardiograph (abbreviated EKG or ECG) technicians. To take a basic EKG, which traces electrical impulses transmitted by the heart, technicians attach electrodes to the patient's chest, arms, and legs, and then manipulate switches on an electrocardiograph machine to obtain a reading. This test is done before most kinds of surgery and as part of a routine physical examination, especially for persons who have reached middle age or have a history of cardiovascular problems.

EKG technicians with advanced training perform Holter monitor and stress testing. For a Holter monitoring, technicians place electrodes on the patient's chest and attach a portable EKG monitor to the patient's belt. Following 24 to 48 hours of normal routine for the patient, the technician removes a cassette tape from the monitor and places it in a scanner. After checking the quality of the recorded impulses on an electronic screen, the technician prints the information from the tape, so a physician can interpret it later. The printed output from the scanner is eventually used by a physician to diagnose heart ailments.

For a treadmill stress test, EKG technicians document the patient's medical history, explain the procedure, connect the patient to an EKG monitor, and obtain a baseline reading and resting blood pressure. Next, they monitor the heart's performance, while the patient is walking on a treadmill, gradually increasing the treadmill's speed to observe the effect of increased exertion. Those cardiovascular technicians who perform EKG and stress tests are known as "noninvasive" technicians, because the techniques they use do not require the insertion of probes or other instruments into the patient's body.

Some cardiovascular technologists and technicians schedule appointments, type doctor interpretations, maintain patient files, and care for equipment.

Working Conditions
Technologists and technicians generally work a 5-day, 40-hour week that may include weekends. Those in catheterization labs tend to work longer hours and may work evenings. They may also be on call during the night and on weekends.

Cardiovascular technologists and technicians spend a lot of time walking and standing. Those who work in catheterization labs may face stressful working conditions, because they are in close contact with patients who have serious heart ailments. Some patients, for example, may encounter complications from time to time that have life or death implications.

Employment

Cardiovascular technologists and technicians held about 33,000 jobs in 1998. Most worked in hospital cardiology departments, whereas some worked in cardiologists' offices, cardiac rehabilitation centers, or ambulatory surgery centers. About one-third were EKG technicians.

Training, Other Qualifications, and Advancement

Although some cardiovascular technologists, vascular technologists, and echocardiographers are currently trained on the job, an increasing number receive training in two to four year programs. Cardiology technologists normally complete a 2-year junior or community college program. One year is dedicated to core courses followed by a year of specialized instruction in either invasive, noninvasive, or noninvasive peripheral cardiology. Those who are qualified in a related allied health profession only need to complete the year of specialized instruction. Graduates from programs accredited by the Joint Review Committee on Education in Cardiovascular Technology are eligible to register as professional technologists with the American Registry of Diagnostic Medical Sonographers or Cardiovascular Credentialing International.

For basic EKGs, Holter monitoring, and stress testing, 1-year certificate programs exist; but most EKG technicians are still trained on the job by an EKG supervisor or a cardiologist. On-the-job training usually lasts about 8 to 16 weeks. Most employers prefer to train people already in the health care field—nursing aides, for example. Some EKG technicians are students enrolled in 2-year programs to become technologists, working part-time to gain experience and make contact with employers.

Cardiovascular technologists and technicians must be reliable, have mechanical aptitude, and be able to follow detailed instructions. A pleasant, relaxed manner for putting patients at ease is an asset.

Job Outlook

Employment of cardiovascular technologists and technicians is expected to grow as fast as the average for all occupations through the year 2008, with technologists and technicians experiencing different patterns of employment change.

Employment of cardiology technologists is expected to grow much faster than the average for all occupations. Growth will occur as the population ages, because older people have a higher incidence of heart problems. Likewise, employment of vascular technologists will grow faster than the average, as advances in vascular technology reduce the need for more costly and invasive procedures.

In contrast, employment of EKG technicians is expected to decline, as hospitals train nursing aides and others to perform basic EKG procedures. Individuals trained in Holter monitoring and stress testing are expected to have more favorable job prospects than those who can only perform a basic EKG.

Some job openings for cardiovascular technologists and technicians will arise from replacement needs, as individuals transfer to other jobs or leave the labor force. Relatively few job openings, due to both growth and replacement needs are expected, however, because the occupation is small.

Earnings

Median annual earnings of cardiology technologists were $35,770 in 1998. The middle 50 percent earned between $29,060 and $42,350 a year. The lowest 10 percent earned less than $23,010 and the highest 10 percent earned more than $49,780 a year. Median annual earnings of cardiology technologists in 1997 were $34,500 in hospitals.

Median annual earnings of EKG technicians were $24,360 in 1998. The middle 50 percent earned between $19,660 and $30,860 a year. The lowest 10 percent earned less than $16,130 and the highest 10 percent earned more than $39,060 a year. Median annual earnings of EKG technicians in 1997 were $23,200 in hospitals.

EKG (ECG) TECHNOLOGISTS & TECHNICIANS

Don't forget! Refer to the general resources listed in Chapter Three.

☤ 📱✓🖱 **Alliance of Cardiovascular Professionals** - 910 Charles Street, Fredericksburg, Virginia 22401; 540/370-0102). Internet Job Opportunities Bank is under construction at **http://www.acp-online.org**. E-mail: SeanMcE@atlanticinteractive.com

☤ 📱📁✓🖱 **American Association of Cardiovascular and Pulmonary Rehabilitation (AACVPR)** - 7600 Terrace Ave., Suite 203, Middletown, WI 53562; 608/831-6989, **http://aacvpr.org**). Homepage has Career Hotline with jobs in these categories: nurse, occupational therapist, exercise physiologist, physician and respiratory therapist. Publications: *Journal of Cardiopulmonary Rehabilitation* (bimonthly), *News and Views of AACVPR* (quarterly newsletter), *Directory Webof Membership and Cardiopulmonary Rehabilitation Programs.*

📱✓🖱 **CathLab.com** - (**http://www.cathlab.com**) Classified section has job ads. Heart 2 Heart lists over 2,000 cath labs and has a chat room.

✓🖱 **CCathNet, Inc.** - 275 Caroline Street, Rochester, NY 14620-2121; 716/461-2013. (**http://www.ccathnet.org**, E-mail: ccathnet@ccathnet.org). Information on Internet site for non-MD cardiovascular professionals.

☤ ✓🖱 **The Society of Invasive Cardiovascular Professionals.** E-mail for publications: cvlraeann@aol.com, URL: **http://www.sicp.com**. Journals of the Society of Invasive Cardiovascular Professionals (SICP) are published by Health Management Publications, Inc., 950 West Valley Road, Suite 2800, Wayne, PA 19087; 610/688-8220 800/237-7285, fax: 610/688-8225. Subscription to *Cath-Lab Digest*, geared specifically to the non-physician cardiac catheterization laboratory professional is free to qualified technical personnel. A three month trial subscription to *The Journal of Invasive Cardiology* is also available. No jobs on the web site.

ELECTRONEURODIAGNOSTIC TECHNOLOGISTS

This career is very similar to cardiovascular technicians who are described above. Only a summary is given here.

Nature of the Work

Electroneurodiagnostic technologists use instruments such as an electroencephalograph (EEG) machine, to record electrical impulses transmitted by the brain and the nervous system. They help physicians diagnose brain tumors, strokes, epilepsy, and sleep disorders. They also measure the effects of infectious diseases on the brain, as well as determine whether individuals with mental or behavioral problems have an organic impairment, such as Alzheimer's disease. Furthermore, they determine cerebral death, the absence of brain activity, and assess the probability of recovery from a coma.

Electroneurodiagnostic technologists who specialize in basic or resting EEGs are called EEG technologists. The range of tests performed by electroneurodiagnostic technologists is broader than, but includes, those conducted by EEG technologists. Because it provides a more accurate description of work typically performed in the field, the title electroneurodiagnostic technologists generally has replaced that of EEG technologist.

Electroneurodiagnostic technologists take patients' medical histories, help patients relax, and then apply electrodes to designated spots on the patient's head. They must choose the most appropriate combination of instrument controls and electrodes, to correct for mechanical and electrical interference from somewhere other than the brain, such as eye movement or radiation from electrical sources.

Increasingly, technologists perform EEGs in the operating room, which requires that they understand anesthesia's effect on brain waves. For special procedure EEGs, technologists may secure electrodes to the chest, arm, leg, or spinal column, to record activity from both the central and peripheral nervous systems.

In ambulatory monitoring, technologists attach small recorders to patients to monitor the brain, and sometimes the heart, while patients carry out normal activities over a 24-hour period. They then remove the recorder and obtain a readout. Technologists review the readouts, selecting sections for the physician to examine.

Using evoked potential testing, technologists measure sensory and physical responses to specific stimuli. After attaching electrodes to the patient, they set the instrument for the type and intensity of the stimulus, increase the intensity until the patient reacts, and note the sensation level.

For nerve conduction tests, used to diagnose muscle and nerve problems, technologists place electrodes on the patient's skin over a nerve and over a muscle. Then they stimulate the nerve with an electrical current and record how long it takes the nerve impulse to reach the muscle.

Technologists who specialize in and administer sleep disorder studies are called polysomnographic technologists. Sleep disorder studies are usually conducted in a clinic called a sleep center. During the procedure, these technologists monitor the patient's respiration and heart and brain wave activity. These workers must know the dynamics of the cardiopulmonary systems during each stage of sleep. They coordinate readings from several organ systems, separate the readings according to the stages of sleep, and relay results to the physician. Polysomnographic technologists may also write technical reports summarizing test results.

Additionally, technologists look for changes in a patient's neurologic, cardiac, and respiratory status, which may indicate an emergency, such as a heart attack, and provide emergency care until help arrives.

Earnings

Median annual earnings of electroneurodiagnostic technologists were $32,070 in 1998. The middle 50 percent earned between $26,610 and $38,500 a year. The lowest 10 percent earned less than $22,200 and the highest 10 percent earned more than $46,620 a year.

EEG TECHNOLOGISTS

Don't forget! Refer to the general resources listed in Chapter Three.

☥ Association   📖 Book   🗁 Directory   🖱 Internet (Web) Site

📑 Job Ads   ✴ E-mail/Hotline   🏷 Job Fairs   📝 Resume Service

☥   **American Board of Registration for Electroencephalographic Technologists** - P.O. Box 916633, Longwood, FL 32791; 407 788-6308, (http://www.abret.org). Certification is voluntary. They give three exams: EEG, evoked potentials and neurophysiologic intraoperative monitoring.

☥ 🗁 📝 🖱   **American Society of Electroneurodiagnostic Technologists (ASET)** - 204 West 7th Street, Carroll, Iowa 51401-2317; 712/792-2978. (http://www.aset.org) *Who's Who*, directory for members only, lists companies and members. Placement service - Subscribers receive lists of available jobs twice per month. Free for ASET Members; $40 fee for a six-month enrollment for non-members. For application call 712-792-2978, fax: 712-792-6962, or E-mail aset@netins.net. A career profile can be found on the web or "A Career in Electroneurodiagnostics: Brain Power in Action" brochure can be ordered for $1.00. A list of schools is included. Free catalog of publications.

☥ **Electroneurodiagnostic Technologists Association of Polysomnographic Technology**, 2025 South Washington, Suite 300, Lansing, MI 48910-0817.

☥   **Joint Review Committee on Electroneurodiagnostic Technology**, Route 1, Box 63A, Genoa, WI 54632.

NUCLEAR MEDICINE TECHNOLOGISTS

Nature of the Work

In nuclear medicine, radionuclides—unstable atoms that emit radiation spontaneously—are used to diagnose and treat disease. Radionuclides are purified and compounded like other drugs to form radiopharmaceuticals. Nuclear medicine technologists administer these radiopharmaceuticals to patients, then monitor the characteristics and functions of tissues or organs in which they localize. Abnormal areas show higher or lower concentrations of radioactivity than normal.

Nuclear medicine technologists operate cameras that detect and map the radioactive drug in the patient's body to create an image on photographic film or a computer monitor. Radiologic technologists also operate diagnostic imaging equipment, but their equipment creates an image by projecting an x ray through the patient. (See the statement on radiologic technologists elsewhere in the Handbook.)

Nuclear medicine technologists explain test procedures to patients. They prepare a dosage of the radiopharmaceutical and administer it by mouth, injection, or other means. When preparing radiopharmaceuticals, technologists adhere to safety standards that keep the radiation dose to workers and patients as low as possible.

Technologists position patients and start a gamma scintillation camera, or "scanner," which creates images of the distribution of a radiopharmaceutical as it localizes in and emits signals from the patient's body. Technologists produce the images on a computer screen or on film for a physician to interpret. Some nuclear medicine studies, such as cardiac function studies, are processed with the aid of a computer.

Nuclear medicine technologists also perform radioimmunoassay studies that assess the behavior of a radioactive substance inside the body. For example, technologists may add radioactive substances to blood or serum to determine levels of hormones or therapeutic drug content.

Technologists keep patient records and record the amount and type of radionuclides received, used, and disposed of.

Working Conditions

Nuclear medicine technologists generally work a 40-hour week. This may include evening or weekend hours in departments that operate on an extended schedule. Opportunities for part-time and shift work are also available. In addition, technologists in hospitals may have on-call duty on a rotational basis.

Because technologists are on their feet much of the day, and may lift or turn disabled patients, physical stamina is important.

Although there is potential for radiation exposure in this field, it is kept to a minimum by the use of shielded syringes, gloves, and other protective devices and adherence to strict radiation safety guidelines. Technologists also wear badges that measure radiation levels. Because of safety programs, however, badge measurements rarely exceed established safety levels.

Employment

Nuclear medicine technologists held about 14,000 jobs in 1998. About 8 out of 10 jobs were in hospitals. The rest were in physicians' offices and clinics, including imaging centers.

Training, Other Qualifications, and Advancement

Nuclear medicine technology programs range in length from 1 to 4 years and lead to a certificate, associate's degree, or bachelor's degree. Generally, certificate programs are offered in hospitals, associate programs in community colleges, and bachelor's programs in 4-year colleges and in universities. Courses cover physical sciences, the biological effects of radiation exposure, radiation protection and procedures, the use of radiopharmaceuticals, imaging techniques, and computer applications.

One-year certificate programs are for health professionals, especially radiologic technologists and ultrasound technologists, who wish to specialize in nuclear medicine. They also attract medical technologists, registered nurses, and others who wish to change fields or specialize. Others interested in the nuclear medicine technology field have three options: A 2-year certificate program, a 2-year associate program, or a 4-year bachelor's program.

The Joint Review Committee on Education Programs in Nuclear Medicine Technology accredits most formal training programs in nuclear medicine technology. In 1999, there were 96 accredited programs.

All nuclear medicine technologists must meet the minimum Federal standards on the administration of radioactive drugs and the operation of radiation detection equipment. In addition, about half of all States require technologists to be licensed. Technologists also may obtain voluntary professional certification or registration. Registration or certification is available from the American Registry of Radiologic Technologists and from the Nuclear Medicine Technology Certification Board. Most employers prefer to hire certified or registered technologists.

Technologists may advance to supervisor, then to chief technologist, and to department administrator or director. Some technologists specialize in a clinical area such as nuclear cardiology or computer analysis or leave patient care to take positions in research laboratories. Some become instructors or directors in nuclear medicine technology programs, a step that usually requires a bachelor's degree or a master's in nuclear medicine technology. Others leave the occupation to work as sales or training representatives for medical equipment and radiopharmaceutical manufacturing firms, or as radiation safety officers in regulatory agencies or hospitals.

Job Outlook

Employment of nuclear medicine technologists is expected to grow about as fast as the average for all occupations through the year 2008. The number of openings each year will be very low because the occupation is small. Growth will arise from an increase in the number of middle-aged and older persons who are the primary users of diagnostic procedures, including nuclear medicine tests. Nonetheless, job seekers will face more competition for jobs than in the recent past. In an attempt to employ fewer technologists and lower labor costs, hospitals continue to merge nuclear medicine and radiologic technology departments. Consequently, opportunities will be best for technologists who can perform both nuclear medicine and radiologic procedures.

Technological innovations may increase the diagnostic uses of nuclear medicine. One example is the use of radiopharmaceuticals in combination with monoclonal antibodies to detect cancer at far earlier stages than is customary today, and without resorting to surgery. Another is the use of radionuclides to examine the heart's ability to pump blood. Wider use of nuclear medical imaging to observe metabolic and biochemical changes for neurology, cardiology, and oncology procedures, will also spur some demand for nuclear medicine technologists.

On the other hand, cost considerations will affect the speed with which new applications of nuclear medicine grow. Some promising nuclear medicine procedures, such as positron emission tomography, are extremely costly, and hospitals contemplating them will have to consider equipment costs, reimbursement policies, and the number of potential users.

Earnings

Median annual earnings of nuclear medicine technologists were $39,610 in 1998. The middle 50 percent earned between $34,910 and $46,570 a year. The lowest 10 percent earned less than $30,590 and the highest 10 percent earned more than $52,770 a year.

NUCLEAR MEDICINE TECHNOLOGISTS

Don't forget! Refer to the general resources listed in Chapter Three. Check the resources for Radiologic Technologists, too.

☤ Association 📖 Book 🗁 Directory 🖱 Internet (Web) Site		
📄 Job Ads ⚡ E-mail/Hotline 🏷 Job Fairs ✐ Resume Service		

📄🖱 **ADVANCE Newsmagazines** - 650 Park Avenue West, Box 61556, King of Prussia, PA 19406-0956; 800/355-1088.   Publishes *ADVANCE for Radiologic Science Professionals* and *ADVANCE for Administrators in Radiation and Radiation Oncology,* free for professionals, with numerous job ads. (**http://www.merion.com/sitemap.html**)

☤🖱 **American Nuclear Society** - 555 North Kensington Ave., La Grange Park, IL 60525;   708/352-6611, fax: 708/352-0499. Members may post resumes and search ads. (**http://www.ans.org**).

☤🗁 **Commission on Accreditation of Allied Health Education Programs** - (**http://www.caahep.org**). The CAAHEP accredits 18 professions, including sonography.

☤🖱 **Nuclear Medicine Technology Certification Board** - 2970 Clairmont Rd., Suite 610, Atlanta, GA 30329; 404/315-1739. Certifies technologists and publishes a*Directory*. (**http://www.nmtcb.org**).

RT IMAGE - Valley Forge Press, 1041 West Bridge Street, Suite 6, Ploenixville, PA 19460; 610/935-3302, 800/9-VF-PRES). Bi-weekly publication. Has pages of employment ads for radiologic science professionals, educators, and administrators. Free to professionals.

Society of Nuclear Medicine (SNM) - 1850 Samuel Morse Drive, Reston, VA 22090; 703/708-9000, fax: 703/708-9015, (**http://www.snm.org**). Technologist members annual dues are $88.00/year plus local chapter fees. *Journal of Nuclear Medicine* and *Journal of Nuclear Medicine Technology* have several job ads per issue. They also run job wanted ads online, available to the public. The web site has an excellent Internet Guide for Allied Health Professionals Links Page.

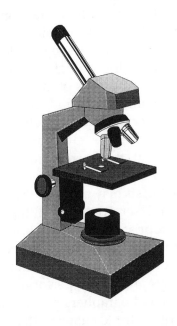

RADIOLOGIC TECHNOLOGISTS

OCCUPATIONAL TITLES:

Radiographers   Sonographers
Radiation Therapy Technologists

Nature of the Work

Perhaps the most familiar use of the x ray is the diagnosis of broken bones. However, medical uses of radiation go far beyond that. Radiation is used not only to produce images of the interior of the body, but to treat cancer as well. At the same time, the use of imaging techniques that do not involve x rays, such as ultrasound and magnetic resonance imaging (MRI), is growing rapidly. The term "diagnostic imaging" embraces these procedures as well as the familiar x ray.

Radiographers produce x ray films (radiographs) of parts of the human body for use in diagnosing medical problems. They prepare patients for radiologic examinations by explaining the procedure, removing articles such as jewelry, through which x rays cannot pass, and positioning patients so that the parts of the body can be appropriately radiographed. To prevent unnecessary radiation exposure, technologists surround the exposed area with radiation protection devices, such as lead shields, or limit the size of the x ray beam. Radiographers position radiographic equipment at the correct angle and height over the appropriate area of a patient's body. Using instruments similar to a measuring tape, technologists may measure the thickness of the section to be radiographed and set controls on the machine to produce radiographs of the appropriate density, detail, and contrast. They place the x ray film under the part of the patient's body to be examined and make the exposure. They then remove the film and develop it.

Experienced radiographers may perform more complex imaging tests. For fluoroscopies, radiographers prepare a solution of contrast medium for the patient to drink, allowing the radiologist, a physician who interprets radiographs, to see soft tissues in the body. Some radiographers, called CT technologists, operate computerized tomography scanners to produce cross sectional views of patients. Others operate machines using giant magnets and radio waves rather than radiation to create an image and are called magnetic resonance imaging (MRI) technologists.

Sonographers, also known as ultrasonographers, direct nonionizing, high frequency sound waves into areas of the patient's body; the equipment then collects reflected echoes to form an image. The image is viewed on a screen and may be recorded on videotape or photographed for interpretation and diagnosis by physicians. Sonographers explain the procedure, record additional medical history, select appropriate equipment settings and use various patient positions as necessary. Viewing the screen as the scan takes place, sonographers look for subtle differences between healthy and pathological areas, decide which images to include, and judge if the images are satisfactory for diagnostic purposes. Sonographers may specialize in neurosonography (the brain), vascular (blood flows), echocardiography (the heart), abdominal (the liver, kidneys, spleen, and pancreas), obstetrics/gynecology (the female reproductive system), and ophthalmology (the eye).

Radiologic technologists must follow physicians' orders precisely and conform to regulations concerning use of radiation to protect themselves, their patients, and coworkers from unnecessary exposure.

In addition to preparing patients and operating equipment, radiologic technologists keep patient records and adjust and maintain equipment. They may also prepare work schedules, evaluate equipment purchases, or manage a radiology department.

Working Conditions

Most full-time radiologic technologists work about 40 hours a week; they may have evening, weekend, or on-call hours.

Technologists are on their feet for long periods and may lift or turn disabled patients. They work at diagnostic machines but may also do some procedures at patients' bedsides. Some radiologic technologists travel to patients in large vans equipped with sophisticated diagnostic equipment.

Although potential radiation hazards exist in this occupation, they are minimized by the use of lead aprons, gloves, and other shielding devices, as well as by instruments monitoring radiation exposure. Technologists wear badges measuring radiation levels in the radiation area, and detailed records are kept on their cumulative lifetime dose.

Employment

Radiologic technologists held about 162,000 jobs in 1998. Most technologists were radiographers, while the rest worked as sonographers. About 1 radiologic technologist in 5 worked part time. More than half of jobs for technologists are in hospitals. Most of the rest are in physicians' offices and clinics, including diagnostic imaging centers.

Training, Other Qualifications, and Advancement

Preparation for this profession is offered in hospitals, colleges and universities, vocational-technical institutes, and the Armed Forces. Hospitals, which employ most radiologic technologists, prefer to hire those with formal training.

Formal training is offered in radiography and diagnostic medical sonography (ultrasound). Programs range in length from 1 to 4 years and lead to a certificate, associate's degree, or bachelor's degree. Two-year associate's degree programs are most prevalent.

Some 1-year certificate programs are available for experienced radiographers or individuals from other health occupations, such as medical technologists and registered nurses, who want to change fields or specialize in sonography. A bachelor's or master's degree in one of the radiologic technologies is desirable for supervisory, administrative, or teaching positions.

The Joint Review Committee on Education in Radiologic Technology accredits most formal training programs for this field. They accredited 602 radiography programs in 1999. The Joint Review Committee on Education in Diagnostic Medical Sonography accredited 77 programs in sonography in 1998.

Radiography programs require, at a minimum, a high school diploma or the equivalent. High school courses in mathematics, physics, chemistry, and biology are helpful. The programs provide both classroom and clinical instruction in anatomy and physiology, patient care procedures, radiation physics, radiation protection, principles of imaging, medical terminology, positioning of patients, medical ethics, radiobiology, and pathology.

For training programs in diagnostic medical sonography, applicants with a background in science, or experience in one of the health professions, generally are preferred. Some programs consider applicants with liberal arts backgrounds, however, as well as high school graduates with courses in math and science.

In 1981, Congress passed the Consumer-Patient Radiation Health and Safety Act, which aims to protect the public from the hazards of unnecessary exposure to medical and dental radiation by ensuring operators of radiologic equipment are properly trained. Under the act, the Federal Government sets voluntary standards that the States, in turn, may use for accrediting training programs and certifying individuals who engage in medical or dental radiography. Because ultrasound does not use ionizing radiation, sonographers are excluded from this act.

In 1999, 35 States and Puerto Rico licensed radiologic technologists. No State requires sonographers to be licensed. Voluntary registration is offered by the American Registry of Radiologic Technologists (ARRT) in radiography. The American Registry of Diagnostic Medical Sonographers (ARDMS) certifies the competence of sonographers. To be eligible for registration, technologists generally must graduate from an accredited program and pass an examination. Many employers prefer to hire registered radiographers and sonographers.

With experience and additional training, staff technologists may become specialists, performing CT scanning, angiography, and magnetic resonance imaging. Experienced technologists may also be promoted to supervisor, chief radiologic technologist, and—ultimately—department administrator or director. Depending on the institution, courses or a master's degree in business or health administration may be necessary for the director's position. Some technologists progress by becoming instructors or directors in radiologic technology programs; others take jobs as sales representatives or instructors with equipment manufacturers.

Radiographers must complete 24 hours of continuing education every other year and provide documentation to prove they have complied with these requirements. Sonographers must complete 30 hours of continuing education every 3 years.

Job Outlook

Employment of radiologic technologists is expected to grow as fast as the average for all occupations through 2008, as the population grows and ages, increasing the demand for diagnostic imaging and therapeutic technology. Although physicians are enthusiastic about the clinical benefits of new technologies, the extent to which they are adopted depends largely on cost and reimbursement considerations. Some promising new technologies may not come into widespread use because they are too expensive and third-party payers may not be willing to pay for their use.

Sonographers should experience somewhat better job opportunities than radiographers. Ultrasound is becoming an increasingly attractive alternative to radiologic procedures. Ultrasound technology is expected to continue to evolve rapidly and spawn many new ultrasound procedures. Furthermore, because ultrasound does not use radiation for imaging, there are few possible side effects.

Radiologic technologists who are educated and credentialed in more than one type of imaging technology, such as radiography and ultrasonography or nuclear medicine, will have better employment opportunities as employers look for new ways to control costs. In hospitals, multi-skilled employees will be the most sought after, as hospitals respond to cost pressures by continuing to merge departments.

Hospitals will remain the principal employer of radiologic technologists. However, employment is expected to grow most rapidly in offices and clinics of physicians, including diagnostic imaging centers. Health facilities such as these are expected to grow very rapidly through 2008 due to the strong shift toward outpatient care, encouraged by third-party payers and made possible by technological advances that permit more procedures to be performed outside the hospital. Some job openings will also arise from the need to replace technologists who leave the occupation.

Earnings

Median annual earnings of radiologic technologists and technicians were $32,880 in 1998. The middle 50 percent earned between $27,560 and $39,420 a year. The lowest 10 percent earned less than $23,650 and the highest 10 percent earned more than $47,610 a year.

RADIOLOGIC TECHNOLOGISTS

Don't forget! Refer to the general resources listed in Chapter Three. Check the resources for nuclear medicine technologists, too.

⚕ Association   📖 Book   🗁 Directory   ⌂ Internet (Web) Site
📱 Job Ads   📧 E-mail/Hotline   📂 Job Fairs   📇 Resume Service

📱⌂ **ADVANCE Newsmagazines** - Publishes *ADVANCE for Radiologic Science Professionals* and *ADVANCE for Administrators in Radiation and Radiation Oncology,* free for professionals, numerous job ads. Located at 650 Park Avenue West, Box 61556, King of Prussia, PA 19406-0956; 800/355-1088, (**http://www.merion.com/sitemap.html**).

⚕ **American Healthcare Radiology Administrator** - 111 Boston Post Rd., Suite 105, P.O. Box 334, Sudbury, MA 01776. For career information, enclose a stamped, self-addressed business size envelope with your request.

⚕📱⌂ **American Institute of Ultrasound in Medicine (AIUM)** - 14750 Sweitzer Lane, Suite 100, Laurel, MD 20707; 301/498-4100, fax: 301/498-4450, (**http://www.aium.org**). *Journal of Ultrasound in Medicine* is issued monthly, $230/yr, and has about 5 jobs ads per issue. Membership consists of more than 9,500 physicians, scientists, engineers, veterinarians, sonographers, technicians, manufacturers, manufacturers' representatives, and medical students. Student membership $50.

⚕📱⌂ **American Registry of Diagnostic Medical Sonographers Directory (ARDMS)** - Suite 360, 600 Jefferson Plaza, Rockville, MD 20852-1150; 301/738-8401, 800/541-9754, fax: 301/738-0312/0313. E-mail for information services: ezigbo@ardms.org. Their Web site at (**http://www.ardms.org**) has job ads Webfor: diagnostic medical sonographers, diagnostic cardiac sonographers, vascular technologists and ophthalmic ultrasound biometrists.

⚕🗁⌂ **American Registry of Radiologic Technologists (ARRT)** - 1255 Northland Drive, St. Paul, MN 55120; 651/687-0048, URL (**http://www.arrt.org**). Directory of Registered Technologists, published every two years. National certifying org. for radiation therapy and radiography and nuclear med. Hand book about exams free.

✼📱⌁ **American Society of Echocardiography** - 4101 Lake Boone Trail, Suite 201, Raleigh, NC 27607; 919/787-5181, fax: 919/787-4916, URL (http://asecho.org). There are 2-3 pages of ads for cardiac sonographers in each issue of the *Journal of American Society of Echocardiography*, published by Mosby. Career in diagnostic medical sonography brochure is available.

✼📱⌁ **American Society of Radiologic Technologists (ASRT)** - 15000 Central Avenue SE, Albuquerque, NM 87123-3917; 800/444-2778, 505/298-4500, fax: 505/298-5063, faxback: 505/298-4500, ext. 298, URL (http://www.asrt.org). *ASRT Scanner*, monthly magazine for members only, has 15-20 job ads per issue. Career information is available on web site.

✼⌁ **Intersocietal Commission for the Accreditation of Echocardiography Laboratories** - (http://www.icael.org) Home site for the ICAEL, echocardiography laboratory accreditation materials and information.

✼🗁 **Joint Review Committee On Education in Diagnostic Medical Sonography** - 7108 S. Alton Way, Bldg C, Englewood, CO 80112; 303/741-3533). Free list of accredited programs in the U.S. (http://www.rit.edu/~hhgscl).

✼📱🗁⌁ **Radiological Society of North America (RSNA)** - 820 Jorie Blvd., Oak Brook, IL 60521; 630/571-2670, fax: 630/571-7837, (http://www.rsna.org). Publishes membership directory. Web site has links to hospitals and university departments of radiological sciences.

📱 **RT IMAGE** - Valley Forge Press, 1041 West Bridge Street, Suite 6, Phoenixville, PA 19460; 610/935-3302, 800/9-VF-PRES. Biweekly publication, free to professionals and students, has many employment ads for radiologic science professionals, educators and administrators.

✼📱🗁⌁ **Society of Diagnostic Medical Sonographers (SDMS)** - 12770 Coit Rd., Suite 708, Dallas, Texas 75251; 972/239-7367, 800/229-9506, fax: 972/239-7378, (http://www.sdms.org). Over 99% of members are sonographers - non-physicians using ultrasound. *Journal of Diagnostic Medical Sonography (JDMS)*, 6/year, is free to members, $107 non-members, with 10-15 job ads per issue. Newsletter also has ads.

SURGICAL TECHNOLOGISTS

Nature of the Work

Surgical technologists, also called surgical or operating room technicians, assist in operations under the supervision of surgeons, registered nurses, or other surgical personnel. Before an operation, surgical technologists help set up the operating room with surgical instruments and equipment, sterile linens, and sterile solutions. They assemble, adjust, and check nonsterile equipment to ensure it is working properly. Technologists also prepare patients for surgery by washing, shaving, and disinfecting incision sites. They transport patients to the operating room, help position them on the operating table, and cover them with sterile surgical "drapes." Technologists also observe patients' vital signs, check charts, and help the surgical team scrub and put on gloves, gowns, and masks.

During surgery, technologists pass instruments and other sterile supplies to surgeons and surgeon assistants. They may hold retractors, cut sutures, and help count sponges, needles, supplies, and instruments. Surgical technologists help prepare, care for, and dispose of specimens taken for laboratory analysis and may help apply dressings. Some operate sterilizers, lights, or suction machines, and help operate diagnostic equipment. Technologists may also maintain supplies of fluids, such as plasma and blood.

After an operation, surgical technologists may help transfer patients to the recovery room and clean and restock the operating room.

Working Conditions

Surgical technologists work in clean, well-lighted, cool environments. They must stand for long periods and remain alert during operations. At times they may be exposed to communicable diseases and unpleasant sights, odors, and materials.

Most surgical technologists work a regular 40-hour week, although they may be on call or work nights, weekends and holidays on a rotating basis.

Employment

Surgical technologists held about 54,000 jobs in 1998. Most are employed by hospitals, mainly in operating and delivery rooms. Others are employed in clinics and surgical centers, and in the offices of physicians and dentists who perform outpatient surgery. A few, known as private scrubs, are employed directly by surgeons who have special surgical teams like those for liver transplants.

Training, Other Qualifications, and Advancement

Surgical technologists receive their training in formal programs offered by community and junior colleges, vocational schools, universities, hospitals, and the military. In 1998, the Commission on Accreditation of Allied Health Education Programs (CAAHEP) recognized 165 accredited programs. High school graduation normally is required for admission. Programs last 9 to 24 months and lead to a certificate, diploma, or associate degree. Shorter programs are designed for students who are already licensed practical nurses or military personnel with the appropriate training.

Programs provide classroom education and supervised clinical experience. Students take courses in anatomy, physiology, microbiology, pharmacology, professional ethics, and medical terminology. Other studies cover the care and safety of patients during surgery, aseptic techniques, and surgical procedures. Students also learn to sterilize instruments; prevent and control infection; and handle special drugs, solutions, supplies, and equipment.

Technologists may obtain voluntary professional certification from the Liaison Council on Certification for the Surgical Technologist by graduating from a formal program and passing a national certification examination. They may then use the designation Certified Surgical Technologist, or CST. Continuing education or reexamination is required to maintain certification, which must be renewed every 6 years. Graduation from a CAAHEP-accredited program will be a prerequisite for certification by March 2000. Most employers prefer to hire certified technologists.

Surgical technologists need manual dexterity to handle instruments quickly. They also must be conscientious, orderly, and emotionally stable to handle the demands of the operating room environment. Technologists must respond quickly and know procedures well to have instruments ready for surgeons without having to be told. They are expected to keep abreast of new developments in the field. Recommended high school courses include health, biology, chemistry, and mathematics.

Technologists advance by specializing in a particular area of surgery, such as neurosurgery or open heart surgery. They may also work as circulating technologists. A circulating technologist is the "unsterile" member of the surgical team who prepares patients; helps with anesthesia; gets, opens, and holds packages for the "sterile" persons during the procedure; interviews the patient before surgery; keeps a written account of the surgical procedure; and answers the surgeon's questions about the patient during the surgery. With additional training, some technologists advance to first assistants, who help with retracting, sponging, suturing, cauterizing bleeders, and closing and treating wounds. Some surgical technologists manage central supply departments in hospitals, or take positions with insurance companies, sterile supply services, and operating equipment firms.

Job Outlook

Employment of surgical technologists is expected to grow much faster than the average for all occupations through the year 2008 as the volume of surgery increases. The number of surgical procedures is expected to rise as the population grows and ages. As the "baby boom" generation enters retirement age, the over 50 population will account for a larger portion of the general population. Older people require more surgical procedures. Technological advances, such as fiber optics and laser technology, will also permit new surgical procedures to be performed.

Hospitals will continue to be the primary employer of surgical technologists, although much faster employment growth is expected in offices and clinics of physicians, including ambulatory surgical centers.

Earnings

Median annual earnings of surgical technologists were $25,780 in 1998. The middle 50 percent earned between $22,040 and $30,230 a year. The lowest 10 percent earned less than $18,930 and the highest 10 percent earned more than $35,020 a year.

SURGICAL TECHNOLOGISTS

Don't forget! Refer to the general resources listed in Chapter Three.

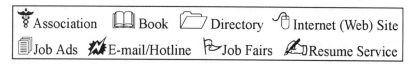

ADVANCE Newsmagazines - Publishes *ADVANCE for Physician Assistants,* free for professionals, numerous job ads. Located at 650 Park Avenue West, Box 61556, King of Prussia, PA 19406-0956; 800/355-1088, (**http://www.merion.com/sitemap.html**).

American Association of Surgical Physician Assistants - PO Box 867, Bernardsville, NJ 07924; 888/882-2772, fax: 732/805-9582, (**http://www.aaspa.org**). Publishes *The Sutureline.* Lists schools with Surgical Physician Assistant programs, including graduate degrees.

American Society of Extra-Corporeal Technology (AMSECT) - 11480 Sunset Hills Road, Suite 210E, Reston, VA 22090; 703/435-8556. (**http://www.amsect.org**) Members are perfusionists, technologists, physicians and nurses that apply extracorporeal technology, the use of heart-lung machines. Information on the profession is on the web site. Offers free placement service for perfusionist members.

Association of Surgical Technologists (AST) - 7108-C S. Alton Way, Englewood, CO 80112; 303/694-9130, 303/694-9169. (**http://www.ast.org**, E-mail: memserv@ast.org) Membership for certified and uncertified technologists. Prepares members for certification. *The Surgical Technologist,* monthly, members free, nonmembers $36/year. Career brochure. Placement service is free for members. Description of career is on the web site.

Liaison Council on Certification for the Surgical Technologist - 7790 East Arapahoe Rd., Suite 240, Englewood, CO 80112-1274. Contact for information on certification.

Chapter

5

HEALTH TECHNICIANS

Patrick Cavanaugh

Patrick Cavanaugh, a certified Paramedic for the Valley Ambulance Authority in Coraopolis, Pennsylvania, began his emergency medical career as an EMT, Emergency Medical Technician. "The differences between an EMT and paramedic are that an EMT can do the splinting of fractures, basic health care, administer CPR, and apply other basic medical procedures," Cavanaugh said. "A paramedic can do more invasive treatment such as starting intravenous fluids, administer drugs, apply heart monitors, and other medical devices. A paramedic functions as the eyes and ears of the doctor in the field."

Training for an EMT is approximately four to five months of class work along with time on the emergency vehicles. Paramedics require eleven months of classroom time plus 200 hours of hospital and emergency vehicle time to obtain certification. Pat said, " All paramedics and EMTs must attend refresher training every month. Hospitals also monitor our activities to insure that we perform a set number of medical procedures each quarter. A minimum number of medical procedures must be completed to retain certification."

Pat recently turned 24 and after 2 ½ years as field paramedic he was promoted to a supervisory position, two days after this interview.

One of the drawbacks of this field are the physical demands placed on EMTs and paramedics. Pat said, "Everyone must pass a lifting test that simulates hoisting a 200-pound stretcher bound patient into an emergency vehicle." Other concerns are over the spread of highly contagious diseases. Paramedics and EMTs are trained to use special protective equipment and they all receive hepatitis immunizations.

Pat said, "This is a good field with excellent potential. Start as an EMT with a reputable company and get as much experience as you can. Then move on to paramedic classes. The best opportunities are in the bigger cities were they have significant turnover."

This chapter features health care technicians. The major occupational groups are:

Dental Hygienists   **Emergency Medical Technicians**
Dental Laboratory Technicians   **Health Information Technicians**
Dispensing Opticians   **Ophthalmic Lab Technicians**

Each specialty is described below. Occupational groups are divided into primary and related occupations so that individuals can investigate other fields for additional job opportunities.

Following each job description are job resource lists: Associations, Books, Directories, Internet Sites, Job Ads, E-mail Job Notification/Job Hotlines, Job Fairs, and Resume/Placement Services with icons to guide you.

DENTAL HYGIENISTS

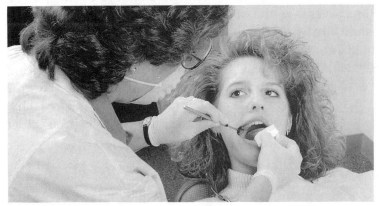

Registered dental hygienist performing an oral exam.
The American Dental Hygienist' Association

Dental hygienists are projected to be one of the 30 fastest growing occupations.

Nature of the Work

Dental hygienists clean teeth and provide other preventive dental care, as well as teach patients how to practice good oral hygiene. Hygienists examine patients' teeth and gums, recording the presence of diseases or abnormalities. They remove calculus, stains, and plaque from teeth; take and develop dental x rays; and apply cavity preventive agents such as fluorides and pit and fissure sealants. In some States, hygienists administer local anesthetics and anesthetic gas; place and carve filling materials, temporary fillings, and periodontal dressings; remove sutures; and smooth and polish metal restorations.

Dental hygienists also help patients develop and maintain good oral health. For example, they may explain the relationship between diet and oral health, inform patients how to select toothbrushes, and show patients how to brush and floss their teeth.

Dental hygienists use hand and rotary instruments, lasers, and ultrasonics to clean teeth; x-ray machines to take dental pictures; syringes with needles to administer local anesthetics; and models of teeth to explain oral hygiene.

Working Conditions

Flexible scheduling is a distinctive feature of this job. Full-time, part-time, evening, and weekend work is widely available. Dentists frequently hire hygienists to work only 2 or 3 days a week, so hygienists may hold jobs in more than one dental office. Dental hygienists work in clean, well-lighted offices. Important health safeguards include strict adherence to proper radiological procedures, and use of appropriate protective devices when administering anesthetic gas. Dental hygienists also wear safety glasses, surgical masks, and gloves to protect themselves from infectious diseases.

Employment

Dental hygienists held about 143,000 jobs in 1998. Because multiple job holding is common in this field, the number of jobs exceeds the number of hygienists. About 3 out of 5 dental hygienists worked part time—less than 35 hours a week.

Almost all dental hygienists work in private dental offices. Some work in public health agencies, hospitals, and clinics.

Training, Other Qualifications, and Advancement

Dental hygienists must be licensed by the State in which they practice. To qualify for licensure, a candidate must graduate from an accredited dental hygiene school and pass both a written and clinical examination. The American Dental Association Joint Commission on National Dental Examinations administers the written examination accepted by all States and the District of Columbia. State or regional testing agencies administer the clinical examination. In addition, most States require an examination on legal aspects of dental hygiene practice. Alabama allows candidates to take its examinations if they have been trained through a State-regulated on-the-job program in a dentist's office.

In 1999, the Commission on Dental Accreditation accredited about 250 programs in dental hygiene. Although some programs lead to a bachelor's degree, most grant an associate degree. Thirteen universities offer master's degree programs in dental hygiene or a related area.

An associate degree is sufficient for practice in a private dental office. A bachelor's or master's degree is usually required for research, teaching, or clinical practice in public or school health programs.

About half of the dental hygiene programs prefer applicants who have completed at least 1 year of college. However, requirements vary from school to school. Schools offer laboratory, clinical, and classroom instruction in subjects such as anatomy, physiology, chemistry, microbiology, pharmacology, nutrition, radiography, histology (the study of tissue structure), periodontology (the study of gum diseases), pathology, dental materials, clinical dental hygiene, and social and behavioral sciences.

Dental hygienists should work well with others and must have good manual dexterity because they use dental instruments within a patient's mouth with little room for error. High school students interested in becoming a dental hygienist should take courses in biology, chemistry, and mathematics.

Job Outlook

Employment of dental hygienists is expected to grow much faster than the average for all occupations through 2008, in response to increasing demand for dental care and the greater substitution of hygienists for services previously performed by dentists. Job prospects are expected to remain very good unless the number of dental hygienist program graduates grows much faster than during the last decade, and results in a much larger pool of qualified applicants.

Population growth and greater retention of natural teeth will stimulate demand for dental hygienists. Older dentists, who are less likely to employ dental hygienists, will leave and be replaced by recent graduates, who are more likely to do so. In addition, as dentists' workloads increase, they are expected to hire more hygienists to perform preventive dental care such as cleaning.

Earnings

Median hourly earnings of dental hygienists were $22.06 in 1998. The middle 50 percent earned between $17.28 and $29.28 an hour. The lowest 10 percent earned less than $12.37 and the highest 10 percent earned more than $38.81 an hour. Benefits vary substantially by practice setting, and may be contingent upon full-time employment. Dental hygienists who work for school systems, public health agencies, the Federal Government, or State agencies usually have substantial benefits.

The State Board of Dental Examiners in each State can supply information on licensing requirements.

Resources for Dental Hygienists and Dental Laboratory Techs are combined. See the end of the Dental Laboratory Technicians section.

DENTAL LABORATORY TECHNICIANS

Nature of the Work

Dental laboratory technicians fill prescriptions from dentists for crowns, bridges, dentures, and other dental prosthetics. First, dentists send a specification of the item to be fabricated, along with an impression (mold) of the patient's mouth or teeth. Then dental laboratory technicians, also called dental technicians, create a model of the patient's mouth, by pouring plaster into the impression and allowing it to set. Next, they place the model on an apparatus that mimics the bite and movement of the patient's jaw. The model serves as the basis of the prosthetic device. Technicians examine the model, noting the size and shape of the adjacent teeth, as well as gaps within the gumline. Based upon these observations and the dentist's specifications, technicians build and shape a wax tooth or teeth model, using small hand instruments called wax spatulas and wax carvers. They use this wax model to cast the metal framework for the prosthetic device.

Once the wax tooth has been formed, dental technicians pour the cast and form the metal, and using small hand-held tools, prepare the surface to allow the metal and porcelain to bond. They then apply porcelain in layers, to arrive at the precise shape and color of a tooth. Technicians place the tooth in a porcelain furnace to bake the porcelain onto the metal framework, then adjust the shape and color, with subsequent grinding and addition of porcelain to achieve a sealed finish. The final product is a near exact replica of the lost tooth or teeth.

In some laboratories, technicians perform all stages of the work, whereas in other labs, each technician does only a few. Dental laboratory technicians can specialize in one of five areas: Orthodontic appliances, crowns and bridges, complete dentures, partial dentures, or ceramics. Job titles can reflect specialization in these areas. For example, technicians who make porcelain and acrylic restorations are called dental ceramists.

Working Conditions

Dental laboratory technicians generally work in clean, well lighted, and well-ventilated areas. Technicians usually have their own workbenches, which can be equipped with Bunsen burners, grinding and polishing equipment, and hand instruments, such as wax spatulas and wax carvers.

The work is extremely delicate and time consuming. Salaried technicians usually work 40 hours a week, but self-employed technicians frequently work longer hours.

Employment
Dental laboratory technicians held about 44,000 jobs in 1998. Most jobs were in commercial dental laboratories, which usually are small, privately owned businesses with fewer than five employees. However, some laboratories are large; a few employ over 50 technicians.

Some dental laboratory technicians worked in dentists' offices. Others worked for hospitals providing dental services, including Department of Veterans Affairs' hospitals. Some technicians work in dental laboratories in their homes, in addition to their regular job. Approximately 1 technician in 5 is self-employed, a higher proportion than in most other occupations.

Training, Other Qualifications, and Advancement
Most dental laboratory technicians learn their craft on the job. They begin with simple tasks, such as pouring plaster into an impression, and progress to more complex procedures, such as making porcelain crowns and bridges. Becoming a fully trained technician requires an average of 3 to 4 years, depending upon the individual's aptitude and ambition; but it may take a few years more to become an accomplished technician.

Training in dental laboratory technology is also available through community and junior colleges, vocational-technical institutes, and the Armed Forces. Formal training programs vary greatly both in length and the level of skill they impart.

In 1998, 34 programs in dental laboratory technology were approved (accredited) by the Commission on Dental Accreditation in conjunction with the American Dental Association (ADA). These programs provide classroom instruction in dental materials science, oral anatomy, fabrication procedures, ethics, and related subjects. In addition, each student is given supervised practical experience in a school or an associated dental laboratory. Accredited programs normally take 2 years to complete and lead to an associate degree.

Graduates of 2-year training programs need additional hands-on experience to become fully qualified. Each dental laboratory owner operates in a different way, and classroom instruction does not necessarily expose students to techniques and procedures favored by individual laboratory owners. Students who have taken enough courses to learn the basics of the craft are usually considered good candidates for training, regardless of whether they have completed a formal program. Many employers will train someone without any classroom experience.

The National Board offers certification, which is voluntary, in five specialty areas: crowns and bridges, ceramics, partial dentures, complete dentures, and orthodontic appliances.

In large dental laboratories, technicians may become supervisors or managers. Experienced technicians may teach or take jobs with dental suppliers in such areas as product development, marketing, and sales. Still, for most technicians, opening one's own laboratory is the way toward advancement and higher earnings.

A high degree of manual dexterity, good vision, and the ability to recognize very fine color shadings and variations in shape are necessary. An artistic aptitude for detailed and precise work is also important. High school students interested in becoming dental laboratory technicians should take courses in art, metal and wood shop, drafting, and sciences. Courses in management and business may help those wishing to operate their own laboratories.

Job Outlook

Job opportunities for dental laboratory technicians should be favorable, despite very slow growth in the occupation. Employers have difficulty filling trainee positions, probably because of relatively low entry-level salaries and lack of familiarity with the occupation.

Although job opportunities are favorable, little or no change in the employment of dental laboratory technicians is expected through the year 2008, due to changes in dental care. The overall dental health of the population has improved because of fluoridation of drinking water, which has reduced the incidence of dental cavities, and greater emphasis on preventive dental care since the early-1960s. As a result, full dentures will be less common, as most people will need only a bridge or crown. However, during the last few years, demand has arisen from an aging public that is growing increasingly interested in cosmetic prosthesis. For example, many dental laboratories are filling orders for composite fillings that are white and look like a natural tooth to replace older, less attractive fillings.

Earnings

Median annual earnings of salaried precision dental laboratory technicians were $25,660 in 1998. The middle 50 percent earned between

$19,410 and $34,600 a year. The lowest 10 percent earned less than $14,720 and the highest 10 percent earned more than $45,980 a year. Median annual earnings of dental laboratory technicians in 1997 were $24,100 in medical and dental laboratories and $25,500 in offices and clinics of dentists.

In general, earnings of self-employed technicians exceed those of salaried workers. Technicians in large laboratories tend to specialize in a few procedures, and, therefore, tend to be paid a lower wage than those employed in small laboratories that perform a variety of tasks.

Resources for Dental Hygienists & Dental Laboratory Techs are combined.

DENTAL HYGIENISTS and
DENTAL LABORATORY TECHNICIANS

Don't forget! Refer to the general resources listed in Chapter Three. Check the dentists resources section in Chapter Nine for more directories.

Association Book Directory Internet (Web) Site
Job Ads E-mail/Hotline Job Fairs Resume Service

American Academy of Dental Group Practice (2525 E. Arizona Biltmore Circle, Suite 127 , Phoenix, AZ 85016; 602/381-1185, fax: 602/381-1093, **http://www.aadgp.org,** E-mail: info@aadgp.org). Members comprised of dentists and dental group practices. Publishes membership directory, $50 to nonmembers.

American Academy of Pediatric Dentistry (211 E. Chicago Avenue, Suite 700, Chicago, Illinois 60611-2663; 312/337-2169, fax 312/337-6329. **http://www.aapd.org**). *American Academy of Pediatric Dentistry Membership Roster,* online for members, provides names and addresses for over 4,600 pediatric dentists. First year membership free to students. Online job ads available to public.

American Association of Dental Schools (AADS) - 1625 Massachusetts Avenue NW, Suite 600, Washington, DC 20036-2212; 202/667-9433, fax: 202/667-0642; **http://www.aads.jhu.edu**, (E-mail: aads@aads.jhu.edu). Members consist of all U.S. and Canadian dental schools, dental education programs and corporations.

American Association of Public Health Dentistry (AAPHD) - 3760 SW Lyle Court, Portland OR. 97221; 503/242-0721, fax: 503/242-0721; (**http://www.pitt.edu/~aaphd**). E-mail natoff@aol.com Organization of dentists and dental hygienists. Membership directory online for members only. Student membership $35. Extensive collection of links.

American Dental Assistant Association - 203 North Lasalle Street, Suite 1320, Chicago, IL 60601-1225; 800/SEE-ADAA, 312/541-1550, fax: 312/541-1496, **http://dentalassistant.org**, E-mail: adaa1@aol.com. *The Dental Assistant Journal*, has 2-3 job ads/issue single issue $6. Internet posting of jobs free to public.

American Dental Association (ADA) - 211 E. Chicago Ave., Chicago, IL 60611; 312/440-2500, fax: 312/440-2800. Offers extensive services to members. Visit their Web site at (**http://www.ada.org**). *American Dental Directory* lists over 141,000 dentists. Web site lists dental associations by state and has excellent links to dental organizations and to Internet search engines. Other Web resources include the Online Career Recruitment Brochure, dental hygiene education facts, dental hygiene licensure facts, classified ads and public health dental hygiene.

American Dental Hygienists' Association (ADHA) - 444 N. Michigan Ave., Suite 3400, Chicago, IL 60611; 312/440-8900; **http://www.adha.org**, E-mail: mail@adha.net). Offers numerous services to members through 375 local chapters, 53 state chapters, and 12 districts. Represents almost 100,000 registered hygienists (RDHs) nationwide. Publishes *Journal of Dental Hygiene*, monthly, free to members. Classifieds section. *Access* 10 issues/yr., free to members, about 5 positions advertised.

America's Finest Dentist Directory This Web site can assist in locating a dentist in your area. Search by state, city and specialty at (**http://www.afdd.com/index.htm**).

Commission on Dental Accreditation, American Dental Association - 211 E. Chicago Ave., Chicago, IL 60611. Contact for infor-mation on certification. Internet: **http://www.ada.org**.

Connecticut Dental Hygienists' Association - 62 Russ St., Hartford, Connecticut 06106; 860/278-5550, fax: 860/244-8287. Web site (**http://www.csda.com**) has information on dental Listservs (e-mail lists) and dental hygiene schools.

⌐⁷ **dentalbytes magEzine** (http://www.dentalbytes.com) Produced by dental bytes, 4319 Medical Drive, Suite 131-135 ,San Antonio, Texas 78229. Excellent site for anyone in the dental field.

▤⌐⁷ **DentalGlobe** (http://dentalglobe.com) This Web site has information on education, student resources and job ads at no charge for dentists and dental hygienists with phone and E-mail addresses for employers. It also has links to dental labs, schools, associations, publications and companies. Provides bulletin boards/chat.

⌐⁷ **Dental Icon - http://www.dentalicon.com** The Dental Yellow List allows searches for any dental product, company or service, including labs. Associated with the American Dentist Guide, a source of information about dentists in Canada, Mexico, and the U.S. at **http://www.dentistguide.com.** This site has links to placement services.

▤⌐⁷ **DentalLogic.com** (http://www.dentallogic.com) Created and maintained by: Stephen J. Charnitski D.M.D. and Robert W. Beadle D.D.S., this site lists dental laboratories and manufacturers, and a wide range of employment ads.

⚕⌐⁷ **Dental Manufacturers of America, Inc.** (Fidelity Building, Suite 2030, 123 South Broad Street, Philadelphia, PA 19109-1020; 215/731-9975, 215/731-9982, fax: 215/731-9984, **http://www.dmanews.org**, E-mail: staff@dmanews.org. The Web site has a member directory.

⌐⁷ **Dental Related Internet Resources** List of dental Listservs (e-mail lists), educational institutions, labs, associations and dental practices. Their URL is(**http://www.dental-resources.com.**

▤⌐⁷ **The Dental Site** (http://www.dentalsite.com) Excellent site for dental patients, dentists, dental assistants, dental hygienists, dental technicians and dental vendors. It has a directory of dental laboratories, links to education, publications, directories, job sources.

▤⁷ **Dental Technology Home Page** Information on subscribing to a Dental Lab Mailing List, a chat channel and a positions available section. URL: **http://scribers.midwest.net/landuze.**

▤⌐✐⁷ **Dental-X-Change** (http://dentalxchange.odont.com) This site has a Companies section which includes laboratories, the Classifieds section has job ads, and you can post your resume free and create a search agent.

Dentist Directory (http://www.dentistdirectory.com) A search engine to locate dentists nationwide.

Dentistinfo.com (853 Sanders Road, Suite 252, Northbrook, IL 60062; 847/564-5329, fax: 847/564-5328, http://www .dentistinfo.com, E-mail: drtooth@dentistinfo.com). Web site has Find a Dentist section and a Job Search section for dentists, hygienists, assistants and sales reps, where you can place a "position wanted" ad free.

Educational Resources (http://www.nyu.edu/Dental/ed.html) Links to U.S. training programs for dental hygienists, dental assistants, dental technologists and to U.S. dentistry associations, including computerized dentistry.

EINet Galaxy - Dental Resources by Specialty Extensive links to information including dental practices. Visit their URL at (http://galaxy.einet.net/galaxy/Medicine/Dentistry.html).

Exploring Careers in Dentistry by Jessica A. Rickert. $16.95. Published by The Rosen Publishing Group, Inc., 29 East 21st St., New York, NY, 10010; 800/237-9932, fax: 888/436-4643. E-mail: rosenpub@tribeca.ios.com.

Guide to Careers in Dentistry Provided by the University of North Carolina at Chapel Hill School of Dentistry. Visit their Web site at (http://www.dent.unc.edu/careers/cidtoc.htm).

National Association of Dental Laboratories (NADL) - 8201 Greensboro Drive, Suite 300, McLean, Virginia 22102; 703/610-9035, 800/950-1150, fax: 703/610-9005. (http:\\www.nadl.org, E-mail: nadl@nadl.org) Organization comprised of state associations representing over 3100 dental laboratories. National Board for Certification certifies lab and technicians. *Journal of Dental Technology* contains 15-20 job ads. $40 for nonmembers, $6 sample issue.

National Board for Certification in Dental Technology, 8201 Greensboro Dr., Suite 300, McLean VA 22101. Contact for information on requirements for certification. The State Board of Dental Examiners in each State can also supply information on licensing requirement.

National Center for Dental Hygiene Research Thomas Jefferson University sponsors this informative site at URL (http://jeffline.tju.edu/DHNet). One page has a list of dental hygiene programs with Web sites.

⌐⍾ **The Tooth Fairy (http://www.toothfairy.org)** Lots of good links for dental hygienists.

⌐⍾ **University of Pittsburgh (http://www.pitt.edu/~cbw/dental.html)** This is an excellent starting point for an Internet search involving the dental profession.

▤⌂⌐⍾ **WebDental (http://www.webdental.com)** Links to Web sites of many dental labs. Classified section allows you to view job ads or post jobs wanted. Links to publications, education and more.

DISPENSING OPTICIANS

Nature of the Work

Dispensing opticians fit eyeglasses and contact lenses, following prescriptions written by ophthalmologists or optometrists and they examine written prescriptions to determine lens specifications. They recommend eyeglass frames, lenses, and lens coatings after considering the prescription and the customer's occupation, habits, and facial features. Dispensing opticians measure clients' eyes, including the distance between the centers of the pupils and the distance between the eye surface and the lens. For customers without prescriptions, dispensing opticians may use a lensometer to record the present eyeglass prescription. They also may obtain a customer's previous record, or verify a prescription with the examining optometrist or ophthalmologist.

Dispensing opticians prepare work orders that give ophthalmic laboratory technicians information needed to grind and insert lenses into a frame. The work order includes lens prescriptions and information on lens size, material, color, and style. Some dispensing opticians grind and insert lenses themselves. After the glasses are made, dispensing opticians verify that the lenses have been ground to specifications. Then they may reshape or bend the frame, by hand or using pliers, so that the eyeglasses fit the customer properly and comfortably. Some also fix, adjust, and refit broken frames. They instruct clients about adapting to, wearing, or caring for eyeglasses.

Some dispensing opticians specialize in fitting contacts, artificial eyes, or cosmetic shells to cover blemished eyes. To fit contact lenses, dispensing opticians measure eye shape and size, select the type of contact lens material, and prepare work orders specifying the prescription and lens size. Fitting contact lenses requires considerable skill, care, and patience. Dispensing opticians observe customers' eyes, corneas, lids, and contact lenses with special instruments and microscopes. During several visits, opticians show customers how to insert, remove, and care for their contacts, and ensure the fit is correct.

Dispensing opticians keep records on customer prescriptions, work orders, and payments; track inventory and sales; and perform other administrative duties.

Working Conditions

Dispensing opticians work indoors in attractive, well-lighted, and well-ventilated surroundings. They may work in medical offices or small stores where customers are served one at a time, or in large stores where several dispensing opticians serve a number of customers at once. Opticians spend a lot of time on their feet. If they prepare lenses, they need to take precautions against the hazards associated with glass cutting, chemicals, and machinery.

Most dispensing opticians work a 40-hour week, although some work longer hours. Those in retail stores may work evenings and weekends. Some work part-time.

Employment

Dispensing opticians held about 71,000 jobs in 1998. About 50 percent worked for ophthalmologists or optometrists who sell glasses directly to patients. Many also work in retail optical stores that offer one-stop shopping. Customers may have their eyes examined, choose frames, and have glasses made on the spot. Some work in optical departments of drug and department stores.

Training, Other Qualifications, and Advancement

Employers usually hire individuals with no background in opticianry or those who have worked as ophthalmic laboratory technicians and then provide the required training. (See the statement on ophthalmic laboratory technicians elsewhere in the Handbook.) Training may be informal, on-the-job or formal apprenticeship. Some employers, however, seek people with postsecondary training in opticianry.

Knowledge of physics, basic anatomy, algebra, geometry, and mechanical drawing is particularly valuable because training usually includes instruction in optical mathematics, optical physics, and the use of precision measuring instruments and other machinery and tools. Dispensing opticians deal directly with the public so they should be tactful, pleasant, and communicate well. Manual dexterity and the ability to do precision work are essential.

Large employers usually offer structured apprenticeship programs, and small employers provide more informal on-the-job training. In the 21 States that offer a license to dispensing opticians, individuals without postsecondary training work from 2 to 4 years as apprentices. Apprenticeship or formal training is offered in most States as well.

Apprentices receive technical training and learn office management and sales. Under the supervision of an experienced optician, optometrist, or ophthalmologist, apprentices work directly with patients, fitting eyeglasses and contact lenses. In the 21 States requiring licensure, information about apprenticeships and licensing procedures is available from the State board of occupational licensing.

Formal opticianry training is offered in community colleges and a few colleges and universities. In 1999, there were 25 programs accredited by the Commission on Opticianry Accreditation that awarded 2-year associate degrees in ophthalmic dispensing or optometric technology. There are also shorter programs of one year or less. Some States that offer a license to dispensing opticians allow graduates to take the licensure exam immediately upon graduation; others require a few months to a year of experience.

Dispensing opticians may apply to the American Board of Opticianry and the National Contact Lens Examiners for certification of their skills. Certification must be renewed every 3 years through continuing education.

Many experienced dispensing opticians open their own optical stores. Others become managers of optical stores or sales representatives for wholesalers or manufacturers of eyeglasses or lenses.

Job Outlook

Employment in this occupation is expected to increase as fast as the average for all occupations through 2008 as demand grows for corrective lenses. The number of middle-aged and elderly persons is projected to increase rapidly. Middle age is a time when many individuals use corrective lenses for the first time, and elderly persons require more vision care, on the whole, than others.

The need to replace those who leave the occupation will result in job openings. Nevertheless, the total number of job openings will be relatively small because the occupation is small. This occupation is vulnerable to changes in the business cycle because eyewear purchases can often be deferred for a time.

Earnings
Median annual earnings of dispensing opticians were $22,440 in 1998. The middle 50 percent earned between $17,680 and $28,560 a year. The lowest 10 percent earned less than $14,240 and the highest 10 percent earned more than $37,080 a year.

Resources for Dispensing Opticians and Ophthalmic Laboratory Technicians are combined as resources serve both professions. See the end of the Ophthalmic Laboratory Technicians section.

OPHTHALMIC LABORATORY TECHNICIANS

Nature of the Work
Ophthalmic laboratory technicians — also known as manufacturing opticians, optical mechanics, or optical goods workers—make prescription eyeglass lenses. Prescription lenses are curved in such a way that light is correctly focused onto the retina of the patient's eye, improving vision. Some ophthalmic laboratory technicians manufacture lenses for other optical instruments, such as telescopes and binoculars. Ophthalmic laboratory technicians cut, grind, edge, and finish lenses according to specifications provided by dispensing opticians, optometrists, or ophthalmologists, and may insert lenses into frames to produce finished glasses. Although some lenses are still produced by hand, technicians increasingly use automated equipment to make lenses.

Ophthalmic laboratory technicians should not be confused with workers in other vision care occupations. Ophthalmologists and optometrists are "eye doctors" who examine eyes, diagnose and treat vision problems, and prescribe corrective lenses. Ophthalmologists are physicians who perform eye surgery. Dispensing opticians, who may also do work described here, help patients select frames and lenses, and adjust finished eyeglasses. (See the statement on physicians, which includes ophthalmologists, and the statements on optometrists and dispensing opticians elsewhere in the Handbook.)

Ophthalmic laboratory technicians read prescription specifications, then select standard glass or plastic lens blanks and mark them to indicate where the curves specified on the prescription should be ground. They place the lens into the lens grinder, set the dials for the prescribed curvature, and start the machine. After a minute or so, the lens is ready to be "finished" by a machine that rotates it against a fine abrasive to grind it and smooth out rough edges. The lens is then placed in a polishing machine with an even finer abrasive, to polish it to a smooth, bright finish.

Next, the technician examines the lens through a lensometer, an instrument similar in shape to a microscope, to make sure the degree and placement of the curve is correct. The technician then cuts the lenses and bevels the edges to fit the frame, dips each lens into dye if the prescription calls for tinted or coated lenses, polishes the edges, and assembles the lenses and frame parts into a finished pair of glasses.

Working Conditions

Ophthalmic laboratory technicians work in relatively clean and well-lighted laboratories and have limited contact with the public. Surroundings are relatively quiet despite the humming of machines. At times, technicians wear goggles to protect their eyes, and may spend a great deal of time standing.

Most ophthalmic laboratory technicians work a 5-day, 40-hour week, which may include weekends, evenings, or occasionally, some overtime. Some work part time.

Ophthalmic laboratory technicians need to take precautions against the hazards associated with cutting glass, handling chemicals, and working near machinery.

Employment

Ophthalmic laboratory technicians held about 23,000 jobs in 1998. Thirty-three percent were in retail optical stores that manufacture and sell prescription glasses. A little over 31 percent were in optical laboratories. These laboratories manufacture eyewear for sale by retail stores that fabricate prescription glasses, and by ophthalmologists and optometrists. Most of the rest were in wholesalers or in optical laboratories that manufacture lenses for other optical instruments, such as telescopes and binoculars.

Training, Other Qualifications, and Advancement

Nearly all ophthalmic laboratory technicians learn their skills on the job. Employers filling trainee jobs prefer applicants who are high school graduates. Courses in science, mathematics, and computers are valuable; manual dexterity and the ability to do precision work are essential.

Technician trainees producing lenses by hand start on simple tasks such as marking or blocking lenses for grinding, then progress to lens grinding, lens cutting, edging, beveling, and eyeglass assembly. Depending on individual aptitude, it may take up to 6 months to become proficient in all phases of the work.

Technicians using automated systems will find computer skills valuable. Training is completed on the job and varies in duration depending on the type of machinery and individual aptitude.

Some ophthalmic laboratory technicians learn their trade in the Armed Forces. Others attend the few programs in optical technology offered by vocational-technical institutes or trade schools. These programs have classes in optical theory, surfacing and lens finishing, and the reading and applying of prescriptions. Programs vary in length from 6 months to 1 year, and award certificates or diplomas.

Job Outlook

Overall employment of ophthalmic laboratory technicians is expected to grow more slowly than average through the year 2008. Employment is expected to increase slowly in manufacturing as firms invest in automated machinery. In retail trade, employment is expected to decline.

Demographic trends make it likely that many more Americans will need vision care in the years ahead. Not only will the population grow, but also the proportion of middle-aged and older adults is projected to increase rapidly. Middle age is a time when many people use corrective lenses for the first time, and elderly persons require more vision care, on the whole, than others.

Fashion, too, influences demand. Frames come in a variety of styles and colors—encouraging people to buy more than one pair. Demand is also expected to grow in response to the availability of new technologies that improve the quality and look of corrective lenses, such as anti-reflective coatings and bifocal lenses without the line visible in traditional bifocals.

Most job openings will arise from the need to replace technicians who transfer to other occupations or leave the labor force. Only a small number of total job openings will occur each year because the occupation is small.

Earnings

Median hourly earnings of ophthalmic laboratory technicians were $9.39 in 1998. The middle 50 percent earned between $7.56 and $11.58 an hour. The lowest 10 percent earned less than $6.48 and the highest 10 percent earned more than $15.74 an hour. Median hourly earnings of ophthalmic laboratory technicians in 1997 were $8.60 in ophthalmic goods and $8.30 in retail stores, not elsewhere classified.

Resources for Dispensing Opticians and Ophthalmic Laboratory Technicians are combined as resources serve both professions.

DISPENSING OPTICIANS & OPHTHALMIC LABORATORY TECHNICIANS

Don't forget! Refer to the general resources listed in Chapter Three.

Association	Book	Directory	Internet (Web) Site
Job Ads	E-mail/Hotline	Job Fairs	Resume Service

20/20 Magazine (Jobson Publishing Corporation, 100 Avenue of the Americas, New York, New York 10013; 212/274-7068, fax: 212/274-0392, **http://www.2020mag.com**, E-mail: 2020@jobson.com, Optician site). Lenses, frames, fashions for eyewear. Whole magazine can be read online.

American Academy of Ophthalmology (AAO) - P.O. Box 7424, San Francisco, CA 94120-7424; phone 415/561-8575. The AAO offers "Find an Ophthalmologist," an online listing of member ophthalmologists in the United States and abroad. Search by city, state or specialty. Visit **http://www.eyenet.org** for more information.

American Board of Opticianry (ABO) and **National Contact Lens Examiners (NCLE)** - 10341 Democracy Lane, Fairfax, VA 22030; 703/691-8355. (**http://www.opticians.org**, E-mail oaa@options.org) ABO and NCLE are national not-for-profit organizations for the voluntary certification of ophthalmic dispensers. The ABO certifies opticians, those who dispense and work with glasses.

⌂⁀ᕼ **Blue Book of Optometrists--Who's Who in Optometry** (Jobson Publishing Corporation, 100 Avenue of the Americas, New York, New York 10013; 212/274-7068, 212/274-7000 fax: 212/274-0392, **http://www.2020mag.com**, E-mail: sbutsch@jobson.com). It includes all optometrists, not just AOA members. This book also includes state optometric association listings and a "yellow pages" of suppliers, manufacturers and import firms

⚕ **Commission on Opticianry Accreditation** - 7023 Little River Turnpike, Suite 207, Annandale, VA 22003, 703/ 941-9110. Contact for general information about a career as an ophthalmic laboratory technician and a list of accredited programs in ophthalmic laboratory technology. Internet: **http://www.coaccreditation.com**.

⚕🖷⁀ᕼ **EyeWorld Online** (http://www.eyeworld.org/statement.html) Sponsored by ASCRS, this site features daily news updates and presentations for eye care professionals. Online classified ads.

⚕⁀ᕼ **The Joint Commission on Allied Health Personnel in Ophthal-mology (JCAHPO)** - 2025 Woodlane Drive, St. Paul, MN 55125-2995; 651/731-2944, 888/284-3937, fax: 651/731-0410, **http://www.jcahpo.org**, E-mail: jcahpo@jcahpo.org). Information on certification.

🖷⁀ᕼ **Journal of Ophthalmic Nursing & Technology** (SLACK, Inc., 6900 Grove Rd., Thorofare, NJ 08086-9447; 856/848-1000, fax: 856/853-5991, **(http://www.slackinc.com/eye)**. Published bimonthly, annual sub-scription $39. Job ads listed under "Classified marketplace." Request a free issue on the Internet site.

⚕🖷⁀ᕼ **National Academy of Opticianry (NAO)** - 8401 Corporate Dr., #605, Landover, MD 20785; 301/577-4828, 800/229-4828, fax: 301/577-3880, **(http://www.nao.org)**. E-mail naoacademy@aol.com. Web site has a job bank.

⚕⁀ᕼ **National Federation of Opticianry Schools (NFOS)** Their Web site at **(http://www.nfos.org**) lists education programs by state and has good links including optical companies.

📖 **Opportunities in Eye Care Careers** by Kathleen Belikoff, 1998, paperback. $11.95. Published by VGM Career Horizons.

⚕⌂⁀ᕼ **Optical Laboratories Association (OLA)** Their Web site at **(http://www.ola-labs.org**) includes optical news and a geographical list of OLA member labs.

🍴 📁 ✍ 🔥 **Opticians Association of America (OAA)** - 10341 Democracy Lane, Fairfax, VA 22030-2521; 703/691-8355, 703/691-3929, URL **http://www.opticians.org,** E-mail: oaa@opticians.org. Members consist of dispensing opticians, state opticians' associations, and retail optical companies. Employment referral service for members only.

📁 🔥 **SLACK Ocular Internet Directory** (SLACK Incorporated, 6900 Grove Road, Thorofare, NJ 08086-9447; 609/848-1000, fax: 609/853-5991). Their site at **http://www.slackinc.com/eye/idirectories/ecnet-xhm** lists related publications with an overview of the Internet for eye care professionals.

EMERGENCY MEDICAL TECHNICIANS

Employment is projected to grow rapidly as paid emergency medical technician positions replace unpaid volunteers.

Nature of the Work

People's lives often depend on the quick reaction and competent care of emergency medical technicians (EMTs) and paramedics. Incidents as varied as automobile accidents, heart attacks, drownings, childbirth, and gunshot wounds all require immediate medical attention. EMTs and paramedics provide this vital attention as they care for and transport the sick or injured to a medical facility.

Depending on the nature of the emergency, EMTs and paramedics typically are dispatched to the scene by a 911 operator and often work with police and fire department personnel. Once they arrive, they determine the nature and extent of the patient's condition while trying to ascertain whether the patient has preexisting medical problems. Following strict procedures, they give appropriate emergency care and transport the patient. Some conditions can be handled following general rules and guidelines, while more complicated problems are carried out under the direction of medical doctors by radio.

EMTs and paramedics may use special equipment such as backboards to immobilize patients before placing them on stretchers and securing them in the ambulance for transport to a medical facility. Usually, one EMT or paramedic drives while the other monitors the patient's vital signs and gives additional care as needed. Some who work for hospital trauma centers, which use helicopters to transport critically ill or injured patients, are part of the flight crew.

At the medical facility, EMTs and paramedics help transfer patients to the emergency department, report their observations and actions to staff, and may provide additional emergency treatment. Some paramedics are trained to treat patients with minor injuries on the scene of an accident or at their home without transporting them to a medical facility. After each run, EMTs replace used supplies and check equipment. If a transported patient had a contagious disease, EMTs decontaminate the interior of the ambulance and report cases to the proper authorities.

Beyond these general duties, the specific responsibilities of EMTs and paramedics depend on their level of qualification and training. To determine this, the National Registry of Emergency Medical Technicians (NREMT) registers emergency medical service (EMS) providers at four levels: First Responder, EMT-Basic, EMT-Intermediate, and EMT-Paramedic. Some States, however, do their own certification and use numeric ratings from 1 to 4 to distinguish levels of proficiency.

The lowest level—First Responders—are trained to provide basic emergency medical care because they tend to be the first persons to arrive at the scene of an incident. Many firefighters, police officers, and other emergency workers have this level of training. The EMT-Basic, also known as EMT-1, represents the first component of the emergency medical technician system. An EMT-1 is trained to care for patients on accident scenes and on transport by ambulance to the hospital under medical direction. The EMT-1 has the emergency skills to assess a patient's condition and manage respiratory, cardiac, and trauma emergencies.

The EMT-Intermediate (EMT-2 and EMT-3) has more advanced training that allows administration of intravenous fluids, use of manual defibrillators to give lifesaving shocks to a stopped heart, and use of advanced airway techniques and equipment to assist patients experiencing respiratory emergencies. EMT-Paramedics (EMT-4) provide the most extensive pre-hospital care. In addition to the procedures already described, paramedics may administer drugs orally and intravenously, interpret electrocardiograms (EKGs), perform endotracheal intubations, and use monitors and other complex equipment.

Working Conditions

EMTs and paramedics work both indoors and outdoors, in all types of weather. They are required to do considerable kneeling, bending, and

heavy lifting. These workers risk noise-induced hearing loss from sirens and back injuries from lifting patients. In addition, EMTs and paramedics may be exposed to diseases such as Hepatitis-B and AIDS, as well as violence from drug overdose victims or psychologically disturbed patients. The work is not only physically strenuous, but also stressful, involving life-or-death situations and suffering patients. Nonetheless, many people find the work exciting and challenging and enjoy the opportunity to help others.

EMTs and paramedics employed by fire departments work about 50 hours a week. Those employed by hospitals frequently work between 45 and 60 hours a week, and those in private ambulance services, between 45 and 50 hours. Some of these workers, especially those in police and fire departments, are on call for extended periods. Because emergency services function 24 hours a day, EMTs and paramedics have irregular working hours that add to job stress.

Employment

EMTs and paramedics held about 150,000 jobs in 1998. In addition, there are many more volunteer EMTs, especially in smaller cities, towns, and rural areas, who work for departments where they may respond to only a few calls for service per month. Most career EMTs and paramedics work in metropolitan areas.

EMTs and paramedics are employed in a number of industries. Nearly half work in local and suburban transportation for private ambulance firms that transport and treat individuals on an emergency or non-emergency basis. About a third of EMTs and paramedics work in local government for fire departments and third service providers, in which emergency medical services are provided by an independent agency. Another fifth are found in hospitals, where they may work full-time within the medical facility or respond to calls in ambulances or helicopters to transport critically ill or injured patients.

Training, Other Qualifications, and Advancement

Formal training and certification is needed to become an EMT or paramedic. All 50 States possess a certification procedure. In 38 States and the District of Columbia, registration with the National Registry is required at some or all levels of certification. Other States administer their own certification examination or provide the option of taking the National Registry examination. EMTs and paramedics must re-register,

usually every 2 years. To re-register, you must be working as an EMT and meet continuing education requirements.

Training is offered at progressive levels: EMT-Basic, also known as EMT-1; EMT-Intermediate, or EMT-2 and EMT-3; and EMT-paramedic, or EMT-4. The EMT-Basic represents the first level of skills required to work in the emergency medical system. Coursework typically emphasizes emergency skills such as managing respiratory, trauma, and cardiac emergencies and patient assessment. Formal courses are often combined with time in an emergency room or ambulance. The program also provides instruction and practice in dealing with bleeding, fractures, airway obstruction, cardiac arrest, and emergency childbirth. Students learn to use and maintain care for common emergency equipment, such as backboards, suction devices, splints, oxygen delivery systems, and stretchers. Graduates of approved EMT basic training programs who pass a written and practical examination administered by the State certifying agency or the National Registry of Emergency Medical Technicians earn the title of Registered EMT-Basic. The course is also a prerequisite for EMT-Intermediate and EMT-Paramedic training.

EMT-Intermediate training requirements vary from State to State. Applicants can opt to receive training in EMT-Shock Trauma, where the caregiver learns to start intravenous fluids and give certain medications, or in EMT-Cardiac, which includes learning heart rhythms and administering advanced medications. Training commonly includes 35-55 hours of additional instruction beyond EMT-Basic coursework and covers patient assessment as well as the use of advanced airway devices and intravenous fluids. Prerequisites for taking the EMT-Intermediate examination include registration as an EMT-Basic, required classroom work, and a specified amount of clinical experience.

The most advanced level of training for this occupation is EMT-Paramedic. At this level, the caregiver receives additional training in body function and more advanced skills. The Paramedic Technology program usually lasts up to 2 years and results in an associate degree in applied science. Such education prepares the graduate to take the National Registry of Emergency Medical Technicians examination and become certified as an EMT-Paramedic. Extensive related coursework and clinical and field experience is required. Due to the longer training requirement, almost all EMT-Paramedics are in paid positions. Refresher courses and continuing education are available at all levels.

EMTs and paramedics should be emotionally stable, have good dexterity, agility, and physical coordination, and be able to lift and carry

heavy loads. They also need good eyesight (corrective lenses may be used) with accurate color vision.

Advancement beyond the EMT-Paramedic level usually means leaving fieldwork. An EMT-Paramedic can become a supervisor, operations manager, administrative director, or executive director of emergency services. Some EMTs and paramedics become instructors, dispatchers, or physician assistants, while others move into sales or marketing of emergency medical equipment. A number of people become EMTs and paramedics to assess their interest in health care. Many return to school to become nurses, physicians, or other health workers.

Job Outlook

Employment of EMTs is expected to grow faster than average for all occupations through 2008. Much of this growth will occur as positions change from volunteer to paid and as the population grows, particularly older age groups that are the greatest users of emergency medical services. In addition to job growth, openings will occur because of replacement needs; some workers leave because of stressful working conditions, limited advancement potential, and the modest pay and benefits in the private sector.

Most opportunities for EMTs and paramedics are expected to arise in hospitals and private ambulance services. Competition will be greater for jobs in local government, including fire, police, and third service rescue squad departments, where job growth for these workers is expected to be slower.

Earnings

Earnings of EMTs depend on the employment setting and geographic location as well as the individual's training and experience. Median annual earnings of EMTs were $20,290 in 1998. The middle 50 percent earned between $15,660 and $26,240. The lowest 10 percent earned less than $12,700 and the highest 10 percent earned more than $34,480. In local and suburban transportation, where private ambulance firms are located, the median salary was $18,300 in 1997. In local government, except education and hospitals, the median salary was $21,900. In hospitals, the median salary was $19,900.

Those in emergency medical services who are part of fire or police departments receive the same benefits as firefighters or police officers. For example, many are covered by pension plans that provide retirement at half pay after 20 or 25 years of service or if disabled in the line of duty.

EMERGENCY MEDICAL TECHNICIANS

Don't forget! Refer to the general resources listed in Chapter Three.

♥ Association   📖 Book   📁 Directory   🖱 Internet (Web) Site

📱 Job Ads   💥 E-mail/Hotline   🏴 Job Fairs   ✒ Resume Service

---

🖱 **Emergency Medical Technicians and Paramedics National Highway Transportation Safety Administration, EMS Division**, 400 7th St. SW., NTS-14, Washington DC.Information on becoming an EMT. Web site located at: **http://www.nhtsa.dot.gov/people/injury/ems.**

📱🖱 **JEMS (Journal of Emergency Medical Services)** - Jems Communications, a subsidiary of Mosby; 800/266-JEMS. JEMS online Web site at (**http://www.jems.com**) has a classified employment ad section.

📱🖱 **MERGInet,** (**http://www.merginet.com**) Resources for emergency, fire and rescue professionals include a CPR-AED discussion list and a WebCrawler customized hot link for Emergency, Fire, Rescue and Medical sites around the Internet. Classified ads included.

📁🖱 **Municipal/County Executive Directory** - Carroll Publishing Company, 1058 Thomas Jefferson Street NW, Washington, DC 20007; 800/336-4240, 202/333-8620, fax: 202-337-7020, E-mail: custsvc-@carrollpub.com, (**http://www.carrollpub.com**). Published annually, it lists over 3000 municipalities and their officials. Check your local library.

♥📱✒📁🖱 **National Association of Emergency Medical Technicians (NAEMT)** - 408 Monroe Street, Clinton, MS 39056; 800/34-NAEMT, 601/924-7744, URL (**http://www.naemt.org**). Membership is for nationally registered or state certified EMTs. Will fax your resume to potential employers. Free job wanted ads for members. Single copy free.

♥📱🖱 **National Flight Paramedics Association (NFPA)** - 383 F Street, Salt Lake City, Utah, 84103; 800/381-NFPA, **http://www.nfpa.rotor.com,** Provides numerous services to members and publishes *Air Medical Journal* and *AIRMED* magazine. The Web site has an Employment Center.

Chapter

6

DIETETICS, PHARMACY and THERAPY OCCUPATIONS

Catherine Palmer

Catherine Palmer is an assistant professor in the Department of Communication Science and Dis-orders in the School of Health and Rehabilitation Sciences at the University of Pittsburgh. I asked her how she got involved in communication rehabilitation. "I became interested in the impact of hearing impairment on communication when I volunteered at a school for the deaf in Massachusetts when I was in high school. I decided to learn sign language and thought I would go into deaf education when I went to college." At the University of Massachusetts, Catherine pursued degrees in Communication Science and Disorders and Elementary Education. "I knew I would have to go to graduate school whether I decided to be a speech-language pathologist, an audiologist, or an educator of the deaf. During my undergraduate degree, I realized that I really enjoyed audiology because determining the degree and impact of a hearing loss is like solving a very important puzzle and treating that hearing loss with hearing aids and/or communication therapy is immediately rewarding."

Catherine went on to complete her master's degree in Audiology at Northwestern University. "During my graduate program, I enjoyed providing hearing solutions to children and adults and I also realized that research held exciting opportunities." Catherine's first job as an audiologist was at the Veteran's Administration Medical Center in Long Beach, California, where she was able to work with patients and participate in research. "I really enjoyed being an audiologist in the VA system. We were able to provide the best hearing aids to people who could really benefit from them." I asked Catherine why she decided to go on for a Ph.D. "The more I worked, the more I realized that research was badly needed in the area of hearing aid development and fitting."

In order to conduct independent research and to obtain funding for that research, an audiologist and/or speech-language pathologist generally needs to have a Ph.D., so Catherine decided to return to school and study for that degree. "Now I teach masters level students in audiology, supervise the research of Ph.D. students, work with patients of all ages in need of hearing aids, and conduct research."

Catherine said "Technology is changing so quickly now that it makes our jobs very exciting. We are constantly involved in continuing education and we are now better able to evaluate an individual's hearing and provide new technological solutions. For example, we can measure the hearing status of a baby only a day old, and we can provide implantable devices for people who are profoundly hearing impaired. Things are changing very quickly. Even though the technology is very exciting, audiologists have the opportunity to work with individuals in a very personal way. I have always enjoyed the mix of high-tech and hands-on work. Communication is essential to every human being and to every aspect of life. Speech-language pathologists and audiologists play an important role in empowering individuals to find solutions to their communication problems."

Catherine updated the chapter on audiology and Speech-Language Pathology in order to reflect current trends and data. She suggests that individuals interested in these fields take the time to observe professionals in both areas and a variety of settings (education, medical, etc.) in order to get a real feeling for what a typical day in the life of an audiologist or speech-language pathologist is like.

This chapter features health care dietetics, pharmacy, and therapy occupations. The major occupational groups are:

Dietitians and Nutritionists	**Recreational Therapists**
Occupational Therapists	**Respiratory Therapists**
Pharmacists	**Speech-Language Audiologists**
Physical Therapists	**Speech-Language Pathologists**

One additional career, **Lactation Consultant,** is profiled on our Web site: **http://www.healthcarejobs.org.**

Each specialty is described below. Occupational groups are divided into primary and related occupations so that individuals can investigate other fields for additional job opportunities.

Following each job description are job resource lists: Associations, Books, Directories, Internet Sites, Job Ads, E-mail Job Notification/Job Hotlines, Job Fairs, and Resume/Placement Services. Job sources are listed alphabetically with the larger sources underlined.

DIETITIANS AND NUTRITIONISTS

Employment of dietitians is expected to grow about as fast as the average for all occupations through the year 2008 due to increased emphasis on disease prevention by improved health habits.

Nature of the Work

Dietitians and nutritionists plan food and nutrition programs and supervise the preparation and serving of meals. They help prevent and treat illnesses by promoting healthy eating habits, scientifically evaluating clients' diets, and suggesting diet modifications, such as less salt for those with high blood pressure or reduced fat and sugar intake for those who are overweight.

Dietitians run food service systems for institutions such as hospitals and schools, promote sound eating habits through education, and conduct research. Major areas of practice are clinical, community, management, research, business and industry, and consultant dietetics.

Clinical dietitians provide nutritional services for patients in institutions such as hospitals and nursing homes. They assess patients' nutritional needs, develop and implement nutrition programs, and evaluate and report the results. They also confer with doctors and other health care professionals in order to coordinate medical and nutritional needs. Some clinical dietitians specialize in the management of overweight patients, care of the critically ill, or of renal (kidney) and diabetic patients. In addition, clinical dietitians in nursing homes, small hospitals, or correctional facilities may also manage the food service department.

Community dietitians counsel individuals and groups on nutritional practices designed to prevent disease and promote good health. Working in places such as public health clinics, home health agencies, and health maintenance organizations, they evaluate individual needs, develop nutritional care plans, and instruct individuals and their families. Dietitians working in home health agencies provide instruction on grocery shopping and food preparation to the elderly, individuals with special needs, and children.

Increased interest in nutrition has led to opportunities in food manufacturing, advertising, and marketing, in which dietitians analyze foods, prepare literature for distribution, or report on issues such as the nutritional content of recipes, dietary fiber, or vitamin supplements.

Management dietitians oversee large-scale meal planning and preparation in health care facilities, company cafeterias, prisons, and schools. They hire, train, and direct other dietitians and food service workers; budget for and purchase food, equipment, and supplies; enforce sanitary and safety regulations; and prepare records and reports.

Consultant dietitians work under contract with health care facilities or in their own private practice. They perform nutrition screenings for their clients, and offer advice on diet-related concerns such as weight loss or cholesterol reduction. Some work for wellness programs, sports teams, supermarkets, and other nutrition-related businesses. They may consult with food service managers, providing expertise in sanitation, safety procedures, menu development, budgeting, and planning.

Working Conditions

Most dietitians work a regular 40-hour week, although some work weekends. Many dietitians work part time.

Dietitians and nutritionists usually work in clean, well-lighted, and well-ventilated areas. However, some dietitians work in warm, congested kitchens. Many dietitians and nutritionists are on their feet for most of the workday.

Employment

Dietitians and nutritionists held about 54,000 jobs in 1998. Over half were in hospitals, nursing homes, or offices and clinics of physicians.

State and local governments provided about 1 job in 6—mostly in health departments and other public health related areas. Other jobs were in restaurants, social service agencies, residential care facilities, diet workshops, physical fitness facilities, school systems, colleges and universities, and the Federal Government—mostly in the Department of Veterans Affairs. Some were employed by firms that provide food services on contract to such facilities as colleges and universities, airlines, correctional facilities, and company cafeterias.

Some dietitians were self-employed, working as consultants to hospitals and nursing homes, and seeing individual clients.

Training, Other Qualifications, and Advancement

High school students interested in becoming a dietitian or nutritionist should take courses in biology, chemistry, mathematics, health, and communications. Dietitians and nutritionists need at least a bachelor's degree in dietetics, foods and nutrition, food service systems management, or a related area. College students in these majors take courses in foods, nutrition, institution management, chemistry, bio-chemistry, biology, microbiology, and physiology. Other suggested courses include business, mathematics, statistics, computer science, psychology, sociology, and economics.

Twenty-seven of the 41 States with laws governing dietetics require licensure, 13 require certification, and 1 requires registration. The Commission on Dietetic Registration of the American Dietetic Association (ADA) awards the Registered Dietitian credential to those who pass a certification exam after completing their academic coursework and supervised experience. Since practice requirements vary by State, interested candidates should determine the requirements of the State in which they want to work before sitting for any exam.

As of 1999, there were 235 bachelor's and master's degree programs approved by the ADA's Commission on Accreditation/Approval for Dietetics Education (CAADE). Supervised practice experience can be acquired in two ways. There are 51 ADA-accredited coordinated programs combining academic and supervised practice experience in a 4- to5-year program. The second option requires completion of 900 hours of supervised practice experience, either in one of the 225 CAADE-accredited internships or in one of the 25 CAADE-approved preprofessional practice programs. Internships and preprofessional practice programs may be full-time programs lasting 9 to 12 months, or part-time programs lasting 2 years. Students interested in research, advanced clinical positions, or public health may need a graduate degree.

Experienced dietitians may advance to assistant, associate, or director of a dietetic department, or become self-employed. Some dietitians specialize in areas such as renal or pediatric dietetics. Others may leave the occupation to become sales representatives for equipment, pharmaceutical, or food manufacturers.

Job Outlook

Employment of dietitians is expected to grow about as fast as the average for all occupations through 2008 due to increased emphasis on disease prevention by improved dietary habits. A growing and aging population will increase the demand for meals and nutritional counseling in nursing homes, schools, prisons, community health programs, and home health care agencies. Public interest in nutrition and the emphasis on health education and prudent lifestyles will also spur demand, especially in management.

The number of dietitian positions in hospitals is expected to grow slowly as hospitals continue to contract out food service operations. However, employment is expected to grow fast in contract providers of food and social services agencies, and offices and clinics of physicians.

Employment growth for dietitians and nutritionists may be somewhat constrained by some employers substituting other workers such as health educators, food service managers, and dietetic technicians.

Earnings

Median annual earnings of dietitians and nutritionists were $35,020 in 1998. The middle 50 percent earned between $28,010 and $42,720 a year. The lowest 10 percent earned less than $20,350 and the highest 10 percent earned more than $51,320 a year.

DIETICIANS and NUTRITIONISTS

Don't forget! Refer to the general resources listed in Chapter Three.

| 🜻 Association | 📖 Book | 🗁 Directory | 🕯 Internet (Web) Site |
| 📱 Job Ads | 💥 E-mail/Hotline | 🏷 Job Fairs | ✍ Resume Service |

📱🗁🕯 **American Diabetes Association** (1701 N. Beauregard Street, Alexandria, VA 22314; Phone 800-342-2303). The web site at URL **http://www.diabetes.org/** has an employment section and a members-only directory.

🜻📱🕯 **The American Dietetic Association (ADA)** - 216 West Jackson Boulevard., Chicago, IL 60606-6995; 312/899-0040. An organization of dietetic professionals and dietitians that scholarship and credentialing information. URL (**http://www.eatright.org**). Publishes the *Journal of the American Dietetic Association,* monthly, $150/yr. Between 35 to 45 job ads appear in each issue. Web site has area on careers in dietetics, including certified schools. "Positions Available" Web area has job ads.

🜻📱✍🕯 **American School Food Service Association (ASFSA)** - 700 S. Washington Street, VA 22314; 703/739-3900, fax: 703/739-3915, (**http://www.asfsa.org**), E-Mail: servicecenter@asfsa.org. "The ASFSA Connection" on the web site, for members only, is for networking and has a Jobline Bulletin Board to post your resume or look for a job. Job ads are available to public.

🕯 **Arbor Nutrition Guide** - (**http://www.arborcom.com**). Sponsored by Dr. Tony Helman, this site's Applied section has extensive links for nutrition professionals.

🕯 **The Blonz Guide, Nutrition, Food & Health Resources** - There is an extensive guide to search engines, and the "It's Academic" area of their web site at (**http://www.blonz.com**) has a list of schools.

🜻🕯 **California Dietetic Association (CDA)** - 7740 Manchester Ave., Suite 102, Playa del Rey, CA 90293-8499; 310/822-0177, fax: 310/823-0264, (**http://www.dietitian.org**), E-mail: cdaep@aol.com. CDA has CE, networking, and a mid-career mentoring program.

California Jobs in Dietetics -P. O. Box 3537, Santa Monica, CA 90408-3537; 310/453-5375. E-mail: carolyn@jobsindietetics@com). Published twice a month. Internet **http://www.jobsindietetics.com.**

Dietitians of Canada - 480 University Avenue, Suite 604, Toronto, Ontario, Canada M5G 1V2; 416/596-0857, fax: 416/596-0603. **(http://www.dietitians.ca).** "Hire a Dietitian" area of site and the newsletter both have classified job ads.

Dietetics.com - **(http://www.dietetics.com).** This site for dietitians' discussion has information on state and local dietetic associations.

Food and Nutrition Information Center of the USDA - Click on their site at **(http://www.nalusda.gov/fnic)** for "Topics A-Z". This section of the web site has links to associations and colleges, directories, and electronic publications.

Institute of Food Technologists - 221 N. LaSalle St., Suite 300, Chicago, IL 60601-1291; 312/782-8424, 800/234-0270. **(http://www.ift.org).** E-mail: customerservice@ift.org) "Employment Services" section on the web lists jobs available, to members. Publishes *ITF Jobs Available Bulletin,* monthly, for members only and *How to Find Your First Job in the Food Sciences,* handbook, $3.00.

National Jobs in Dietetics - (P.O. Box 3537, Santa Monica, CA 90408-3537; 310/453-5375. Every state except California is covered. E-mail: carolyn@jobsindietetics.com, Internet **(http://www.jobsindietetics.com.** Published twice monthly. Subscriptions are $42 for 2 months, $58 for 3 months, and $144 for 12 months.

Nutrition Navigator - **(http://navigator.tufts.edu).** Provided by Tufts University, this award-winning site rates the nutrition web sites.

West Virginia Dietetic Association's "Dietetic Jobs" National Database - **(http://www.wvda.org/jobs)** Easy to use job site.

PHARMACISTS

OCCUPATIONAL TITLES:

Nutrition support pharmacists	Pharmacotherapists
Pharmacists	Radiopharmacists

RELATED OCCUPATIONS
Pharmacy Technicians and Assistants

Pharmacy technicians and assistants help licensed pharmacists provide medication and other health care products to patients. Technicians usually perform routine tasks to help prepare prescribed medication for patients, such as counting and labeling. Assistants are often clerks or cashiers who primarily answer telephones, handle money, stock shelves, and perform other clerical duties. Opportunities for pharmacy technicians and assistants are expected to be good, especially for those with formal training or previous work experience. Although most pharmacy technicians receive informal on-the-job training, employers are beginning to favor those who have completed formal training. Median hourly earnings of pharmacy technicians in 1998 were $8.54. Certified technicians may earn more. For information, contact the Pharmacy Technician Certification Board, 2215 Constitution Ave. NW., Washington DC 20037 (**http://www.ptcb.org**) and check the resource section for pharmacists below.

Nature of the Work

Pharmacists dispense drugs prescribed by physicians and other health practitioners and provide information to patients about medications and their use. They advise physicians and other health practitioners on the selection, dosages, interactions, and side effects of medications. Pharmacists must understand the use, composition, and clinical effects of drugs. Compounding—the actual mixing of ingredients to form powders, tablets, capsules, ointments, and solutions—is only a small part of a pharmacist's practice, because most medicines are produced by pharmaceutical companies in a standard dosage and drug delivery form.

Pharmacists in community or retail pharmacies counsel patients, as well as answer questions about prescription drugs, such as possible adverse reactions or interactions. They provide information about over-the-counter drugs and make recommendations after asking a series of health questions, such as whether the customer is taking any other medications. They also give advice about durable medical equipment and home health care supplies. Those who own or manage community pharmacies may sell non-health-related merchandise, hire and supervise personnel, and oversee the general operation of the pharmacy. Some community pharmacists provide specialized services to help patients manage conditions such as diabetes, asthma, smoking cessation, or high blood pressure.

Pharmacists in hospitals and clinics dispense medications and advise the medical staff on the selection and effects of drugs. They may make sterile solutions and buy medical supplies. They also assess, plan, and monitor drug regimens. They counsel patients on the use of drugs while in the hospital, and on their use at home when they are discharged. Pharmacists may also evaluate drug use patterns and outcomes for patients in hospitals or managed care organizations.

Pharmacists who work in home health care monitor drug therapy and prepare infusions—solutions that are injected into patients—and other medications for use in the home.

Most pharmacists keep confidential computerized records of patients' drug therapies to ensure that harmful drug interactions do not occur. They frequently teach pharmacy students serving as interns in preparation for graduation and licensure.

Some pharmacists specialize in specific drug therapy areas, such as psychiatric disorders, intravenous nutrition support, oncology, nuclear pharmacy, and pharmacotherapy.

Working Conditions

Pharmacists usually work in clean, well-lighted, and well-ventilated areas. Many pharmacists spend most of their workday on their feet. When working with sterile or potentially dangerous pharmaceutical products, pharmacists wear gloves and masks and work with other special protective equipment. Many community and hospital pharmacies are open for extended hours or around the clock, so pharmacists may work evenings, nights, weekends, and holidays. Consultant pharmacists may travel to nursing homes or other facilities to monitor people's drug therapy.

About 1 out of 7 pharmacists worked part time in 1998. Most full-time salaried pharmacists worked about 40 hours a week. Some, including most self-employed pharmacists, worked more than 50 hours a week.

Employment

Pharmacists held about 185,000 jobs in 1998. About 3 out of 5 worked in community pharmacies, either independently owned or part of a drug store chain, grocery store, department store, or mass merchandiser. Most community pharmacists were salaried employees, but some were self–employed owners. About one-quarter of salaried pharmacists worked in hospitals, clinics, mail-order pharmacies, pharmaceutical wholesalers, home health care agencies, or the Federal Government.

Some pharmacists hold more than one job. They may work a standard week in one work setting, and also work part time elsewhere.

Training, Other Qualifications, and Advancement

A license to practice pharmacy is required in all States, the District of Columbia, and U.S. territories. To obtain a license, one must serve an internship under a licensed pharmacist, graduate from an accredited college of pharmacy, and pass a State examination. Most States grant a license without extensive reexamination to qualified pharmacists already licensed by another State—check with State boards of pharmacy for details. Many pharmacists are licensed to practice in more than one State. States may require continuing education for license renewal.

In 1998, 81 colleges of pharmacy were accredited to confer degrees by the American Council on Pharmaceutical Education. Nearly all pharmacy programs grant the degree of Doctor of Pharmacy (Pharm.D.) which requires at least 6 years of postsecondary study. A small number of pharmacy schools continue to award the 5-year Bachelor of Science (B.S.) in pharmacy degree. However, all accredited pharmacy schools are expected to graduate their last B.S. class by the year 2005. Either a Pharm.D. or B.S. degree currently fulfills the requirements to take the licensure examination of a state board of pharmacy.

Requirements for admission to colleges of pharmacy vary. A few colleges admit students directly from high school. Most colleges of pharmacy, however, require 1 or 2 years of college-level prepharmacy education. Entry requirements usually include mathematics and basic sciences, such as chemistry, biology, and physics, as well as courses in the humanities and social sciences. Some colleges require the applicant to take the Pharmacy College Admissions Test.

All colleges of pharmacy offer courses in pharmacy practice, designed to teach students to dispense prescriptions, communicate with patients and other health professionals, and to strengthen their understanding of professional ethics and practice management responsibilities. Pharmacists' training increasingly emphasizes direct patient care, as well as consultative services to other health professionals.

In the 1997-1998 academic year, 60 colleges of pharmacy awarded the Master of Science degree or the Ph.D. degree. Although a number of pharmacy graduates interested in further training pursue an advanced degree in pharmacy, there are other options. Some complete 1- or 2-year residency programs or fellowships. Pharmacy residencies are postgraduate training programs in pharmacy practice. Pharmacy fellowships are highly individualized programs designed to prepare participants to work in research laboratories.

Areas of graduate study include pharmaceutics and pharmaceutical chemistry (physical and chemical properties of drugs and dosage forms), pharmacology (effects of drugs on the body), and pharmacy administration, including pharmacoeconomics and social-behavioral aspects of patient care.

Prospective pharmacists should have scientific aptitude, good communication skills, and a desire to help others. They must also be conscientious and pay close attention to detail, because the decisions they make affect human lives.

In community pharmacies, pharmacists usually begin at the staff level. After they gain experience and secure the necessary capital, some become owners or part owners of pharmacies. Pharmacists in chain drug stores may be promoted to pharmacy supervisor or manager at the store level, then to the district or regional level, and later to an executive position within the chain's headquarters.

Hospital pharmacists may advance to supervisory or administrative positions. Pharmacists in the pharmaceutical industry may advance in marketing, sales, research, quality control, production, packaging, and other areas.

Job Outlook

Employment of pharmacists is expected to grow slower than the average for all occupations through the year 2008, despite the increased pharmaceutical needs of a larger and older population, and greater use of medication.

Retail pharmacies are taking steps to increase their prescription volume to make up for declining dispensing fees. Automation of drug dispensing and greater use of pharmacy technicians will help them to dispense more prescriptions. The number of community pharmacists needed in the future will depend on the expansion rate of chain drug stores and the willingness of insurers to reimburse pharmacists for providing clinical services to patients taking prescription medications. With its emphasis on cost control, managed care encourages growth of lower-cost prescription drug distributors such as mail-order firms for certain medications. Slower employment growth is expected in traditional chain and independent pharmacies.

Employment in hospitals is also expected to grow slowly, as hospitals reduce inpatient stays, downsize, and consolidate departments. Pharmacy services are shifting to long-term, ambulatory, and home care settings, where opportunities for pharmacists will be best. New opportunities for pharmacists are emerging in managed care organizations, where pharmacists analyze trends and patterns in medication use for their populations of patients. Fast growth is also expected for pharmacists trained in research, disease management, and pharmacoeconomics—determining the costs and benefits of different drug therapies.

Cost-conscious insurers and health systems may continue to emphasize the role of pharmacists in primary and preventive health services. They realize that the expense of using medication to treat diseases and conditions is often considerably less than the potential costs for patients whose conditions go untreated. Pharmacists can also reduce the expenses resulting from unexpected complications due to allergic reactions or medication interactions.

The increased number of middle aged and elderly people will spur demand for pharmacists in all practice settings. The number of prescriptions influences the demand for pharmacists, and the middle aged and elderly populations use more prescription drugs, on average, than younger people.

Other factors likely to increase the demand for pharmacists through the year 2008 include the likelihood of scientific advances that will make more drug products available, new developments in administering medication, and increasingly sophisticated consumers seeking more information about drugs.

Earnings

Median annual earnings of pharmacists in 1998 were $66,220. The middle 50 percent earned between $52,310 and $80,250 a year. The lowest 10 percent earned less than $42,550 and the highest 10 percent more than $88,670 a year.

According to a survey by Drug Topics magazine, published by Medical Economics Co., average base salaries of full-time, salaried pharmacists were about $59,700 a year in 1998. Pharmacists working in chain drug stores had an average base salary of about $62,300 a year, while pharmacists working in independent drug stores averaged about $56,300, and hospital pharmacists averaged about $59,500 a year. Overall, salaries for pharmacists were highest on the West coast. Many pharmacists also receive compensation in the form of bonuses, overtime, and profit-sharing.

PHARMACISTS

Don't forget! Refer to the general resources listed in Chapter Three.

⚕ Association   📖 Book   🗁 Directory   🖰 Internet (Web) Site

📋 Job Ads   🕮 E-mail/Hotline   🖂 Job Fairs   ✒ Resume Service

---

⚕📋🗁🖰 **Academy of Managed Care Pharmacy (AMCP)** - 100 N. Pitt Street, Suite 400, Alexandria, VA 22314; 800/TAP-AMCP, 703/683-8416, fax: 703/683-8417, (**www.amcp.org**). Annual membership directory $350.

📋🖰 **Advanstar Publications** - 859 Willamette Street, Eugene, OR 97401; 541/343-1200). All publications are free to qualified professionals. *Pharmaceutical Technology* **http://www.pharmtech.com** is an excellent publication with display job ads.

⚕🗁✒🖰 **American Association of Colleges of Pharmacy (AACP)** - 1426 Prince St., Alexandria, VA 22314-2841; 703/739-2330, fax: 703/836-8982, (**http://www.aacp.org**). Members can use the employment service on the net, which also features links to Pharmacy Schools and other related sites. Publishes booklet, *Pharmacy School Admission Requirements* and List of Colleges and Schools of Pharmacy.

⚕📋🗁✒🖰 **American College of Clinical Pharmacy (ACCP)** - 3101 Broadway, Suite 650, Kansas City, MO 64111; 816/531-2177, URL (**http://www.accp.com**). *ACCP News* is free and contains job ads which also appear on the web site. *The ACCP Membership Directory* also is available along with a placement service. Ask for the free ICSA information packet on grants, loans, scholarships, residencies and fellowships.

American Pharmaceutical Association (APhA) - 2215 Constitution Avenue NW, Washington, DC 20037; 202/628-4410, fax: 202/783-2351, (**http://www.aphanet.org**). Membership categories for pharmacists, pharmacy scientists, and others.

American Society of Health-System Pharmacists (ASHP) - 7272 Wisconsin Avenue, Bethesda, MD 20814; 301/657-3000, (http://www.ashp.com), E-mail: info@ashp.org. Publishes a career brochure. Student membership is $25. Free placement service for members. Fill out a form and you will be mailed lists of employers who have placed ads. View career opportunities by state on the Internet site.

California Pharmacists Association (CphA) - 1112 I Street, Suite 300, Sacramento, CA 95814; 916/444-7811, 800/444-3851, fax: 916/444-7929, (**http://www.cpha.com/cpha**). For employment ads, see the "CphA Job Market" area on the web site.

International Society for Pharmaceutical Engineering (ISPE) - 3816 W. Linebaugh Ave., Suite 412, Tampa, FL 33624; 813/960-2105, (**www.ispe.org**). *Pharmaceutical Engineering,* published bimonthly, subscriptions free. Twenty or more ads for process engineers and pharmaceutical specialists. Links to North American chapters on web.

National Association of Chain Drug Stores (NACDS) - 413 N. Lee Street, P. O. Box 1417, Alexandria, VA 22313-1480. NACDS has general information on careers in pharmacy. (**http://www.nacds.org/front2.html**).

Pharmaceutical Online - "Employment Opportunities" allows you to view ads, post your resume and enter discussion forums at URL (**http://www.pharmaceuticalonline.com**).

Pharmacy Times - (**http://www.pharmacytimes.com**) 1065 Old Country Road, Suite 213, Westbury NY 11590; 516/997-0377. The web site has continuing education, student center, career information and classified job ads.

PharmWeb - (**http://www.pharmweb.net**) To find out about job possibilities, click on "PharmWeb Appointments"; then you can join the Alert mailing list.

U.S. Pharmacist - 100 Avenue of the Americas, NY, NY 10013-1678, 212/274-7000, fax: 212/219-7835, (**http://www.uspharmacist.com**)This site has continuing education, a classified ads area which has jobs ads.

INTERVIEW WITH AN
OCCUPATIONAL THERAPIST

Tamara Theodore

Tamara Theodore is a Pediatric Occupational Therapist in private practice in Encino, California. "I always wanted to do something in the health field. I thought of being a pediatrician but felt that I wanted a family and didn't think I could properly devote time to both. I had a blind date once, which turned out to be a man who was going to be an Occupational Therapist. He told me that it was a field in which the course of study was a blend of art, psychology and medicine. That really intrigued me and so I began to pursue it."

She graduated from the University of Southern California with a B. S. in 1972. "After college, I took two required internships, one in Mental Health and one in Physical Disabilities. These were full time positions and, in the second one, I specialized in pediatrics at Children's Hospital of Los Angeles."

When asked for advice to people just starting out, Tamara replied, "Decide what area you want to work in and put your mind to it! When I started school, there were lots of jobs available. When I graduated there were very few. I decided I wanted to work in pediatrics, which was the hardest to get into. I volunteered after my internship was over until they created a position for me." Later, she needed field work experience for a Master's Program. "I went to a special school for children who could not be handled in the regular public school and asked for a volunteer position. They offered me a position as Director of Sensory Integration Therapy because I was an O.T. trained in this specialty. So hang in there!"

Currently, Tamara explains, the job market for Occupational Therapists is excellent. "The field is wide open, gives professional status, good income and plenty of challenge and variety. The thing that is great about this field is that there are never two days the same. One can create almost any kind of job environment they want, but the premise is always the same: helping people to develop, maintain or achieve maximum function for their developmental level."

The great variety in employment possibilities makes this career especially appealing. Tamara explains, "This job usually includes working closely with nursing and doing a lot of parent training and education. There are Early Intervention Programs across the nation for birth to three that are educationally based and state funded. These provide assistance to families with special needs children to help them to learn and develop in areas that are deficient in gross and fine motor skills, cognitive skills, language skills, social and emotional skills. Occupational Therapists work with all types of people, ages and problems from premature infants to geriatrics and everything in-between. Therapists work with adolescents and adults with all types of problem to help them adjust and return to school or work. There are therapists who work in the school system or in rehabilitation or private practice settings who work with children with a variety of deficits that limit their ability to learn and or function. Therapists enjoy working with the elderly who need to learn new ways to cope after stroke, heart attack or accident."

"I have been in this field for 25 years and really love it as much today as I did when I first started. I love working with small children. I love the mix of psychology, medicine and art. I love the opportunity to be creative. In 25 years of continuous learning, I still have so much more to learn."

Tamara emphasizes the personality traits needed for success in this field. "I think it is important to want to help people and to have a genuine interest in their well being and a true caring for humankind to be a success in this field. Therapists have to be 'adaptive' and creative and need to enjoy problem solving. If you are that kind of person, go for it! The possibilities are almost endless; thus one can change jobs within the field, keeping it interesting and varied."

OCCUPATIONAL THERAPISTS

RELATED OCCUPATIONS
Occupational Therapy Assistants and Aides

Occupational therapy assistants and aides work under the direction of occupational therapists to provide rehabilitative services to persons with mental, physical, emotional, or developmental impairments. Occupational therapy assistants help clients with rehabilitative activities and exercises outlined in a treatment plan developed in collaboration with an occupational therapist. Occupational therapy aides typically prepare materials and assemble equipment used during treatment and are responsible for a range of clerical tasks. Persons must complete an associate's degree or certificate program from an accredited community college or technical school to qualify for occupational therapy assistant jobs. In contrast, occupational therapy aides usually receive most of their training on the job. Employment of occupational therapy assistants and aides is expected to grow much faster than the average for all occupations through 2008. Median annual earnings of occupational therapy assistants and aides were $28,690 in 1998. Information on a career as an occupational therapy assistant and a list of accredited programs can be obtained by sending a self-addressed label and $5.00 to the American Occupational Therapy Association listed in the resources section.

Nature of the Work

Occupational therapists help people improve their ability to perform tasks in their daily living and working environments. They work with individuals who have conditions that are mentally, physically, developmentally, or emotionally disabling. They also help them to develop, recover, or maintain daily living and work skills. Occupational therapists not only help clients improve basic motor functions and reasoning abilities, but also compensate for permanent loss of function. Their goal is to help clients have independent and satisfying lives.

Occupational therapists assist clients in performing activities of all types, ranging from using a computer, to caring for daily needs such as dressing, cooking, and eating. Physical exercises may be used to increase strength and dexterity, while paper and pencil exercises may be chosen to improve visual acuity and the ability to discern patterns. A client with short-term memory loss, for instance, might be encouraged to make lists to aid recall. A person with coordination problems might be assigned exercises to improve hand-eye coordination. Occupational therapists also use computer programs to help clients improve decision making, abstract reasoning, problem solving, and perceptual skills, as well as memory, sequencing, and coordination—all of which are important for independent living.

For those with permanent functional disabilities, such as spinal cord injuries, cerebral palsy, or muscular dystrophy, therapists instruct in the use of adaptive equipment such as wheelchairs, splints, and aids for eating and dressing. They also design or make special equipment needed at home or at work. Therapists develop computer-aided adaptive equipment and teach clients with severe limitations how to use it. This equipment enables clients to communicate better and to control other aspects of their environment.

Some occupational therapists, called industrial therapists, treat individuals whose ability to function in a work environment has been impaired. They arrange employment, plan work activities, and evaluate the client's progress.

Occupational therapists may work exclusively with individuals in a particular age group, or with particular disabilities. In schools, for example, they evaluate children's abilities, recommend and provide therapy, modify classroom equipment, and in general, help children participate as fully as possible in school programs and activities. Occupational therapy is also beneficial to the elderly population. Therapists help senior citizens lead more productive, active and independent lives through a variety of methods, including the use of adaptive equipment.

Occupational therapists in mental health settings treat individuals who are mentally ill, mentally retarded, or emotionally disturbed. To treat these problems, therapists choose activities that help people learn to cope with daily life. Activities include time management skills, budgeting, shopping, homemaking, and use of public transportation. They may also work with individuals who are dealing with alcoholism, drug abuse, depression, eating disorders, or stress related disorders.

Recording a client's activities and progress is an important part of an occupational therapist's job. Accurate records are essential for evaluating clients, billing, and reporting to physicians and others.

Working Conditions

Occupational therapists in hospitals and other health care and community settings usually work a 40-hour week. Those in schools may also participate in meetings and other activities, during and after the school day. More than one-fourth of occupational therapists work part-time.

In large rehabilitation centers, therapists may work in spacious rooms equipped with machines, tools, and other devices generating noise. The job can be tiring, because therapists are on their feet much of the time. Those providing home health care may spend time driving from appointment to appointment. Therapists also face hazards such as back strain from lifting and moving clients and equipment.

Therapists are increasingly taking on supervisory roles. Due to rising health care costs, third party payers are beginning to encourage occupational therapy assistants and aides to take more hands-on responsibility. By having assistants and aides work more closely with clients under the guidance of a therapist, the cost of therapy should be more modest.

Employment

Occupational therapists held about 73,000 jobs in 1998; about 1 in 4 worked part time. About 1 in 10 occupational therapists held more than one job in 1998. The largest number of jobs was in hospitals, including many in rehabilitation and psychiatric hospitals. Other major employers include offices and clinics of occupational therapists and other health practitioners, school systems, home health agencies, nursing homes, community mental health centers, adult daycare programs, job training services, and residential care facilities.

Some occupational therapists are self-employed in private practice. They see clients referred by physicians or other health professionals, or provide contract or consulting services to nursing homes, schools, adult daycare programs, and home health agencies.

Employment is projected to increase over the 1998-2008 period, but due to the effects of Federal limits on reimbursement for therapy services, the majority of expected employment growth is expected to occur during the second half of the projection period.

Training, Other Qualifications, and Advancement

A bachelor's degree in occupational therapy is the minimum requirement for entry into this field. All States, Puerto Rico, and the District of Columbia regulate occupational therapy. To obtain a license, applicants must graduate from an accredited educational program, and pass a national certification examination. Those who pass the test are awarded the title of registered occupational therapist.

In 1999, entry-level education was offered in 88 bachelor's degree programs; 11 post-bachelor's certificate programs for students with a degree other than occupational therapy; and 53 entry-level master's degree programs. Nineteen programs offered a combined bachelor's and master's degree and 2 offered an entry-level doctoral degree. Most schools have full-time programs, although a growing number also offer weekend or part-time programs.

Occupational therapy coursework includes physical, biological, and behavioral sciences, and the application of occupational therapy theory and skills. Completion of 6 months of supervised fieldwork is also required.

Persons considering this profession should take high school courses in biology, chemistry, physics, health, art, and the social sciences. College admissions offices also look favorably at paid or volunteer experience in the health care field.

Occupational therapists need patience and strong interpersonal skills to inspire trust and respect in their clients. Ingenuity and imagination in adapting activities to individual needs are assets. Those working in home health care must be able to successfully adapt to a variety of settings.

Job Outlook

Employment of occupational therapists is expected to increase faster than the average for all occupations through 2008. However, Federal legislation imposing limits on reimbursement for therapy services may continue to adversely affect the job market for occupational therapists in the near term. Because of the effects of these provisions, the majority of expected employment growth for occupational therapists is expected to occur in the second half of the projection period.

Over the long run, the demand for occupational therapists should continue to rise as a result of growth in the number of individuals with disabilities or limited function requiring therapy services. The baby-boom generation's movement into middle age, a period when the incidence of heart attack and stroke increases, will increase the demand for therapeutic services. The rapidly growing population 75 years of age and above (an age that suffers from a high incidence of disabling conditions), will also demand additional services. Medical advances now enable more patients with critical problems to survive. These patients may need extensive therapy.

Hospitals will continue to employ a large number of occupational therapists to provide therapy services to acutely ill inpatients. Hospitals will also need occupational therapists to staff their outpatient rehabilitation programs.

Employment growth in schools will result from expansion of the school-age population and extended services for disabled students. Therapists will be needed to help children with disabilities prepare to enter special education programs.

Earnings

Median annual earnings of occupational therapists were $48,230 in 1998. The middle 50 percent earned between $39,140 and $68,570 a year. The lowest 10 percent earned less than $30,850 and the highest 10 percent earned more than $86,540 a year.

Resources for occupational therapists and physical therapists are combined as many resources serve both professions. See the end of the Physical Therapist section.

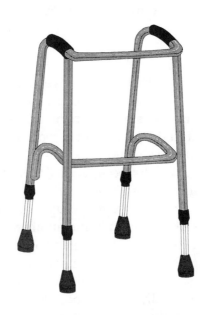

PHYSICAL THERAPISTS

RELATED OCCUPATIONS

Physical Therapist Assistants and Aides

Physical therapist assistants and aides perform components of physical therapy procedures and related tasks selected and delegated by a supervising physical therapist. Physical therapist assistants perform a variety of tasks. Treatment procedures delegated to these workers, under the direction of therapists, involve exercises, massages, electrical stimulation, paraffin baths, hot and cold packs, traction, and ultrasound. Physical therapist assistants record the patient's responses to treatment and report to the physical therapist the outcome of each treatment. Physical therapist aides are trained on the job, but physical therapist assistants typically have earned an associate's degree from an accredited physical therapist assistant program. Employment of physical therapist assistants and aides is expected to grow much faster than the average through the year 2008. Median annual earnings of physical therapist assistants and aides were $21,870 in 1998. Information on a career as a physical therapist assistant and a list of accredited schools can be obtained from The American Physical Therapy Association, listed in the resources section.

Nature of the Work

Physical therapists provide services that help restore function, improve mobility, relieve pain, and prevent or limit permanent physical disabilities of patients suffering from injuries or disease. They restore, maintain, and promote overall fitness and health. Their patients include accident victims and individuals with disabling conditions such as low back pain, arthritis, heart disease, fractures, head injuries, and cerebral palsy.

Therapists examine patients' medical histories, then test and measure their strength, range of motion, balance and coordination, posture, muscle performance, respiration, and motor function. They also determine patients' ability to be independent and reintegrate into the community or workplace after injury or illness. Next, they develop treatment plans describing a treatment strategy, the purpose, and anticipated outcome. Physical therapist assistants, under the direction and supervision of a physical therapist, may be involved in the implementation of the treatment plan. Physical therapist aides perform routine support tasks, as directed by the therapist.

Treatment often includes exercise for patients who have been immobilized and lack flexibility, strength, or endurance. They encourage patients to use their own muscles to further increase flexibility and range of motion before finally advancing to other exercises improving strength, balance, coordination, and endurance. Their goal is to improve how an individual functions at work and home.

Physical therapists also use electrical stimulation, hot packs or cold compresses, and ultrasound to relieve pain and reduce swelling. They may use traction or deep-tissue massage to relieve pain. Therapists also teach patients to use assistive and adaptive devices such as crutches, prostheses, and wheelchairs. They may also show patients exercises to do at home to expedite their recovery.

As treatment continues, physical therapists document progress, conduct periodic examinations, and modify treatments when necessary. Such documentation is used to track the patient's progress, and identify areas requiring more or less attention.

Physical therapists often consult and practice with a variety of other professionals, such as physicians, dentists, nurses, educators, social workers, occupational therapists, speech-language pathologists, and audiologists.

Some physical therapists treat a wide range of ailments; others specialize in areas such as pediatrics, geriatrics, orthopedics, sports medicine, neurology, and cardiopulmonary physical therapy.

Working Conditions

Physical therapists practice in hospitals, clinics, and private offices that have specially equipped facilities or they treat patients in hospital rooms, homes, or schools.

Most physical therapists work a 40-hour week, which may include some evenings and weekends. The job can be physically demanding because therapists often have to stoop, kneel, crouch, lift, and stand for long periods of time. In addition, physical therapists move heavy equipment and lift patients or help them turn, stand, or walk.

Employment

Physical therapists held about 120,000 jobs in 1998; about 1 in 4 worked part time. The number of jobs is greater than the number of practicing physical therapists because some physical therapists hold two or more jobs. For example, some may have a private practice, but also work part time in another health facility. About 1 in 10 physical therapists held more than one job in 1998.

Over two-thirds of physical therapists were employed in either hospitals or offices of physical therapists. Other jobs were in home health agencies, outpatient rehabilitation centers, offices and clinics of physicians, and nursing homes. Some physical therapists are self-employed in private practices. They may provide services to individual patients or contract to provide services in hospitals, rehabilitation centers, nursing homes, home health agencies, adult daycare programs, and schools. They may be in solo practice or be part of a consulting group. Physical therapists also teach in academic institutions and conduct research.

Although the effects of Federal limits on reimbursement for therapy services will cause keen competition for jobs during the first half of the projection period, employment is expected to increase over the 1998-2008 period.

Training, Other Qualifications, and Advancement

All States require physical therapists to pass a licensure exam after graduating from an accredited physical therapist educational program before they can practice.

According to the American Physical Therapy Association, there were 189 accredited physical therapist programs in 1999. Of the accredited programs, 24 offered bachelor's degrees, 157 offered master's degrees, and 8 offered doctoral degrees. By 2002, all physical therapist programs seeking accreditation will be required to offer degrees at the master's degree level and above, in accordance with the Commission on Accreditation in Physical Therapy Education.

Physical therapist programs start with basic science courses such as biology, chemistry, and physics, and then introduce specialized courses such as biomechanics, neuroanatomy, human growth and development, manifestations of disease, examination techniques, and therapeutic procedures. Besides classroom and laboratory instruction, students receive supervised clinical experience. Individuals who have a 4-year degree in another field and want to be a physical therapist, should enroll in a master's or a doctoral level physical therapist educational program.

Competition for entrance into physical therapist educational programs is very intense, so interested students should attain superior grades in high school and college, especially in science courses. Courses useful when applying to physical therapist educational programs include anatomy, biology, chemistry, social science, mathematics, and physics. Before granting admission, many professional education programs require experience as a volunteer in a physical therapy department of a hospital or clinic.

Physical therapists should have strong interpersonal skills to successfully educate patients about their physical therapy treatments. They should also be compassionate and posses a desire to help patients. Similar traits are also needed to interact with the patient's family.

Physical therapists are expected to continue professional development by participating in continuing education courses and workshops. A number of States require continuing education to maintain licensure.

Job Outlook

Employment of physical therapists is expected to grow faster than the average for all occupations through 2008. However, Federal legislation imposing limits on reimbursement for therapy services may continue to adversely affect the job market for physical therapists in the near term. Because of the effects of these provisions, the majority of expected employment growth for physical therapists will occur in the second half of the projection period.

Over the long run, the demand for physical therapists should continue to rise as a result of growth in the number of individuals with disabilities or limited function requiring therapy services. The rapidly growing elderly population is particularly vulnerable to chronic and debilitating conditions that require therapeutic services. Also, the baby-boom generation is entering the prime age for heart attacks and strokes, increasing the demand for cardiac and physical rehabilitation. More young people will need physical therapy as technological advances save the lives of a larger proportion of newborns with severe birth defects.

Future medical developments should also permit a higher percentage of trauma victims to survive, creating additional demand for rehabilitative care. Growth may also result from advances in medical technology which permit treatment of more disabling conditions.

Widespread interest in health promotion should also increase demand for physical therapy services. A growing number of employers are using physical therapists to evaluate work sites, develop exercise programs, and teach safe work habits to employees in the hope of reducing injuries.

Earnings

Median annual earnings of physical therapists were $56,600 in 1998. The middle 50 percent earned between $44,460 and $77,810 a year. The lowest 10 percent earned less than $35,700 and the highest 10 percent earned more than $90,870 a year.

OCCUPATIONAL THERAPISTS and PHYSICAL THERAPISTS

Don't forget! Refer to the general resources listed in Chapter Three and the Home Health Care Chapter.

ADVANCE Newsmagazines - Free to qualified professionals, *ADVANCE for Physical Therapists and PT Assistants, ADVANCE for Directors in Rehabilitation,* and *ADVANCE for Occupational Therapy Practitioners,* have extensive classified ads and meeting lists. Call 800/355-1088 or view Web site at **(http://www.merion.com)**.

American Massage Therapy Association (AMTA) - 820 Davis St., Suite 100, Evanston, IL 60201-4444; Phone: 847/864-0123, Fax: 847/864-1178, E-mail: info@inet.amtamassage.org. Web site has career, school and certification information. Members only can post resumes on the Job Network. URL: **http://www.amtamassage.org**.

American Occupational Therapy Association (AOTA) - 4720 Montgomery Lane, P.O. Box 31220, Bethesda, MD 20824-1220; 800/377-8555, 301/652-2682, **(http://www.aota.org)**. Some state chapters have employment services. "AOTA area" of the web site lists state chapters. "Student area" has a guide to accredited programs. *American Journal of Occupational Therapy* $50/year nonmembers. *OT Practice* is published 22 times per year, $35 for student members, $75 to nonmember students and member non-students, with job ads.

♈ 🗐↶ **American Society of Hand Therapists (ASHT)** - 401 North Michigan Avenue, Chicago, IL 60611; 312/321-6866, (**http://www.asht.org**) ASHT offers free job ads in their newsletter, *ASHT Times* (quarterly). *ASHT Membership Directory* is online. Occupational therapists and physical therapists can become certified in hand therapy after 5 years in practice, but certification is voluntary.

♈ 🗐↶ **National Rehabilitation Association (NRA)** - 633 S. Washington St., Alexandria, VA 22314; 703/836-0850, (**http://www.nationalrehab.org**). Members are counselors and job trainers. The NRA is an umbrella organization for seven associations including the National Association of Rehabilitation Instructors and the National Association of Private Rehabilitation. *Contemporary Rehab* includes list of employment opportunities. Free to members, 8/year. Student memberships cost $20.

♈ 🗐🗲↶**National Strength and Conditioning Association (NSCA)** - 1955 N. Union Blvd., Colorado Springs, CO 80909; 719/632-6722, 800/815-6826 fax: 719/ 632-6367, (**http://www.nsca-lift.org/menu.asp**). Members are personal trainers, PTs and OTs. *NSCA Career Hotline* online, available to members only, has job ads. On-site Career Fair available at annual conferences.

🗐🗁↶ **OccupationalTherapist.com** - This web site has a job data bank at (**http://www.occupationaltherapist.com**).Use the global directory to find an OT practice, clinic, school or association by area. The site has many useful links.

🗐🗁↶ Occupational Therapy Internet World - Provided by Richard Powell, MA, OTR, (**http://www.mother.com/~ktherapy/ot**) includes excellent networking opportunities: message board, chat information, Listservs and a directory of occupational therapists with e-mail addresses and short descriptions. Many are looking to converse with others by e-mail. The Occupational Therapy Online Peach Pages is a listing of occupational therapists by state and city. The OT Internet Directory is for therapists, assistants, and students. Award-winning site has a job advertizing page under construction.

📖 **Opportunities in Occupational Therapy Careers** by Marguerite Abbott and **Opportunities in Physical Therapy Careers** by Bernice R. Krumhans are Published by VGM Career Horizons, 4255 Touhy Ave., Lincolnwood, IL 60646-1975; 800/323-4900.

✒ **Physical Therapy -The Web Space** - (http://automailer.com/tws) E:mail: you@physio.zzn.com. This site has excellent resources: journals, schools, organizations, commercial sites (job recruiters, companies and clinics), job   sites, e-lists and chat.   They offer great resources for Canadian and U.S. physical therapists and PT students.

▤▱✒ **Physical Therapist Online** - (http://physicaltherapist.com) Find a school, a job or a physical therapist around the world.

▤✐✒ **RehabWorld** - (http://www.rehabworld.com) This site provides information for OT, PT, mental health and speech therapy: job searches, rehab links, and e-mail lists. Post your resume.

▥✒ **SLACK Incorporated** - 6900 Grove Road, Thorofare, NJ 08086-1000; Phone: 856-848-1000. (http://www.slackbooks.com). Publishes many books in the health care field, including *OT Student Primer: A Guide to College Success*.   Web site has, extensive links in three categories: "Occupational Therapy", "Physical Therapy", and "Athletic Training." Job ads site links are within each category.

▱✒ **The Therapy Directory** - (http://www.therapydirectory.com) Use this search site to find a specialist in massage therapy, occupational therapy, physical therapy, psychology/counseling, speech-language, or therapeutic recreation, by city, state, or zip code.

RECREATIONAL THERAPISTS

RELATED OCCUPATIONS:
Recreational therapists design activities to help people with disabilities lead more fulfilling and independent lives. Other workers who have similar jobs are:

Art Therapists	Occupational Therapists
Drama Therapists	Orientation Therapists for the Blind
Dance Therapists	Rehabilitation Counselors
Music Therapists	

Employment of recreational therapists is expected to increase, due to expansion in long-term care, physical and psychiatric rehabilitation, and services for people with disabilities.

Nature of the Work
Recreational therapists, also referred to as therapeutic recreation specialists, provide treatment services and recreation activities to individuals with disabilities, illnesses, or other disabling conditions. These therapists use a variety of techniques to treat or maintain the physical, mental, and emotional well-being of clients. Treatments may include the use of arts and crafts, animals, sports, games, dance and movement, drama, music, and community outings. Therapists help individuals reduce depression, stress, and anxiety. They also help individuals recover basic motor functioning and reasoning abilities, build confidence, and socialize effectively to enable greater independence, as well as to reduce or eliminate the effects of illness or disability. Additionally, they help integrate people with disabilities into the community, by helping them use community resources and recreational activities. Recreational therapists should not be confused with recreation workers, who organize recreational activities primarily for enjoyment. (Recreation workers are discussed elsewhere in the Handbook.)

In acute health care settings, such as hospitals and rehabilitation centers, recreational therapists treat and rehabilitate individuals with specific health conditions, usually in conjunction or collaboration with physicians, nurses, psychologists, social workers, and physical and occupational therapists. In long-term care facilities and residential facilities, recreational therapists use leisure activities—especially structured group programs—to improve and maintain general health and well-being. They may also treat clients and provide interventions to prevent further medical problems and secondary complications related to illness and disabilities.

Recreational therapists assess clients, based on information from standardized assessments, observations, medical records, medical staff, family, and clients themselves. They then develop and carry out therapeutic interventions consistent with client needs and interests. For example, clients isolated from others, or with limited social skills, may be encouraged to play games with others, or right-handed persons with right-side paralysis may be instructed to adapt to using their non-affected left side to throw a ball or swing a racket. Recreational therapists may instruct patients in relaxation techniques to reduce stress and tension, stretching and limbering exercises, proper body mechanics for participation in recreation activities, pacing and energy conservation techniques, and individual as well as team activities. Additionally, therapists observe and document patients' participation, reactions, and progress.

Community based therapeutic recreation specialists may work in park and recreation departments, special education programs for school districts, or programs for older adults and people with disabilities. Included in the latter group are programs and facilities such as assisted living, adult day service centers and substance abuse rehabilitation centers. In these programs, therapists use interventions to develop specific skills while providing opportunities for exercise, mental stimulation, creativity, and fun. Although most therapists are employed in other areas, those who work in schools help counselors, teachers, and parents address the special needs of students—most importantly, easing the transition into adult life for disabled students.

Working Conditions

Recreational therapists provide services in special activity rooms but also plan activities and prepare documentation in offices. When working with clients during community integration programs, they may travel locally to instruct clients on the accessibility of public transportation and other public areas, such as parks, playgrounds, swimming pools, restaurants, and theaters.

Therapists often lift and carry equipment as well as lead recreational activities. Recreational therapists generally work a 40-hour week that may include some evenings, weekends, and holidays.

Employment

Recreational therapists held about 39,000 jobs in 1998. About 38 percent of salaried jobs for therapists were in hospitals, and 26 percent were in nursing and personal care facilities. Others worked in residential facilities, community mental health centers, adult day care programs, correctional facilities, community programs for people with disabilities, and substance abuse centers. About 1 out of 3 therapists was self-employed, generally contracting with long-term care facilities or community agencies to develop and oversee programs.

Training, Other Qualifications, and Advancement

A bachelor's degree in therapeutic recreation, or in recreation with a concentration in therapeutic recreation, is the usual requirement for entry-level positions. Persons may qualify for paraprofessional positions with an associate degree in therapeutic recreation or a health care related field. An associate degree in recreational therapy; training in art, drama, or music therapy; or qualifying work experience may be sufficient for activity director positions in nursing homes.

Most employers prefer to hire candidates who are certified therapeutic recreation specialists (CTRS). The National Council for Therapeutic Recreation Certification (NCTRC) certifies therapeutic recreation specialists. To become certified, specialists must have a bachelor's degree, pass a written certification examination, and complete an internship of at least 360 hours, under the supervision of a certified therapeutic recreation specialist. A few colleges or agencies may require 600 hours of internship.

There are approximately 150 programs that prepare recreational therapists. Most offer bachelors degrees, although some offer associate, master's, or doctoral degrees. As of 1998, there were 43 recreation programs with options in therapeutic recreation accredited by the National Council on Accreditation.

Recreational therapy programs include courses in assessment, treatment and program planning, intervention design, and evaluation. Students also study human anatomy, physiology, abnormal psychology, medical and psychiatric terminology, characteristics of illnesses and disabilities, professional ethics, and the use of assistive devices and technology.

Recreational therapists should be comfortable working with persons who are ill or have disabilities. Therapists must be patient, tactful, and persuasive when working with people who have a variety of special needs. Ingenuity, a sense of humor, and imagination are needed to adapt activities to individual needs; and good physical coordination is necessary to demonstrate or participate in recreational activities.

Therapists may advance to supervisory or administrative positions. Some teach, conduct research, or perform contract consulting work.

Job Outlook

Employment of recreational therapists is expected to grow as fast as the average for all occupations through the year 2008, because of anticipated expansion in long-term care, physical and psychiatric rehabilitation, and services for people with disabilities. However, the total number of job openings will be relatively low, because the occupation is small. Opportunities should be best for persons with a bachelor's degree in therapeutic recreation or in recreation with an option in therapeutic recreation.

Health care facilities will provide a growing number of jobs in hospital-based adult day care and outpatient programs and in units offering short-term mental health and alcohol or drug abuse services. Rehabilitation, home-health care, transitional programs, and psychiatric facilities will provide additional jobs.

The rapidly growing number of older adults is expected to spur job growth for therapeutic recreation specialists and recreational therapy paraprofessionals in assisted living facilities, adult day care programs, and social service agencies. Continued growth is also expected in community residential facilities, as well as day care programs for individuals with disabilities.

Earnings

Median annual earnings of recreational therapists were $27,760 in 1998. The middle 50 percent earned between $21,580 and $35,000 a year. The lowest 10 percent earned less than $16,380 and the highest 10 percent earned more than $42,440 a year. Median annual earnings for recreational therapists in 1997 were $29,700 in hospitals and $21,900 in nursing and personal care facilities.

RECREATIONAL THERAPISTS

Don't forget! Refer to the general resources listed in Chapter Three. Look in the Occupational Therapists / Physical Therapists section of this chapter for **National Rehabilitation Association, RehabWorld, SLACK Incorporated** and **The Therapy Directory**.

| 🜊 Association | 📖 Book | 📂 Directory | 🖱 Internet (Web) Site |
| 📑 Job Ads | 💥 E-mail/Hotline | 🏷 Job Fairs | 📎 Resume Service |

🜊📑🏷🖱 **American Alliance for Health, Physical Education, Recreation and Dance (AAHPERD)** - 1900 Association Drive, Reston, VA 22091; 703/476-3400, 800/213-7193, (**http://www.aahperd.org**), E-mail: webmaster@aahperd.org. AAHPERD consists of 6 associations: American Association for Active Lifestyles and Fitness (AAALF), American Association for Health Education (AAHE), American Association for Leisure and Recreation (AALR), National Association for Girls and Women in Sport (NAGWS), National Association for Sport and Physical Education (NASPE), and National Dance Association (NDA). AAHPERD publishes many career brochures. Student memberships are $45.

🜊🖱 **American Art Therapy Association, Inc. (AATA)** - 1202 Allanson Road, Mundelein, Illinois 60060; 888/290-0878. Affiliate chapters have been established in many states; contact information through their web site at (**http://www.arttherapy.org**), E-mail: estygariii@aol.com. The AATA publishes *Art Therapy Model Job Description, Art Therapy: Journal of the American Art Therapy Association*, and *AATA Newsletter*.

🜊🖱 **American Horticultural Therapy Association (AHTA)** - 909 York Street, Denver, CO 80206; 720/865-3616. Web site (**http://www.ahta.org**) has career description and guide to education programs. Publishes *People Plant Connection* newsletter, sample issue $3.00. E-Mail: ahta@ahta.org.

🜊📑🖱 **American Therapeutic Recreation Association (ATRA)** - 1414 Prince Street, Alexandria, VA 22314; (**http://www.atra-tr.org/atra.htm**). ATRA has a newsletter and career information, job ads, and employment updates on their web site.

Art Therapy in Canada - (http://www.home.ican.net/~phansen). Provides an Art Therapy Newsgroup, e-mail lists, and a description of the profession; very informative.

National Association for Drama Therapy (NADT) - 5505 Connecticut Ave., N.W. #280 Washington, D.C. 20015; 202/966-7409, fax: 202/966-2283. (http://www.nadt.org), E-mail: nadt@danielgrp.com. Informative website, with job ads as one feature.

National Association for Music Therapy - 8455 Colesville Road, Suite 1000, Silver Spring, MD 20910. A web site (http://www.namt.com) with career information, members-only page, including job posting, to start March 1, 2001.

National Coalition of Arts Therapies Associations (NCATA) - c/o ADTA, 8455 Colesville Rd., Suite 1000, Silver Spring MD 20910; 714/751-0103, (http://www.ncata.com). The council is an alliance of professional associations dedicated to the advancement of the arts as therapeutic modalities. Site provides links to six creative arts therapies organizations, with contact information: American Association for Music Therapy, American Art Therapy Association, American Dance Therapy Association, National Association for Drama Therapy, American Society for Group Psychotherapy & Psychodrama, and National Association for Poetry Therapy.

National Council for Therapeutic Recreation Certification (NCTRC) - P. O. Box 479, Thiells, NY 10984-049, (http://www.nctrc.org) Certification standards and applications are available here.

National Therapeutic Recreation Society (NTRS) - 22377 Belmont Ridge Road, Ashburn, VA 20148; 703/858-0784, fax: 703/858-0794, (http://www.nrpa.org/branches/ntrs.htm), E-mail: NTRSNRPA@aol.com. NTRS is a branch of the National Recreation and Park Association (NRPA). *Preparing for a Career in Therapeutic Recreation*, a booklet, is available to members, $5.25/non-members, $7.50. Career description is on the web site. Access to the *Job Bulletin* on the web is $55/yr.

Project TRAIN (Therapeutic Recreation Access to the Internet) - Presents Listserv groups at (http://perth.uwlax.edu/train). An excellent collection of links to sites of interest in all aspects of RT.

Therapeutic Recreation Directory Numerous resources include networking opportunities in chat room and on bulletin board;

directory of therapeutic recreation associations, colleges with TR programs, e-mail addresses of recreation therapists. Visit their site at (**www.recreationtherapy.com/rt.htm**). Includes job ads.

⌐ **Therapeutic Recreation Web Ring** - Fourteen TR organizations linked their Internet sites to each other through the following URL (**http://www.webring.org/cgi-bin/webring?ring=txrec;list**).

RESPIRATORY THERAPISTS

Job opportunities will be best for therapists who work with newborns and infants.

Nature of the Work

Respiratory therapists evaluate, treat, and care for patients with breathing disorders. To evaluate patients, therapists test the capacity of the lungs and analyze oxygen and carbon dioxide concentration. They also measure the patient's potential of hydrogen (pH), which indicates the acidity or alkalinity level of the blood. To measure lung capacity, therapists have patients breathe into an instrument that measures the volume and flow of oxygen during inhalation and exhalation. By comparing the reading with the norm for the patient's age, height, weight, and sex, respiratory therapists can determine whether lung deficiencies exist. To analyze oxygen, carbon dioxide, and pH levels, therapists draw an arterial blood sample, place it in a blood gas analyzer, and relay the results to a physician.

Respiratory therapists treat all types of patients, ranging from premature infants whose lungs are not fully developed, to elderly people whose lungs are diseased. These workers provide temporary relief to patients with chronic asthma or emphysema and emergency care for patients who suffered heart failure or a stroke or are victims of drowning or shock. Respiratory therapists most commonly use oxygen or oxygen mixtures, chest physiotherapy, and aerosol medications. To increase a patient's concentration of oxygen, therapists place an oxygen mask or nasal cannula on a patient and set the oxygen flow at the level prescribed by a physician. Therapists also connect patients who cannot breathe on their own to ventilators that deliver pressurized oxygen into the lungs. They insert a tube into a patient's trachea, or windpipe; connect the tube to the ventilator; and set the rate, volume, and oxygen concentration of the oxygen mixture entering the patient's lungs.

Therapists regularly check on patients and equipment. If the patient appears to be having difficulty, or if the oxygen, carbon dioxide, or pH level of the blood is abnormal, they change the ventilator setting, according to the doctor's order or check equipment for mechanical problems. In home care, therapists teach patients and their families to use ventilators and other life support systems. Additionally, they visit several times a month to inspect and clean equipment and ensure its proper use and make emergency visits, if equipment problems arise.

Respiratory therapists perform chest physiotherapy on patients to remove mucus from their lungs and make it easier for them to breathe. For example, during surgery, anesthesia depresses respiration, so this treatment may be prescribed to help get the patient's lungs back to normal and to prevent congestion. Chest physiotherapy also helps patients suffering from lung diseases, such as cystic fibrosis, that cause mucus to collect in the lungs. In this procedure, therapists place patients in positions to help drain mucus, thump and vibrate patients' rib cages, and instruct them to cough.

Respiratory therapists also administer aerosols—generally liquid medications suspended in a gas that forms a mist which is inhaled—and teach patients how to inhale the aerosol properly to assure its effectiveness.

Therapists are increasingly asked to perform tasks that fall outside their traditional role. Tasks are expanding into cardiopulmonary procedures like electrocardiograms and stress testing, as well as other tasks like drawing blood samples from patients. Therapists also keep records of materials used and charges to patients. Additionally, some teach or supervise other respiratory therapy personnel.

Working Conditions

Respiratory therapists generally work between 35 and 40 hours a week. Because hospitals operate around the clock, therapists may work evenings, nights, or weekends. They spend long periods standing and walking between patients' rooms. In an emergency, therapists work under a great deal of stress.

Because gases used by respiratory therapists are stored under pressure, they are potentially hazardous. However, adherence to safety precautions and regular maintenance and testing of equipment minimize the risk of injury. As with many health occupations, respiratory therapists run a risk of catching infectious diseases, but carefully following proper procedures minimizes this risk, as well.

Employment

Respiratory therapists held about 86,000 jobs in 1998. About 9 out of 10 jobs were in hospital departments of respiratory care, anesthesiology, or pulmonary medicine. Home health agencies, respiratory therapy clinics, and nursing homes accounted for most of the remaining jobs.

Training, Other Qualifications, and Advancement

Formal training is necessary for entry to this field. Training is offered at the postsecondary level by hospitals, medical schools, colleges and universities, trade schools, vocational-technical institutes, and the Armed Forces. Some programs prepare graduates for jobs as registered respiratory therapists (RRT); other, shorter programs lead to jobs as certified respiratory therapists (CRT). According to the Committee on Accreditation for Respiratory Care (CoARC), there were 327 registered respiratory therapist programs and 134 certified respiratory therapist programs in the United States in 1999.

Formal training programs vary in length and in the credential or degree awarded. Most of the CoARC-accredited registered respiratory therapist programs last 2 years and lead to an associate degree. Some, however, are 4-year bachelor's degree programs. Areas of study for respiratory therapy programs include human anatomy and physiology, chemistry, physics, microbiology, and mathematics. Technical courses deal with procedures, equipment, and clinical tests.

More and more therapists receive on-the-job training, allowing them to administer electrocardiograms and stress tests, as well as draw blood samples from patients.

Therapists should be sensitive to patients' physical and psychological needs. Respiratory care workers must pay attention to detail, follow instructions, and work as part of a team. In addition, operating complicated respiratory therapy equipment requires mechanical ability and manual dexterity.

High school students interested in a career in respiratory care should take courses in health, biology, mathematics, chemistry, and physics. Respiratory care involves basic mathematical problem solving and an understanding of chemical and physical principles. For example, respiratory care workers must be able to compute medication dosages and calculate gas concentrations.

Over 40 States license respiratory care personnel. The National Board for Respiratory Care offers voluntary certification and registration to graduates of CoARC-accredited programs. Two credentials are awarded to respiratory therapists who satisfy the requirements: Registered Respiratory Therapist (RRT) and Certified Respiratory Therapist (CRT). All graduates—those from 2- and 4-year programs in respiratory therapy, as well as those from 1-year CRT programs—may take the CRT examination. CRTs who meet education and experience requirements can take a separate examination, leading to the award of the RRT.

Individuals who have completed a 4-year program in a non-respiratory field but have college level courses in anatomy, physiology, chemistry, biology, microbiology, physics, and mathematics can become a CRT, after graduating from an accredited 1- or 2-year program. After they receive 2 years of clinical experience, they are eligible to take the registry exam to become an RRT.

Most employers require applicants for entry-level or generalist positions to hold the CRT or be eligible to take the certification examination. Supervisory positions and those in intensive care specialties usually require the RRT (or RRT eligibility).

Respiratory therapists advance in clinical practice by moving from care of general to critical patients who have significant problems in other organ systems, such as the heart or kidneys. Respiratory therapists, especially those with 4-year degrees, may also advance to supervisory or managerial positions in a respiratory therapy department. Respiratory therapists in home care and equipment rental firms may become branch managers.

Job Outlook

Job opportunities are expected to remain good. Employment of respiratory therapists is expected to increase much faster than the average for all occupations through the year 2008, because of substantial growth of the middle-aged and elderly population—a development that will heighten the incidence of cardiopulmonary disease.

Older Americans suffer most from respiratory ailments and cardiopulmonary diseases such as pneumonia, chronic bronchitis, emphysema, and heart disease. As their numbers increase, the need for respiratory therapists will increase, as well. In addition, advances in treating victims of heart attacks, accident victims, and premature infants (many of whom are dependent on a ventilator during part of their treatment) will increase the demand for the services of respiratory care practitioners.

Opportunities are expected to be highly favorable for respiratory therapists with cardiopulmonary care skills with infant experience.

Although hospitals will continue to employ the majority of thera-pists, a growing number of therapists can expect to work outside of hospitals in home health agencies, clinics, or nursing homes.

Earnings

Median annual earnings for respiratory therapists were $34,830 in 1998. The middle 50 percent earned between $30,040 and $39,830 a year. The lowest 10 percent earned less than $25,910 and the highest 10 percent earned more than $46,760 a year.

RESPIRATORY THERAPISTS

Don't forget! Refer to the general resources listed in Chapter Three, the OT/PT section of this Chapter and Home Health Chapter, too.

   ⚕Association   📖 Book   📁 Directory   Internet (Web) Site

   Job Ads   E-mail/Hotline   Job Fairs   Resume Service

ADVANCE - 650 Park Avenue West, Box 61556, King of Prussia, PA 19406-0956; 800/355-1088. (**http://www.merion.com/sitemap.html**) Publishes *ADVANCE for Managers of Respiratory Care* and *ADVANCE for Respiratory Care Practitioners*, free for professionals.

American Association for Respiratory Care (AARC) - 11030 Ables Ln., Dallas, TX 75229; 972/243-2272, fax: 972/484-2720, (**http://www.aarc.org**), E-mail: info@aarc.org. *AARC Times* is online. The web site has job listings and information on the career. Members can post position wanted ads on the site.

California Society for Respiratory Care (CSRC) - 660 J Street, Suite 481, Sacramento, CA 95814, (**http://www.csrc.org**). Web site has a member directory, a list of schools offering respiratory care programs in California, employment ads, and links to other state societies for respiratory care.

Canadian Society of Respiratory Therapists (CSRT) - URL (**http://www.csrt.com**), E-mail: info@csrt.com. The professional area has newsgroups, bulletin board, job listings and CSRT newsletter.

☤ **Committee on Accreditation for Respiratory Care (CoARC)** - 1248 Harwood Rd., Bedford, TX 76021-4244. **(http://www.coarc.com).** Contact for a current list of CoARC-accredited educationl programs for respiratory therapy occupations.

🖱 **MedMark Respiration Medicine** - Impressive collection of links by Ildo Shin, M.D. at **(http://user.iworld.net/medmark/rm)**.

☤ 🗁🖱 **National Board for Respiratory Care (NBRC)** - 8310 Nieman Rd., Lenexa, KS 66214; 913/599-4200. Publishes *NBRC Annual Directory.* URL **(http://www.nbrc.org),** E-mail: nbrc-info@nbrc.org.

🖱 **National Jewish Medical and Research Center** - 1400 Jackson St., Denver, Colorado 80206; 303/388-4461, 800/222-LUNG. Their web site at **(http://www.nationaljewish.org)** has information about a career in pulmonary rehabilitation.

🗁🖱 **The RCsourcePAGES®** - McPeck Consulting Services, 32 Spencer Lane, Stony Brook, NY 11790-3139; voice mail 516/689-7251. **(http://www.sourcepages.com)** E-mail: mmcpeck@sourcepages.com.

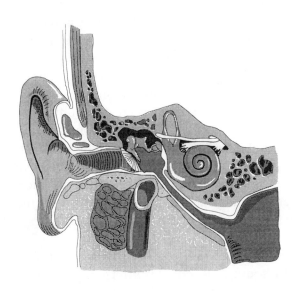

SPEECH-LANGUAGE PATHOLOGISTS AND AUDIOLOGISTS

Nature of the Work

Speech-language pathologists assess, treat, and help to prevent speech, language, cognitive, communication, voice, swallowing, fluency, and other related disorders; audiologists identify, assess, and manage auditory, balance, and other neural systems.

Speech-language pathologists work with people who cannot make speech sounds, or cannot make them clearly; those with speech rhythm and fluency problems, such as stuttering; people with voice quality problems, such as inappropriate pitch or harsh voice; those with problems understanding and producing language; and those with cognitive communication impairments, such as attention, memory, and problem solving disorders. They may also work with people who have oral motor problems causing eating and swallowing difficulties.

Speech and language problems can result from hearing loss, brain injury or deterioration, cerebral palsy, stroke, cleft palate, voice pathology, mental retardation, or emotional problems. Problems can be congenital, developmental, or acquired. Speech-language pathologists use written and oral tests, as well as special instruments, to diagnose the nature and extent of impairment and to record and analyze speech, language, and swallowing irregularities. Speech-language pathologists develop an individualized plan of care, tailored to each patient's needs. For individuals with little or no speech capability, speech-language pathologists select augmentative alternative communication methods, including automated devices and sign language, and teach their use. They teach these individuals how to make sounds, improve their voices, or increase their language skills to communicate more effectively. Speech-language pathologists help patients develop, or recover, reliable communication skills so patients can fulfill their educational, vocational, and social roles.

Most speech-language pathologists provide direct clinical services to individuals with communication disorders. In speech and language clinics, they may independently develop and carry out treatment programs. In medical facilities, they may work with physicians, social workers, psychologists, and other therapists to develop and execute treatment plans. Speech-language pathologists in schools develop individual or group programs, counsel parents, and may assist teachers with classroom activities.

Speech-language pathologists keep records on the initial evaluation, progress, and discharge of clients. This helps pinpoint problems, tracks client progress, and justifies the cost of treatment when applying for reimbursement. They counsel individuals and their families concerning communication disorders and how to cope with the stress and misunderstanding that often accompany them. They also work with family members to recognize and change behavior patterns that impede communication and treatment and show them communication enhancing techniques to use at home.

Some speech-language pathologists conduct research on how people communicate. Others design and develop equipment or techniques for diagnosing and treating speech problems.

Audiologists work with people who have hearing, balance, and related problems. They use audiometers, computers, and other testing devices to measure the loudness at which a person begins to hear sounds, the ability to distinguish between sounds, and the nature and extent of hearing loss. Audiologists interpret these results and may coordinate them with medical, educational, and psychological information to make a diagnosis and determine a course of treatment.

Hearing disorders can result from a variety of causes including trauma at birth, viral infections, genetic disorders, exposure to loud noise, or aging. Treatment may include examining and cleaning the ear canal, fitting and dispensing hearing aids or other assistive devices, and audiologic rehabilitation (including auditory training or instruction in speech or lip reading). Audiologists may recommend, fit, and dispense personal or large area amplification systems, such as hearing aids and alerting devices. Audiologists provide fitting and tuning of cochlear implants and provide the necessary rehabilitation for adjustment to listening with implant amplification systems. They also measure noise levels in workplaces and conduct hearing protection programs in industry, as well as in schools and communities.

Audiologists provide direct clinical services to individuals with hearing or balance disorders. In audiology (hearing) clinics, they may independently develop and carry out treatment programs. Audiologists, in a variety of settings, work as members of interdisciplinary professional teams in planning and implementing service delivery for children and adults, from birth to old age. Similar to speech-language pathologists, audiologists keep records on the initial evaluation, progress, and discharge of clients. These records help pinpoint problems, track client progress, and justify the cost of treatment, when applying for reimbursement.

Audiologists may conduct research on types of, and treatment for, hearing, balance, and related disorders. Others design and develop equipment or techniques for diagnosing and treating these disorders.

Working Conditions

Speech-language pathologists and audiologists usually work at a desk or table in clean comfortable surroundings. The job is not physically demanding but does require attention to detail and intense concentration. The emotional needs of clients and their families may be demanding. Most full-time speech-language pathologists and audiologists work about 40 hours per week; some work part-time. Those who work on a contract basis may spend a substantial amount of time traveling between facilities.

Employment

Speech-language pathologists and audiologists held about 105,000 jobs in 1998. About one-half provided services in preschools, elementary and secondary schools, or colleges and universities. Others were in offices of speech-language pathologists and audiologists; hospitals; offices of physicians; speech, language, and hearing centers; home health agencies; or other facilities.

Some speech-language pathologists and audiologists are self-employed in private practice. They contract to provide services in schools, physician's offices, hospitals, or nursing homes, or work as consultants to industry. Audiologists are more likely to be employed in independent healthcare offices, while speech-language pathologists are more likely to work in school settings.

Training, Other Qualifications, and Advancement

Of the States that regulate licensing (44 for speech-language pathologists and 49 for audiologists), almost all require a master's degree or equivalent. Other requirements are 300 to 375 hours of supervised clinical experience, a passing score on a national examination, and 9 months of postgraduate professional clinical experience. Thirty-six States have continuing education requirements for licensure renewal. Medicaid, medicare, and private health insurers generally require a practitioner to be licensed to qualify for reimbursement.

About 235 colleges and universities offer graduate programs in speech-language pathology. Courses cover anatomy and physiology of the areas of the body involved in speech, language, and hearing; the development of normal speech, language, and hearing; the nature of disorders; acoustics; and psychological aspects of communication. Graduate students also learn to evaluate and treat speech, language, and hearing disorders and receive supervised clinical training in communication disorders.

About 115 colleges and universities offer graduate programs in audiology in the United States. Course work includes anatomy; physiology; basic science; math; physics; genetics; normal and abnormal communication development; auditory, balance and neural systems assessment and treatment; audiologic rehabilitation; and ethics.

Speech-language pathologists can acquire the Certificate of Clinical Competence in Speech-Language Pathology (CCC-SLP) offered by the American Speech-Language-Hearing Association, and audiologists can earn the Certificate of Clinical Competence in Audiology (CCC-A). To earn a CCC, a person must have a graduate degree and 375 hours of supervised clinical experience, complete a 36-week postgraduate clinical fellowship, and pass a written examination. According to the American Speech-Language Hearing Association, as of 2007, audiologists will need to have a bachelor's degree and complete 75 hours of credit toward a doctoral degree in order to seek certification. As of 2012, audiologists will have to earn a doctoral degree in order to be certified.

Speech-language pathologists and audiologists should be able to effectively communicate diagnostic test results, diagnoses, and proposed treatment in a manner easily understood by their clients. They must be able to approach problems objectively and provide support to clients and their families. Because a client's progress may be slow, patience, compassion, and good listening skills are necessary.

Job Outlook

Employment of speech-language pathologists and audiologists is expected to grow much faster than the average for all occupations through the year 2008. Because hearing loss is strongly associated with aging, rapid growth in the population age 55 and over will cause the number of persons with hearing impairment to increase markedly. In addition, baby boomers are now entering middle age, when the possibility of neurological disorders and associated speech, language, and hearing impairments increases. Medical advances are also improving the survival rate of premature infants and trauma and stroke victims, who then need assessment and possible treatment.

Employment growth in health services would be even faster except for Federal legislation imposing limits on reimbursement for therapy services that may continue to adversely affect the job market for therapy providers over the near term. Because of the effects of these provisions, the majority of expected employment growth in health services will occur in the second half of the projection period.

Employment in schools will increase along with growth in elementary and secondary school enrollments, including enrollment of special education students. Federal law guarantees special education and related services to all eligible children with disabilities. Greater awareness of the importance of early identification and diagnosis of speech, language, and hearing disorders will also increase employment.

The number of speech-language pathologists and audiologists in private practice will rise due to the increasing use of contract services by hospitals, schools, and nursing homes. In addition to job openings stemming from employment growth, some openings for speech-language pathologists and audiologists will arise from the need to replace those who leave the occupation.

Earnings

Median annual earnings of speech-language pathologists and audiologists were $43,080 in 1998. The middle 50 percent earned between $34,580 and $55,260 a year. The lowest 10 percent earned less than $27,460 and the highest 10 percent earned more than $80,720 a year.

According to a 1999 survey by the American Speech Language and Hearing Association, the median annual salary for full-time certified speech-language pathologists or audiologists who worked 11 or 12 months annually was $44,000. For those who worked 9 or 10 months annually, median annual salaries for speech-language pathologists were $40,000; for audiologists, $42,000.

SPEECH-LANGUAGE PATHOLOGISTS
and AUDIOLOGISTS

Don't forget! There are many good general resources listed in Chapter Three. Look in the Occupational Therapists / Physical Therapists section of this chapter for **National Rehabilitation Association, RehabWorld,** and **The Therapy Directory.**

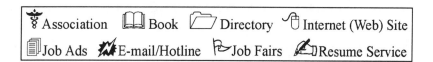

Association   Book   Directory   Internet (Web) Site
Job Ads   E-mail/Hotline   Job Fairs   Resume Service

Academy of Dispensing Audiologists® (ADA) - 3008 Millwood Avenue, Columbia, South Carolina 29205; 800/445-8629, 803/252-5646, fax: 803/765-0860, **http://www.audiologist.org/**, E-Mail: info@audiologist.org. Web site has forums and a directory by state.

ADVANCE Newsmagazines - *ADVANCE for Speech-Language Pathologists and Audiologists,* URL (**www.merion.com/sitemap.html**). Free to qualified professionals, these publications have extensive classified ads and meeting lists. Call 800/355-1088 for additional information.

The Alexander Graham Bell Association for the Deaf - 3417 Volta Place N.W., Washington, DC 20007-2778; 202/337-5220, voice and TTY, fax: 202/337-8314, (**http://www.agbell.org**). Professional programs and services department. Job liting is free online.

American Academy of Audiology (AAA) - 8300 Greensboro Drive, Suite 750, McLean, VA 22102; 703/610-9022, 800/AAA-2336, fax: 703/790-8631, (**http://www.audiology.com**).

American Academy of Private Practice in Speech Pathology and Audiology (AAPPSPA) - 100 West Fairway Drive, Valdosta, GA 31605, (http://www.aappspa.org). This site has a listing of private practitioners by area. Has a newsgroup.

American Speech-Language-Hearing Association (ASHA) - 10801 Rockville Pike, Rockville, MD 20852; 800/498-2071, 301/571-0457 (TTY), fax: 877/541-5035, (**http://www.asha.org**). Career Kit ($3.50) contains career descriptions, accredited school listing and salary ranges.

Publishes *Tools for a Successful Job Search*, $24/members, $33/nonmembers. (E-mail: careers@asha.org).

Better Hearing Institute - 5021-B Backlick Road, Annandale, VA 22003; Hearing HelpLine at 800-EAR WELL, E-mail: mail@ betterhearing.org, (**http://www.betterhearing.org**). Web site has a searchable list of audiologists, hearing instrument dispensers, and otolaryngologists. Links to other organizations to contact for jobs.

California Speech Language and Hearing Association (CSHA) - 825 University Avenue, Sacramento, CA 95825; 916/921-1568, fax: 916/921-0127, (**http://www.caspeechhearing.org**).

Canadian Association of Speech Language Pathologists & Audiologists (CASLPA) - (**http://www.caslpa.ca**) Career ads.

Council of Academic Programs in Communication Sciences and Disorders (CGPCSD) - PO Box 26532, Minneapolis, MN 55426; 612/920-0966, fax: 612/920-6098, (**http://www.capcsd.org**) E-mail: cgp@cgpcsd.org.

Educational Audiology Association (EAA) - 4319 Ehrlich Road, Tampa, FL 33624; 800/460-7EAA, (**http://edaud.org**). E-mail: eaa@l-tgraye.com. Listserv and *Educational Audiology Association Newsletter*.

National Institute on Deafness and Other Communication Disorders (NIDCD) - This web site has Employment Opportunities at the NIDCD & NIH posted on (**http://www.nidcd.nih.gov**).

National Student Speech Language Hearing Association (NSSLHA) - Internet URL: (**http://pegasus.cc.ucf.edu/~nsslha96**). E-mail: nsslha@asha.org. Sponsors a Job Fair.

University Programs in Speech-language Pathology and Audiology - (**http://facstaff.uww.edu/bradleys/cdprograms.html**) This site lists state programs and certification organization information.

Chapter 7

NURSING CAREERS

Desiree H. Griffith

Desiree Griffith, a post-anesthesia care registered nurse at the Sewickley Hospital in Western Pennsylvania, was born in Guyana, South America on April 5, 1947. She came to America in 1968 just before turning 21. Desiree was a tax assesor in Guyana. Math and science were always her strong points and in New York she landed a job as a claims adjuster.

"I met a friend in New York that was in nursing school. She was having a great time and really loved what she was doing", said Desiree. "I wanted to deal more with people so I followed my friend's example and entered the Brooklyn Jewish Hospital's nursing program in 1969." Mrs. Griffith did very well in school and she said, "I loved it. I enjoyed working with people and it was always challenging."

Mrs. Griffith started working in a medical surgery unit and stayed there for six months. Then she went on maternity leave to have her first child. After returning from maternity leave she requested a recovery room assignment and has worked in this area since 1973. "Post-anesthesia Care is the section that you're taken to after surgery to recover patients from the effects of anesthesia," said Desiree, "This used to be called the recovery room."

In 1977 Desiree and her family moved to Charlotte, North Carolina and she landed a job in a cardiovascular recovery unit at the Charlotte Memorial Hospital. The last eighteen months at Charlotte Desiree worked in post-anesthesia care.

"One of the advantages of the nursing field is the ability to work diverse schedules depending on your personal circumstances," said Desiree. "In 1980 we moved to Pittsburgh where I worked casual (part-time) at the Sewickley Hospital due to my husband's work schedule. After my second child was born I opted to work on weekends only for a period of time. For several years I shared a job with another nurse; I worked Monday, Tuesday and a half day on Wednesday, my partner worked the remainder of the week."

"Nursing is a great field to work in - it's hard work without a doubt. The field is wide open with many career options. Also, as a registered nurse everyone in my unit is fully qualified to do the same function. Therefore, when I need a day off it isn't difficult to get someone to work for me."

"There are other things to consider," said Desiree, "You may be required to work rotating shifts, weekends, and holidays. The stress involved when you deal with life and death situations on a daily basis can get to you. If something is happening in recovery you don't have the option to just leave at the end of your shift. You must be willing to stay no matter what you have planned. Your patients depend on you entirely."

Desiree said, "You can always find a job in nursing if you really want to work. You may not find one with all daylight work and no weekends but you will find a job. Most of it is up to you."

This chapter features nursing. The major occupational groups are:

Licensed Practical Nurses   **Registered Nurses**
Nursing Aides and Psychiatric Aides

Each specialty is described below. Following all of the job descriptions are job resource lists: Associations, Books, Directories, Internet Sites, Job Ads, E-mail Job Notification/Job Hotlines, Job Fairs, and Resume and Placement Services with icons guide you.

LICENSED PRACTICAL NURSES

Training lasting about 1 year is available in about 1,100 State-approved programs, mostly in vocational or technical schools.

Nature of the Work

Licensed practical nurses (L.P.N.s), or licensed vocational nurses as they are called in Texas and California, care for the sick, injured, convalescent, and disabled under the direction of physicians and registered nurses. (The work of registered nurses is described elsewhere in the Handbook.)

Most L.P.N.s provide basic bedside care. They take vital signs such as temperature, blood pressure, pulse, and respiration. They also treat bedsores, prepare and give injections and enemas, apply dressings, give alcohol rubs and massages, apply ice packs and hot water bottles, and insert catheters. L.P.N's observe patients and report adverse reactions to medications or treatments. They collect samples from patients for testing, perform routine laboratory tests, feed them, and record food and liquid intake and output. They help patients with bathing, dressing, and personal hygiene, keep them comfortable, and care for their emotional needs. In States where the law allows, they may administer prescribed medicines or start intravenous fluids. Some L.P.N.s help deliver, care for, and feed infants. Some experienced L.P.N.s supervise nursing assistants and aides.

L.P.N.s in nursing homes, in addition to providing routine bedside care, may also help evaluate residents' needs, develop care plans, and supervise the care provided by nursing aides. In doctors' offices and clinics, they may also make appointments, keep records, and perform other clerical duties. L.P.N.s who work in private homes may also prepare meals and teach family members simple nursing tasks.

Working Conditions

Most licensed practical nurses in hospitals and nursing homes work a 40-hour week, but because patients need round-the-clock care, some work nights, weekends, and holidays. They often stand for long periods and help patients move in bed, stand, or walk.

L.P.N.s may face hazards from caustic chemicals, radiation, and infectious diseases such as hepatitis. They are subject to back injuries when moving patients and shock from electrical equipment. They often must deal with the stress of heavy workloads. In addition, the patients they care for may be confused, irrational, agitated, or uncooperative.

Employment

Licensed practical nurses held about 692,000 jobs in 1998. Thirty-two percent of L.P.N.s worked in hospitals, 28 percent worked in nursing homes, and 14 percent in doctors' offices and clinics. Others worked for temporary help agencies, home health care services, residential care facilities, schools, or government agencies. About 1 in 4 worked part time.

Training, Other Qualifications, and Advancement

All States require L.P.N.s to pass a licensing examination after completing a State-approved practical nursing program. A high school diploma is usually required for entry, but some programs accept people without a diploma.

In 1998, approximately 1,100 State-approved programs provided practical nursing training. Almost 6 out of 10 students were enrolled in technical or vocational schools, while 3 out of 10 were in community and junior colleges. Others were in high schools, hospitals, and colleges and universities.

Most practical nursing programs last about 1 year and include both classroom study and supervised clinical practice (patient care). Classroom study covers basic nursing concepts and patient-care related subjects, including anatomy, physiology, medical-surgical nursing, pediatrics, obstetrics, psychiatric nursing, administration of drugs, nutrition, and first aid. Clinical practice is usually in a hospital, but sometimes includes other settings.

L.P.N.s should have a caring, sympathetic nature. They should be emotionally stable because work with the sick and injured can be stressful. As part of a health care team, they must be able to follow orders and work under close supervision.

Job Outlook

Employment of L.P.N.s is expected to grow as fast as the average for all occupations through 2008 in response to the long-term care needs of a rapidly growing population of very old people and to the general growth of health care. However, L.P.N.s seeking positions in hospitals may face competition, as the number of hospital jobs for L.P.N.s declines; the number of inpatients, with whom most L.P.N.s work, is not expected to increase much. As in most other occupations, replacement needs will be a major source of job openings.

Employment in nursing homes is expected to grow faster than the average. Nursing homes will offer the most new jobs for L.P.N.s as the number of aged and disabled persons in need of long-term care rises. In addition to caring for the aged, nursing homes will be called on to care for the increasing number of patients who have been released from the hospital and have not recovered enough to return home.

Much faster than average growth is expected in home health care services. This is in response to a growing number of older persons with functional disabilities, consumer preference for care in the home, and technological advances, which make it possible to bring increasingly complex treatments into the home.

An increasing proportion of sophisticated procedures, which once were performed only in hospitals, are being performed in physicians' offices and clinics, including ambulatory surgicenters and emergency medical centers, thanks largely to advances in technology. As a result, employment is projected to grow much faster than average in these places as health care in general expands.

Earnings

Median annual earnings of licensed practical nurses were $26,940 in 1998. The middle 50 percent earned between $23,160 and $31,870 a year. The lowest 10 percent earned less than $20,210 and the highest 10 percent earned more than $37,540 a year.

NURSING AIDES AND PSYCHIATRIC AIDES

OCCUPATIONAL TITLES:

Geriatric Aides	Nursing Assistants
Hospital Attendants	Psychiatric Nursing Assistants
Mental Health Assistants	Ward Attendants

Job prospects for nursing aides will be good because of fast growth and high turnover in this large occupation.

Nature of the Work

Nursing and psychiatric aides help care for physically or mentally ill, injured, disabled, or infirm individuals confined to hospitals, nursing or residential care facilities, and mental health settings. (Home health and personal care aides, whose duties are similar but who work in clients' homes, are discussed elsewhere in the Handbook.)

Nursing aides, also known as nursing assistants, geriatric aides, unlicenced assistive personnel, or hospital attendants, perform routine tasks under the supervision of nursing and medical staff. They answer patients' call bells, deliver messages, serve meals, make beds, and help patients eat, dress, and bathe. Aides may also provide skin care to patients; take temperatures, pulse, respiration, and blood pressure; and help patients get in and out of bed and walk. They may also escort patients to operating and examining rooms, keep patients' rooms neat, set up equipment, or store and move supplies. Aides observe patients' physical, mental, and emotional conditions and report any change to the nursing or medical staff.

Nursing aides employed in nursing homes are often the principal caregivers, having far more contact with residents than other members of the staff. Since some residents may stay in a nursing home for months or even years, aides develop ongoing relationships with them and interact with them in a positive, caring way.

Psychiatric aides are also known as mental health assistants and psychiatric nursing assistants. They care for mentally impaired or emotionally disturbed individuals. They work under a team that may include psychiatrists, psychologists, psychiatric nurses, social workers, and therapists. In addition to helping patients dress, bathe, groom, and eat, psychiatric aides socialize with them and lead them in educational and recreational activities. Psychiatric aides may play games such as cards with the patients, watch television with them, or participate in group activities such as sports or field trips. They observe patients and report any physical or behavioral signs which might be important for the professional staff to know. They accompany patients to and from wards for examination and treatment. Because they have the closest contact with patients, psychiatric aides have a great deal of influence on their outlook and treatment.

Working Conditions

Most full-time aides work about 40 hours a week, but because patients need care 24 hours a day, some aides work evenings, nights, weekends, and holidays. Many work part-time. Aides spend many hours standing and walking, and they often face heavy workloads. Because they may have to move patients in and out of bed or help them stand or walk, aides must guard against back injury. Nursing aides may also face hazards from minor infections and major diseases such as hepatitis, but can avoid infections by following proper procedures.

Nursing aides often have unpleasant duties; they empty bed pans and change soiled bed linens. The patients they care for may be disoriented, irritable, or uncooperative. Psychiatric aides must be prepared to care for patients whose illness may cause violent behavior. While their work can be emotionally demanding, many aides gain satisfaction from assisting those in need.

Employment

Nursing aides held about 1.4 million jobs in 1998, and psychiatric aides held about 95,000 jobs. About one-half of all nursing aides worked in nursing homes, and about one-fourth worked in hospitals. Others worked in residential care facilities, such as halfway houses and homes for the aged or disabled, or in private households. Most psychiatric aides worked in psychiatric units of general hospitals, psychiatric hospitals, State and county mental institutions, homes for mentally retarded and psychiatric patients, and community mental health centers.

Training, Other Qualifications, and Advancement

In many cases, neither a high school diploma nor previous work experience is necessary for a job as a nursing or psychiatric aide. A few employers, however, require some training or experience. Hospitals may require experience as a nursing aide or home health aide. Nursing homes often hire inexperienced workers who must complete a minimum of 75 hours of mandatory training and pass a competency evaluation program within 4 months of employment. Aides who complete the program are placed on the State registry of nursing aides. Some States require psychiatric aides to complete a formal training program.

These occupations can offer individuals an entry into the world of work. The flexibility of night and weekend hours also provides high school and college students a chance to work during the school year.

Nursing aide training is offered in high schools, vocational-technical centers, some nursing homes, and community colleges. Courses cover body mechanics, nutrition, anatomy and physiology, infection control, communication skills, and resident rights. Personal care skills such as how to help patients bathe, eat, and groom are also taught.

Some facilities, other than nursing homes, provide classroom instruction for newly hired aides, while others rely exclusively on informal on-the-job instruction from a licensed nurse or an experienced aide. Such training may last several days to a few months. From time to time, aides may also attend lectures, workshops, and in-service training.

Applicants should be healthy, tactful, patient, understanding, emotionally stable, dependable, and have a desire to help people. They should also be able to work as part of a team, have good communication skills, and be willing to perform repetitive, routine tasks.

Opportunities for advancement within these occupations are limited. To enter other health occupations, aides generally need additional formal training. Some employers and unions provide opportunities by simplifying the educational paths to advancement. Experience as an aide can also help individuals decide whether to pursue a career in the health care field.

Job Outlook

Job prospects for nursing aides should be good through the year 2008. Numerous openings will arise from a combination of fast growth and high turnover for this large occupation. Employment of nursing aides is expected to grow faster than the average for all occupations in response to an emphasis on rehabilitation and the long-term care needs of a rapidly growing elderly population. Employment will increase as a result of the expansion of nursing homes and other long-term care facilities for people with chronic illnesses and disabling conditions, many of whom are elderly. Financial pressure on hospitals to release patients as soon as possible should produce more nursing home admissions. Modern medical technology will also increase the employment of nursing aides. This technology, while saving and extending more lives, increases the need for long-term care provided by aides. As a result, nursing and personal care facilities are expected to grow rapidly and to provide most of the new jobs for nursing aides.

Employment of psychiatric aides is expected to grow slower than the average for all occupations. Employment will rise in response to the sharp increase in the number of older persons—many of whom will require mental health services. Employment of aides in outpatient community mental health centers is likely to grow because of increasing public acceptance of formal treatment for drug abuse and alcoholism, and a lessening of the stigma attached to those receiving mental health care. However, employment in hospitals—where one-half of psychiatric aides work—is likely to decline due to attempts to contain costs by limiting inpatient psychiatric treatment.

Replacement needs will constitute the major source of openings for aides. Turnover is high, a reflection of modest entry requirements, low pay, and lack of advancement opportunities.

Earnings

Median hourly earnings of nursing aides, orderlies, and attendants were $7.99 in 1998. The middle 50 percent earned between $6.72 and $9.54 an hour. The lowest 10 percent earned less than $5.87 and the highest 10 percent earned more than $11.33 an hour.

Median hourly earnings of psychiatric aides were $10.66 in 1998. The middle 50 percent earned between $8.33 and $13.36 an hour. The lowest 10 percent earned less than $6.87 and the highest 10 percent earned more than $15.28 an hour. Median hourly earnings of psychiatric aides in 1997 were $11.20 in State government and $9.80 in hospitals.

Aides in hospitals generally receive at least 1 week's paid vacation after 1 year of service. Paid holidays and sick leave, hospital and medical benefits, extra pay for late-shift work, and pension plans also are available to many hospital and some nursing home employees.

REGISTERED NURSES

The largest health care occupation, with over 2 million jobs. One of the 10 occupations projected to have the largest numbers of new jobs.

Nature of the Work

Registered nurses (R.N.s) work to promote health, prevent disease, and help patients cope with illness. They are advocates and health educators for patients, families, and communities. When providing direct patient care, they observe, assess, and record symptoms, reactions, and progress; assist physicians during treatments and examinations; administer medications; and assist in convalescence and rehabilitation. R.N.s also develop and manage nursing care plans; instruct patients and their families in proper care; and help individuals and groups take steps to improve or maintain their health. While State laws govern the tasks R.N.s may perform, it is usually the work setting, which determines their day-to-day job duties.

Hospital nurses form the largest group of nurses. Most are staff nurses, who provide bedside nursing care and carry out medical regimens. They may also supervise licensed practical nurses and aides. Hospital nurses usually are assigned to one area such as surgery, maternity, pediatrics, emergency room, intensive care, or treatment of cancer patients. Some may rotate among departments.

Office nurses care for outpatients in physicians' offices, clinics, surgicenters, and emergency medical centers. They prepare patients for and assist with examinations, administer injections and medications, dress wounds and incisions, assist with minor surgery, and maintain records. Some also perform routine laboratory and office work.

Nursing home nurses manage nursing care for residents with conditions ranging from a fracture to Alzheimer's disease. Although they usually spend most of their time on administrative and supervisory tasks, R.N.s also assess residents' medical condition, develop treatment plans, supervise licensed practical nurses and nursing aides, and perform difficult procedures such as starting intravenous fluids. They also work in specialty-care departments, such as long-term rehabilitation units for strokes and head-injuries.

Home health nurses provide periodic services, prescribed by a physician, to patients at home. After assessing patients' home environments, they care for and instruct patients and their families. Home health nurses care for a broad range of patients, such as those recovering from illnesses and accidents, cancer, and child birth. They must be able to work independently and may supervise home health aides.

Public health nurses work in government and private agencies and clinics, schools, retirement communities and other community settings. They focus on populations, working with individuals, groups, and families to improve the overall health of communities. They also work as partners with communities to plan and implement programs. Public health nurses instruct individuals, families, and other groups in health education, disease prevention, nutrition, and child care. They arrange for immunizations, blood pressure testing, and other health screening. These nurses also work with community leaders, teachers, parents, and physicians in community health education.

Occupational health or industrial nurses provide nursing care at worksites to employees, customers, and others with minor injuries and illnesses. They provide emergency care, prepare accident reports, and arrange for further care if necessary. They also offer health counseling, assist with health examinations and inoculations, and assess work environments to identify potential health or safety problems.

Head nurses or nurse supervisors direct nursing activities. They plan work schedules and assign duties to nurses and aides, provide or arrange for training, and visit patients to observe nurses and to insure that care is proper. They may also insure records are maintained and equipment and supplies are ordered.

At the advanced level, nurse practitioners provide basic primary health care. They diagnose and treat common acute illnesses and injuries. Nurse practitioners can prescribe medications in all States and the District of Columbia. Other advanced practice nurses include clinical nurse specialists, certified registered nurse anesthetists, and certified nurse-midwives. Advanced practice nurses have met higher educational and clinical practice requirements beyond the basic nursing education and licensing required of all R.N.s.

Working Conditions

Most nurses work in well-lighted, comfortable health care facilities. Home health and public health nurses travel to patients' homes and to schools, community centers, and other sites. Nurses may spend considerable time walking and standing. They need emotional stability to cope with human suffering, emergencies, and other stresses. Because patients in hospitals and nursing homes require 24-hour care, nurses in these institutions may work nights, weekends, and holidays. They may also be on-call; available to work on short notice. Office, occupational health, and public health nurses are more likely to work regular business hours. Almost 1 in 10 R.N.s held more than one job in 1998.

Nursing has its hazards, especially in hospitals, nursing homes, and clinics where nurses may care for individuals with infectious diseases such as hepatitis. Nurses must observe rigid guidelines to guard against these and other dangers such as radiation, chemicals used for sterilization of instruments, and anesthetics. In addition, they are vulnerable to back injury when moving patients, shocks from electrical equipment, and hazards posed by compressed gases.

Employment

As the largest health care occupation, registered nurses held about 2.1 million jobs in 1998. About 3 out of 5 jobs were in hospitals, in inpatient and outpatient departments. Others were mostly in offices and clinics of physicians and other health practitioners, home health care agencies, nursing homes, temporary help agencies, schools, and government agencies. The remainder worked in residential care facilities, social service agencies, religious organizations, research facilities, management and public relations firms, insurance agencies, and private households. About 1 out of 4 R.N.s worked part time.

Training, Other Qualifications, and Advancement

In all States, students must graduate from a nursing program and pass a national licensing examination to obtain a nursing license. Nurses may be licensed in more than one State, either by examination or endorsement of a license issued by another State. Licenses must be periodically renewed. Some States require continuing education for licensure renewal.

In 1998, there were over 2,200 entry level R.N. programs. There are three major educational paths to nursing: Associate degree in nursing (A.D.N.), bachelor of science degree in nursing (B.S.N.), and diploma. A.D.N. programs, offered by community and junior colleges, take about 2 years. About half of all R.N. programs in 1998 were at the A.D.N. level. B.S.N. programs, offered by colleges and universities, take 4 or 5 years. About one-fourth of all programs in 1998 offered degrees at the bachelor's level. Diploma programs, given in hospitals, last 2 to 3 years. Only a small number of programs, about 4 percent, offer diploma level degrees. Generally, licensed graduates of any of the three program types qualify for entry level positions as staff nurses.

There have been attempts to raise the educational requirements for an R.N. license to a bachelor's degree and, possibly, create new job titles. These changes, should they occur, will probably be made State by State, through legislation or regulation. Changes in licensure requirements would not affect currently licensed R.N.s, who would be "grandfathered" in, no matter what their educational preparation. However, individuals considering nursing should carefully weigh the pros and cons of enrolling in a B.S.N. program, since their advancement opportunities are broader. In fact, many career paths are open only to nurses with bachelor's or advanced degrees. A bachelor's degree is usually necessary for administrative positions and is a prerequisite for admission to graduate nursing programs in research, consulting, teaching, or a clinical specialization.

Many A.D.N. and diploma-trained nurses enter bachelor's programs to prepare for a broader scope of nursing practice. They can often find a hospital position and then take advantage of tuition reimbursement programs to work toward a B.S.N.

Nursing education includes classroom instruction and supervised clinical experience in hospitals and other health facilities. Students take courses in anatomy, physiology, microbiology, chemistry, nutrition, psychology and other behavioral sciences, and nursing. Coursework also includes liberal arts classes.

Supervised clinical experience is provided in hospital departments such as pediatrics, psychiatry, maternity, and surgery. A growing number of programs include clinical experience in nursing homes, public health departments, home health agencies, and ambulatory clinics.

Nurses should be caring and sympathetic. They must be able to accept responsibility, direct or supervise others, follow orders precisely, and determine when consultation is required.

Experience and good performance can lead to promotion to more responsible positions. Nurses can advance, in management, to assistant head nurse or head nurse. From there, they can advance to assistant director, director, and vice president. Increasingly, management level nursing positions require a graduate degree in nursing or health services administration. They also require leadership, negotiation skills, and good judgment. Graduate programs preparing executive level nurses usually last 1 to 2 years.

Within patient care, nurses can advance to clinical nurse specialist, nurse practitioner, certified nurse-midwife, or certified registered nurse anesthetist. These positions require 1 or 2 years of graduate education, leading in most instances to a master's degree, or to a certificate.

Some nurses move into the business side of health care. Their nursing expertise and experience on a health care team equip them to manage ambulatory, acute, home health, and chronic care services. Some are employed by health care corporations in health planning and development, marketing, and quality assurance. Other nurses work as college and university faculty or do research.

Job Outlook

Employment of registered nurses is expected to grow faster than the average for all occupations through 2008 and because the occupation is large, many new jobs will result. There will always be a need for traditional hospital nurses, but a large number of new nurses will be employed in home health, long-term, and ambulatory care.

Faster than average growth will be driven by technological advances in patient care, which permit a greater number of medical problems to be treated, and an increasing emphasis on primary care. In addition, the number of older people, who are much more likely than younger people to need medical care, is projected to grow very rapidly. Many job openings also will result from the need to replace experienced nurses who leave the occupation, especially as the median age of the registered nurse population continues to rise.

Employment in hospitals, the largest sector, is expected to grow more slowly than in other health-care sectors. While the intensity of nursing care is likely to increase, requiring more nurses per patient, the number of inpatients (those who remain overnight) is not likely to increase much. Patients are being released earlier and more procedures are being done on an outpatient basis, both in and outside hospitals. Most rapid growth is expected in hospitals' outpatient facilities, such as same-day surgery, rehabilitation, and chemotherapy.

Employment in home health care is expected to grow rapidly. This is in response to a growing number of older persons with functional disabilities, consumer preference for care in the home, and technological advances which make it possible to bring increasingly complex treatments into the home. The type of care demanded will require nurses who are able to perform complex procedures.

Employment in nursing homes is expected to grow much faster than average due to increases in the number of people in their eighties and nineties, many of whom will require long-term care. In addition, the financial pressure on hospitals to release patients as soon as possible should produce more nursing home admissions. Growth in units to provide specialized long-term rehabilitation for stroke and head injury patients or to treat Alzheimer's victims will also increase employment.

An increasing proportion of sophisticated procedures, which once were performed only in hospitals, are being performed in physicians' offices and clinics, including ambulatory surgicenters and emergency medical centers. Accordingly, employment is expected to grow faster than average in these places as health care in general expands.

In evolving integrated health care networks, nurses may rotate among employment settings. Since jobs in traditional hospital nursing positions are no longer the only option, R.N.s will need to be flexible.

Opportunities will be good for nurses with advanced education and training, such as nurse practitioners.

Earnings

Median annual earnings of registered nurses were $40,690 in 1998. The middle 50 percent earned between $34,430 and $49,070 a year. The lowest 10 percent earned less than $29,480 and the highest 10 percent earned more than $69,300 a year. Median annual earnings in the industries employing the largest numbers of registered nurses in 1997 were as follows: Personnel supply services $43,000, Hospitals 39,900, Home health care services 39,200, Offices and clinics of medical doctors 36,500, Nursing and personal care facilities 36,300. Many employers offer flexible work schedules, child care, educational benefits, and bonuses.

NURSING CAREER RESOURCES

Don't forget! Refer to the general resources listed in Chapter Three and the Home Health Care Chapter.

💉 Association   📖 Book   🗁 Directory   🕯 Internet (Web) Site
📱 Job Ads   📠 E-mail/Hotline   🏷 Job Fairs   📇 Resume Service

📱🕯 **ADVANCE Newsmagazines** -*ADVANCE for Nurse Practitioners* is free to qualified professionals. (**http://www.merion.com/sitemap.html**) Includes extensive classified ads and meeting lists. Call 800/355-1088.

📖 **Advancing Your Career : Concepts of Professional Nursing** - by Rose Kearney Nunnery, $36.95. Published by F A Davis Co., 2001.

💉🕯 **Air and Transport Nurses Association** - 915 Lee Street, Des Plaines, IL 60016-4001; 847/460-4001, 800-897-NFNA, Fax: 847/460-4001, (**http://www.nfna.org**). Offers speakers bureau, publishes various news-etters and journals.

💉📱🗁🕯 **American Association of Colleges of Nursing (AACN)** - One Dupont Circle, NW, Suite 530, Washington, DC 20036; 202/463-6930. (**http://www.aacn.nche.edu**) Publishes *Journal of the American Colleges of Nursing.* The Web site has information on nursing education, and nursing careers and ads for lots of jobs.

💉📱🕯 **American Association of Critical-Care Nurses (AACN)** - 101 Columbia, Aliso Viejo, CA 92656-1491; 800/809-2226, 714/362-2000. (**http://www.aacn.org**) Publishes *Critical Care Nurse,* $30/yr or $8/single issue, with about 8 display ads. *American Journal of Critical Care,* $48/yr, has up to 12 classified ads. Contact ajcc@aol.com.

💉📱🕯 **American Association of Neuroscience Nurses (AANN)** - 4700 W. Lake Ave. Glenview, IL 60025; 847/375-4733, 888/557-2266. (**http://www.aann.org**) Membership consists of 3,400 registered nurses and other health care professionals. Use Web site to find jobs through the AANN career advancement program.

💉📱🕯 **American Association of Nurse Anesthetists (AANA)** - 222 South Prospect, Park Ridge, IL 60068-4001; 847/692-7050. They have an E-mail news hotline. Their Web site is **http://www.aana.com**. The *AANA Journal* has about 10 employment ads per issue.

♀ 📘✍📱 **American Association of Occupational Health Nurses (AAOHN)** - 2920 Brandywine Road, Suite 100Atlanta, GA 30341; 707/455-7757, fax: 707/455-7271. **(http://www.aaohn.org)** Organization consists of nurses employed by businesses. Employment Information Service is free to members, (nonmember rate is $150 for two months) and will publish brief resumes (100 words). The Web site contains links to information on employment, certification, and continuing education.

♀📱 **American Holistic Nurses Association (AHNA)** - P. O. Box 2130, Flagstaff, AZ 86003; 800/278-AHNA. Their Web site is **http://ahna.org**. Provides a network for nurses interested in entering the holistic field. Publishes "Beginnings" (monthly newsletter), *Journal of Holistic Nursing* (quarterly) and educational material.

♀📱 **American Licensed Practical Nurses Association (ALPNA)** - 1090 Vermont Ave., NW, Ste. 1200, Washington, DC 20005; 202/682-9000. **(http://www.nursingcenter.com)** Publishes nursing standards and pamphlets. Provides continuing education courses for members. Lots of valuable links to journals, associations, and other Web sites.

♀📘📱 **American Nephrology Nurses Association (ANNA)** - Box 56, E. Holly Ave., Pitman, NJ 08071; 609/256-2320. Membership includes registered nurses. Publishes newsletters, several journals, and guides. Visit their Web site at **http://anna.inurse.com**. Web site includes job ads.

♀📘📁📱 **American Nurses Association** (ANA) - 600 Maryland Avenue, SW , Suite 100 West, Washington, DC 20024; 800/274-4ANA, 202/554-4444. **(http://www.nursingworld.org)** The ANA, established in 1896, is a full-service professional organization for the nation's registered nurse population. State association contact information can be obtained by mail or found on the Web site. Send for the ANA catalog listing dozens of publications. Members receive *The American Nurse* and *American Journal of Nursing*. *The American Nurse* is $10/yr for students. *The 1998 Career Guide*, published annually, free at 800/638-3030, lists hospitals and health care centers, also offers career guidance and job hunting advice. *Preparing For A Career In Nursing* is a free 9 page pamphlet with a question and answer format.

📖 **Anatomy of a Job Search - A Nurse's Guide to Finding and Landing the Job You Want** - by Jeanna Bozell, Paperback, 146 pages, $22.95.

Published by Springhouse, 1999. The author is a nurse recruiter. Features advice on resumes and marketing yourself.

Association of Operating Room Nurses, Inc. (AORN) - 2170 S. Parker Rd., Suite 300, Denver, CO 80231-5711; 303/755-6300, 800/755-2676, fax on demand: 800/755-7980. (**http://www.aorn.org**) Search their very informative Web site for perioperative job opportunities. Publishes books, and pamphlets.

Association of Rehabilitation Nurses (ARN) - 4700 W. Lake Avenue, Glenview, IL 60025; 800/229-7530 or 847/375-4710, fax: 877/734-9384, E-mail: info@rehabnurse.org, Internet **http://www.rehabnurse.org**. Membership consists of over 7000 registered nurses interested in rehailitation nursing. E-mail: info@rehabnurse.org). Web site has job ads.

Association of Women's Health, Obstetric and Neonatal Nurses 2000 L Street NW, Suite 740, Washington, DC 20036; 800/673-8499. (**http://www.awhonn.org**) *AWHONN Lifelines* has up to 20 job ads per issue. JOGNN is published by Lippincott. Continuing education curses are offered online, as are job ads.

The Canadian Nurse - 50 Driveway, Ottawa, Ontario, Canada K2P 1E2; 613/237-2133, 800/361-8404, fax: 613/237-3520. Bilingual. Journal has about 12 ads per issue. E-mail: cnj@cna-nurses.CA.

The Discipline of Nursing : An Introduction - by Margaret O'Bryan Doheny, Christina Benson Cook & Mary Consta Stopper, 1997, $35.60. 4th Edition, paperback, 300 pages. Published by Appleton & Lange. ISBN: 0838517161. Chapters include: nursing history, nursing practice in various settings, ethical and legal considerations, and future directions in nursing.

Dollars for College: the Quick Guide to Financial Aid for Nursing and Other Health Fields - Garrett Park Press, P.O.Box 190, Garrett Park, MD 20896; 301/946-2553. $6.95.

Healthweek - 1156 Aster Ave., Suite C, Sunnyvale, CA 94086; 800/859-2091. (**http://www.nurseweek.com**) Newsletter covering the health care industry. Has classified ads for registered nurses, respiratory therapists and physical therapists. Free for RNs in most states. Subscriptions for non-RNs is $45.

HomeCare - P. O. Box 12924, Overland Park, KS 66282, fax 913/967-1903. (**http://www.homecaremag.com**, E-mail: marilyn@miramar.com)

Publication has information on the industry and products for home care, published monthly, subscriptions free.

📖 **Kaplan Careers in Nursing: Manage Your Future in the Changing World of Healthcare** - by Annette Vallano, Paperback, 256 pages, $16.00. Published by Kaplan, 1999. Includes profiles of real nurses, advice on marketing yourself and information on changes in the field.

✒ **Lippincott's Nursing Center** - Lippincott Williams & Wilkins (http://www.nursingcenter.com) This site has AJN Career Center with educational opportunities (interactive online CE courses), contact information for many hospitals and the full text of the AJN Career Guide for the current year. Provides links to many nursing associations.

📑✒ **Medical - AdMart - (http://www.medical-admart.com)** Compiles classified ads from medical publications. Call 800/237-9851 for additional information, or check Web site for lots of job ads and other information.

✍✒ **MED OPTIONS USA** - 6542 Hypoluxo Road, Suite 294, Lakeworth, FL, 33467;   Phone: 800/357-8314, fax: 800/357-8684, **(http://www.medoptions.com)**. Free nurse practitioner and physician assistant job service.

📑✒ **Mosby-Year Book, Inc.** - 11830 Westline Industrial Dr., St. Louis, MO 63146; 800/325-4177, 314/872-8370. Mosby publishes many nursing and other medical   journals *including: Geriatric Nursing, Journal of Emergency Nursing* and *Nursing Outlook* published bimonthly. Visit their Internet Web site at **http://www.harcourthealth.com.**

⚕✒ **National Black Nurses Association (NBNA)** - 8630 Fenton Street, Suite 330, Silver Springs, MD 20910, 301/589-3200, fax: 301/5893223. **(http://www.nbna.org)** More than 5000 members comprised of registered nurses, LPNs, vocational nurses, and students. Publishes annual reports, various journals and the *NBNA quarterly* newsletter.

⚕📑📁✒ **National Federation of Licensed Practical Nurses** - 893 US Highway 70 West, Suite 202, Gardner, NC 27529; 919/779-0046, 800/948-2511, fax: 919/779-5642. **(http://www.nflpn.org)** Membership consists of vocational and licensed practical nurses.

⚕ **National Federation for Specialty Nursing Organizations** - East Holly Avenue, Box 56 , Pitman, NJ 08071; 856/ 256-2333. Contact for addresses of nursing specialty organizations. **(http://www.nfsno.org)**

☥ 📖📑✍ **National League for Nursing (NLN)** - 61 Broadway, #33rd Floor, NY 40006, 212/363-5555, 800/669-1656. (**http://www.nln.org**) Over 10,000members in 46 state groups. Publishes a weekly newsletter and an annual journal for licensed practical nurses. Weekly job postings online.

☥✍ **National Student Nurses' Association (NSNA)** - 555 W. 57th St., New York, NY 10019; 212/581-2211. (**http://www.nsna.org**, E-mail: nsna@nsna.org) Group consists of over 36,000 students. Publishes *Imprint Magazine*, ($18), a newsletter, and handbooks. Job counseling is available at conferences. Has a scholarship foundation.

✍✍ **Nurse Options USA** - 6542 Hypoluxo Road, Suite 294, Lake Worth, FL 33467; 800/828-0665. (**http://www.nurseoptions.com**) Registered Nurse and Nurse Management permanent, temporary, and travel positions throughout the USA. Part of Med Options USA.

📑✍✍ **Nurse Practitioner Support Services** - 10024 S.E 240 Street, Suite #102, Kent, WA 98031; 253/852-9042, fax: 253/852-7725. (**http://www.nurse.net/jobs/index.html**, E-mail: npss@nurse.net) Web site has job listings, extensive resources, and a service to e-mail the listings to you.

📖 **The Nurses' Career Guide : Discovering New Horizons in Health Care** - by Zardoya Eagles, Paperback, $21.56. Published by Sovereignty Press, 1997.

📑✍ **NURSEWEEK** - 1156 Aster Ave., Suite C, Sunnyvale, CA 94086; 800/859-2091. (**http://www.nurseweek.com**) Free publication listing jobs for registered nurses in California.

📑✍ **Nursing & Allied Healthweek** - *HealthWeek Magazine*, 3001 LBJ Freeway, Suite 211, Dallas, TX 75234, E-mail: editor@healthweek.com. (**http://www.healthweek.com/jobinfo.html**)

✍ **Nursing HealthWeb** - (**http://www.healthweb.org**) This page is sponsored by the Taubman Medical Library, the School of Nursing at The University of Michigan, and the HealthWeb project. It has information on careers in nursing, electronic discussion groups, links to nursing schools, information about professional societies, and resources in allied health.

📑✍✍ **Nursing Jobs** - (**http://www.langara.bc.ca/vnc/htm**)Job search assistance with links to sites to help prepare you for a search, write a resume and rehearse interviewing.

NursingNet - (http://www.nursingnet.org) Provides information about nursing and related subjects, including publications, associations and employment. Has a message board.

NurseZone.com - (http://www.nursezone.com) This very well-organized site organizes your job search by specialty and region, then state. Career advice and resume creation center. Provides information about state licensing, nursing, and Nurse lifestyle stories.

Oncology Nursing Society - (http://www.ons.org) Membership directory for members only, $20. Free brochure "Career Resources in the United States."

Peterson's Guide to Nursing Programs - Peterson's Guides, P.O. Box 2123, Princeton, NJ 08543; 800/338-3282. $26.95. Good information and many publications. Web site at **http://www.petersons.com**.

Prime National Publishing Corporation - 470 Boston Post Rd., Weston, MA 02193; 800/869-2700, 781/899-2702. (**http://pnpco.com**) This company runs about 14 yearly job fairs for experienced nurses. Web site has job ads and advice on writing resumes.

SLACK, Inc. - (**http://www.slackinc.com/allied/allnet.htm**) This publisher's Internet site has extensive links to nursing resources.

Springhouse Corporation - Customer Service Dept., 1111 Bethlehem Pike, Springhouse, PA 19477-0908; 800/346-7844. Free Nursing Career Directory will put you directly in touch with health care recruiters that need your services. Internet **http://www.springnet.com**.

Chapter

8

HEALTH & SOCIAL SERVICES OCCUPATIONS

Sabrina R. Damp

Sabrina Damp started out as a Medical Assistant with the High-Mark Blue Cross Blue Shield Primary Care Center in Pittsburgh's North Hills. In 1999 she transferred within the same company to the practice of Dr. Paul Zubritzky and Associates in Robinson Township, PA. She graduated with honors from North Hills School of Health Occupations in October of 1997. "I became interested in the medical field while I was hospitalized during my first semester of college. Shortly thereafter, I decided not to return to college for the second semester. Instead, I enrolled in the Medical Assisting program at the North Hills School of Health Occupations in April of 1997," said Sabrina.

I asked Sabrina if she had difficulty finding employment after graduation. She said, "Opportunities were plentiful. I had four or five interviews the first month and two job offers. I selected Blue Cross Blue

Shield because the job they offered was interesting with prospects for advancement as I gained job experience and successfully completed various training programs. Coincidently, I started this job on my 20th birthday, January 12, 1998."

North Hills School of Health Occupations offered excellent placement opportunities. She received calls for interviews for months after accepting a position with HighMark. Their externship program was very helpful. She said that the six-week externship helped her build the confidence that she needed to succeed. Sabrina passed the (RMA) Registered Medical Assistant exam in December of 1998.

Sabrina started working in the front office answering telephones, setting up appointments, collecting co-payments, filing, and calling to confirm next day appointments at Northern Area Family Medicine. After working four months she began rotating to patient care in the back office taking patient pulse rates, blood pressure, temperature, giving injections, taking blood and administering electrocardiograms. She said, "I enjoy the diversity of working both front and back office. The day goes very fast and I enjoy helping patients and the doctors and physician's assistants." Currently, at Dr. Paul M. Zubritzky and Associates office, she was hired as a front office person. Her job entails answering phones, preparing the schedule for the doctors, calling in prescriptions, taking messages, filing, and billing. At this office she was hired specifically for front office duties which she enjoys very much. Sabrina decided to go back to school to pursue her degree in business and HighMark Blue Cross Blue Shield, her direct employer, is paying for her tuition at Robert Morris College. Sabrina Says " I have been with HighMark for three years now and they offer great advancement and I plan to take advantage of it and work my way up through the company."

Many health care facilities are recruiting medical assistants. "Four months after I started, two of my classmates were hired by the same company. The starting pay is good and the benefits are excellent," Ms. Damp said. "The medical assistant field is an excellent career choice and I was able to complete school and start work in less than a year."

She recommends that to be successful you must be yourself and reflect a positive attitude toward coworkers and patients. "It's important to deal professionally with everyone at all levels and you must be sensitive to patients' needs at all times," Ms. Damp said.

This chapter presents occupations that are in the health services group. The occupations are:

Medical Assistants   **Human Service Worker**
Social Workers

See chapter 10 for health service careers involving home health care, including **Homemaker - Home Health Aides.**

Following each job description is a list of job resources: Associations, Books, Directories, Internet Sites, Job Ads, E-mail Job Notification/Job Hotlines, Job Fairs, and Resume/Placement Services with icons to guide you.

MEDICAL ASSISTANTS

Medical assistants is expected to be one of the 10 fastest growing occupations through the year 2008.

Nature of the Work

Medical assistants perform routine administrative and clinical tasks to keep the offices and clinics of physicians, podiatrists, chiropractors, and optometrists running smoothly. They should not be confused with physician assistants who examine, diagnose, and treat patients under the direct supervision of a physician. (Physician assistants are discussed elsewhere in the Handbook.)

The duties of medical assistants vary from office to office, depending on office location, size, and specialty. In small practices, medical assistants are usually "generalists," handling both administrative and clinical duties and reporting directly to an office manager, physician, or other health practitioner. Those in large practices tend to specialize in a particular area under the supervision of department administrators.

Medical assistants perform many administrative duties. They answer telephones, greet patients, update and file patient medical records, fill out insurance forms, handle correspondence, schedule appointments, arrange for hospital admission and laboratory services, and handle billing and bookkeeping.

Clinical duties vary according to State law and include taking medical histories and recording vital signs, explaining treatment procedures to patients, preparing patients for examination, and assisting the physician during the examination. Medical assistants collect and prepare laboratory specimens or perform basic laboratory tests on the premises, dispose of contaminated supplies, and sterilize medical instruments. They instruct patients about medication and special diets, prepare and administer medications as directed by a physician, authorize drug refills as directed, telephone prescriptions to a pharmacy, draw blood, prepare patients for x rays, take electrocardiograms, remove sutures, and change dressings.

Medical assistants may also arrange examining room instruments and equipment, purchase and maintain supplies and equipment, and keep waiting and examining rooms neat and clean.

Assistants who specialize have additional duties. Podiatric medical assistants make castings of feet, expose and develop x rays, and assist podiatrists in surgery. Ophthalmic medical assistants help ophthalmologists provide medical eye care. They administer diagnostic tests, measure and record vision, and test the functioning of eyes and eye muscles. They also show patients how to use eye dressings, protective shields, and safety glasses, and how to insert, remove, and care for contact lenses. Under the direction of the physician, they may administer medications, including eye drops. They also maintain optical and surgical instruments and assist the ophthalmologist in surgery.

Working Conditions

Medical assistants work in well-lighted, clean environments. They constantly interact with other people, and may have to handle several responsibilities at once.

Most full-time medical assistants work a regular 40-hour week. Some work part-time, evenings, or weekends.

Employment

Medical assistants held about 252,000 jobs in 1998. Sixty-five percent were in physicians' offices, and 14 percent were in offices of other health practitioners such as chiropractors, optometrists, and podiatrists. The rest were in hospitals, nursing homes, and other health care facilities.

Training, Other Qualifications, and Advancement

Most employers prefer to hire graduates of formal programs in medical assisting. Such programs are offered in vocational-technical high schools, post-secondary vocational schools, community and junior colleges, and in colleges and universities. Post-secondary programs usually last either 1 year, resulting in a certificate or diploma, or 2 years, resulting in an associate degree. Courses cover anatomy, physiology, and medical terminology as well as typing, transcription, record-keeping, accounting, and insurance processing. Students learn laboratory techniques, clinical and diagnostic procedures, pharmaceutical principles, medication administration, and first aid. They study office practices, patient relations, medical law, and ethics. Accredited programs include an internship that provides practical experience in physicians' offices, hospitals, or other health care facilities.

Although formal training in medical assisting is available, such training—while generally preferred—is not always required. Some medical assistants are trained on the job, although this is less common than in the past. Applicants usually need a high school diploma or the equivalent. Recommended high school courses include mathematics, health, biology, typing, bookkeeping, computers, and office skills. Volunteer experience in the health care field is also helpful.

Two agencies recognized by the U.S. Department of Education accredit programs in medical assisting: the Commission on Accreditation of Allied Health Education Programs (CAAHEP) and the Accrediting Bureau of Health Education Schools (ABHES). In 1999, there were about 450 medical assisting programs accredited by CAAHEP and over 140 accredited by ABHES. The Committee on Accreditation for Ophthalmic Medical Personnel accredited 14 programs in ophthalmic medical assisting.

Although there is no licensing for medical assistants, some States require them to take a test or a short course before they can take x rays or perform other specific clinical tasks. Employers prefer to hire experienced workers or certified applicants who have passed a national examination, indicating that the medical assistant meets certain standards of competence. The American Association of Medical Assistants awards the Certified Medical Assistant credential; the American Medical Technologists awards the Registered Medical Assistant credential; the American Society of Podiatric Medical Assistants awards the Podiatric Medical Assistant Certified credential; and the Joint Commission on Allied Health Personnel in Ophthalmology awards the Ophthalmic Medical Assistant credential at three levels: Certified Ophthalmic Assistant, Certified Ophthalmic Technician, and Certified Ophthalmic Medical Technologist.

Because medical assistants deal with the public, they must be neat and well-groomed and have a courteous, pleasant manner. Medical assistants must be able to put patients at ease and explain physicians' instructions. They must respect the confidential nature of medical information. Clinical duties require a reasonable level of manual dexterity and visual acuity.

Medical assistants may be able to advance to office manager. They may qualify for a variety of administrative support occupations, or may teach medical assisting. Some, with additional education, enter other health occupations such as nursing and medical technology.

Job Outlook

Employment of medical assistants is expected to grow much faster than the average for all occupations through the year 2008 as the health services industry expands due to technological advances in medicine, and a growing and aging population. It is one of the fastest growing occupations.

Employment growth will be driven by the increase in the number of group practices, clinics, and other health care facilities that need a high proportion of support personnel, particularly the flexible medical assistant who can handle both administrative and clinical duties. Medical assistants primarily work in outpatient settings, where much faster than average growth is expected.

In view of the preference of many health care employers for trained personnel, job prospects should be best for medical assistants with formal training or experience, particularly those with certification.

Earnings

The earnings of medical assistants vary, depending on experience, skill level, and location. Median annual earnings of medical assistants were $20,680 in 1998. The middle 50 percent earned between $17,020 and $24,340 a year. The lowest 10 percent earned less than $14,020 and the highest 10 percent earned more than $28,640 a year.

MEDICAL ASSISTANTS

Don't forget! Refer to the general resources listed in Chapter Three.

Accrediting Bureau of Health Education Schools (ABHES) - 803 W. Broad St., Suite 730, Falls Church, VA 22046. 703/533-2082. **(http://www.abhes.org)** E-mail: abhes@erols.com. Provides a list of accredited educational programs in medical assisting.

The American Association of Medical Assistants (AAMA) 20 North Wacker Drive, Suite 1575, Chicago, IL 60606-2963; 312/899-1500. **(http://www.aama-ntl.org)** The AAMA offers a national examination leading to the Certified Medical Assistant (CMA) credential, and with the AMA, accredits educational programs, most of which have placement services. A career packet is available. The web has career information, a members only networking area, local chapter information, and discussion forum. CAAHEP accredited medical assisting programs are listed on the site.

American Medical Technologists (AMT) - 710 Higgins Road, Park Ridge, IL 60068; 847/873-5169, fax: 847/823-0458, E-mail: Amtmail@aol.com, **http://www.amt1.com**. The AMT administers the Registered Medical Assistant certification exam. Classes to prepare for the exam are also offered here. Member dues: $48/year for RMA. *AMT Events*, 6/year plus 3 newsletters, $70 for non-members, has a few classified ads. Classes available online from web site.

American Society of Podiatric Medical Assistants - 2124 S. Austin Blvd., Cicero, IL 60804. 708/863-6303, 888/88SDPMS. E-mail SandraPMAC@aol.com, **http://aspma.org/aboutus.html**. Web site has job ads for members and career information.

Association of Technical Personnel in Ophthalmology 2025 Woodlane Drive, St Paul, MN 55125-2995, 651/731-7239, 800/482 4858, fax 651/731-0410. **(http://www.atpo.com** E-mail: ATPOmembership@ cahpo.org) Placement service for all ophthalmic personnel is free for members, nonmembers $10. Information about careers and training programs is available.

☤ ⌂ **Joint Commission on Allied Health Personnel in Ophthalmology (JCAHPO)** - 2025 Woodlane Dr., St. Paul, MN 55125-2995, 651/731-2944. (http://www.jcahpo.org, E-mail: jcahpo@jcahpo.org) Certifies assistants, technicians and technologists. Career brochures are online. The web site has "What is Ophthalmic Medical Assisting?" and offers several audio tape classes for credit.

📖 **Medical Technicians** Published by Ferguson Pub-lishing Company, 1998. $13.95. Careers covered include biomedical equipment technicians, dialysis technicians, medical assistants, psychiatric technicians and surgical technologists.

☤ **Registered Medical Assistants of American Medical Technologists**, 710 Higgins Rd., Park Ridge, IL 60068-5765. Internet: (**www.amt1.com**) Information about career opportunities and the Registered Medical Assistant certification exam is available.

SOCIAL AND HUMAN SERVICE ASSISTANTS

OCCUPATIONAL TITLES:

Social Service Technician	**Mental Health Technician**
Case Management Aide	**Child Abuse Worker**
Social Work Assistant	**Community Outreach Worker**
Residential Counselor	**Gerontology Aide**
Alcohol or Drug Abuse Counselor	

Human service worker and assistant occupations are projected to be among the fastest growing.

Nature of the Work

Human service workers and assistants is a generic term for people with various job titles, including social service assistant, case management aide, social work assistant, community support worker, alcohol or drug abuse counselor, mental health aide, community outreach worker, life skill counselor, and gerontology aide. They usually work under the direction of professionals from a variety of fields, such as nursing, psychiatry, psychology, rehabilitative or physical therapy, or social work. The amount of responsibility and supervision they are given varies a great deal. Some have little direct supervision; others work under close direction.

Human service workers and assistants provide direct and indirect client services. They assess clients' needs, establish their eligibility for benefits and services, and help clients obtain them. They examine financial documents such as rent receipts and tax returns to determine whether the client is eligible for food stamps, Medicaid, welfare, and other human service programs. They also arrange for transportation and escorts, if necessary, and provide emotional support. Human service workers and assistants monitor and keep case records on clients and report progress to supervisors and case managers. Human service workers and assistants also may transport or accompany clients to group meal sites, adult daycare centers, or doctors' offices. They may telephone or visit clients' homes to make sure services are being received, or to help resolve disagreements, such as those between tenants and landlords. They also may help clients complete insurance or medical forms, as well as applications for financial assistance. Additionally, social and human service workers and assistants may assist others with daily living needs.

Human service workers and assistants play a variety of roles in a community. They may organize and lead group activities, assist clients in need of counseling or crisis intervention, or administer a food bank or emergency fuel program. In halfway houses, group homes, and government-supported housing programs, they assist adults who need supervision with personal hygiene and daily living skills. They review clients' records, ensure that they take correct doses of medication, talk with family members, and confer with medical personnel and other care givers to gain better insight into clients' backgrounds and needs. Human service workers and assistants also provide emotional support and help clients become involved in their own well being, in community recreation programs, and in other activities.

In psychiatric hospitals, rehabilitation programs, and outpatient clinics, human service workers and assistants work with professional care providers, such as psychiatrists, psychologists, and social workers to help clients master everyday living skills, to teach them how to communicate more effectively, and to get along better with others. They support the client's participation in a treatment plan, such as individual or group counseling or occupational therapy.

Working Conditions

Working conditions of human service workers and assistants vary. Some work in offices, clinics, and hospitals, while others work in group homes, shelters, sheltered workshops, and day programs. Many spend their time in the field visiting clients. Most work a 40-hour week, although some work in the evening and on weekends.

The work, while satisfying, can be emotionally draining. Understaffing and relatively low pay may add to the pressure. Turnover is reported to be high, especially among workers without academic preparation for this field.

Employment

Human service workers and assistants held about 268,000 jobs in 1998. Almost half worked in private social or human services agencies, offering a variety of services, including adult daycare, group meals, crisis intervention, counseling, and job training. Many human service workers and assistants supervised residents of group homes and halfway houses. About one-third were employed by State and local governments, primarily in public welfare agencies and facilities for mentally disabled and developmentally challenged individuals. Human service workers and assistants also held jobs in clinics, detoxification units, community mental health centers, psychiatric hospitals, day treatment programs, and sheltered workshops.

Training, Other Qualifications, and Advancement

Although a bachelor's degree usually is not required for this occupation, employers increasingly are seeking individuals with relevant work experience or education beyond high school. Certificates or associate degrees in subjects such as social work, human services, or one of the social or behavioral sciences meet most employers' requirements.

Human services programs have a core curriculum that trains students to observe patients and record information, conduct patient interviews, implement treatment plans, employ problem-solving techniques, handle crisis intervention matters, and use proper case management and referral procedures. General education courses in liberal arts, sciences, and the humanities also are part of the curriculum. Many degree programs require completion of a supervised internship.

Educational attainment often influences the kind of work an employee may be assigned and the degree of responsibility that may be entrusted to them. For example, workers with no more than a high school education are likely to receive extensive on-the-job training to work in direct-care services, while employees with a college degree might be assigned to do supportive counseling, coordinate program activities, or manage a group home. Human service workers and assistants with proven leadership ability, either from previous experience or as a volunteer in the field, often receive greater autonomy in their work. Regardless of the academic or work background of employees, most employers provide some form of in-service training, such as seminars and workshops, to their employees.

Hiring requirements in group homes tend to be more stringent than in other settings. For example, employers may require employees to have a valid driver's license or to submit to a criminal background investigation.

Employers try to select applicants who have effective communication skills, a strong sense of responsibility, and the ability to manage time effectively. Many human services jobs involve direct contact with people who are vulnerable to exploitation or mistreatment; therefore, patience, understanding, and a strong desire to help others, are highly valued characteristics.

Formal education almost always is necessary for advancement. In general, advancement requires a bachelor's or master's degree in counseling, rehabilitation, social work, human services management, or a related field.

Job Outlook

Opportunities for human service workers and assistants are expected to be excellent, particularly for applicants with appropriate post-secondary education. The number of human service workers and assistants is projected to grow much faster than the average for all occupations between 1998 and 2008—ranking among the most rapidly growing occupations. The need to replace workers who move into new positions due to advancement, retirement, or for other reasons will create many additional job opportunities. This occupation, however, is not attractive to everyone. It can be draining emotionally and the pay is relatively low. Qualified applicants should have little difficulty finding employment.

Faced with rapid growth in the demand for social and human services, employers are developing new strategies for delivering and funding services. Many employers increasingly will rely on human service workers and assistants to undertake greater responsibility in delivering services to clients.

Opportunities are expected to be best in job training programs, residential care facilities, and private social service agencies, which include such services as adult daycare and meal delivery programs. Demand for these services will expand with the growing number of elderly, who are more likely to need services. In addition, social and human service workers and assistants will continue to be needed to provide services to pregnant teenagers, the homeless, the mentally disabled and developmentally challenged, and those with substance abuse problems.

Job training programs are expected to require additional human service workers and assistants. As social welfare policies shift focus from benefit-based programs to work-based initiatives, there will be an increased demand for people to teach job skills to the people who are new to or re-entering the workforce. Additionally, streamlined and downsized businesses create increased demand for persons with job retraining expertise. Human service workers and assistants will help companies to cope with new modes of conducting business and employees to master new job skills.

Residential care establishments should face increased pressures to respond to the needs of the chronically and mentally ill. Many of these patients have been deinstitutionalized and lack the knowledge or the ability to care for themselves. Also, more community-based programs, supported independent living sites, and group residences are expected to be established to house and assist the homeless, and the chronically, and mentally, ill. As a result, demand for human service workers and assistants will increase.

The number of jobs for human service workers and assistants will grow more rapidly than overall employment in State and local governments. State and local governments employ many of their human service workers and assistants in corrections and public assistance departments. Although employment in corrections departments is growing, employment of social and human service workers and assistants is not expected to grow as rapidly as employment in other corrections jobs, such as guards or corrections officers. Public assistance programs have been employing more human service workers and assistants in an attempt to employ fewer social workers, who are more educated, thus more highly paid.

Earnings

Median annual earnings of human service workers and assistants were $21,360 in 1998. The middle 50 percent earned between $16,620 and $27,070. The top 10 percent earned more than $33,840, while the lowest 10 percent earned less than $13,540.

SOCIAL AND HUMAN SERVICE ASSISTANTS

Resources for social and human service assistants are combined with social workers, as many resources serve both professions. See the end of the social workers section.

Information on job openings may be available from State employment service offices or directly from city, county, or State departments of health, mental health and mental retardation, and human resources.

SOCIAL WORKER

Employment is projected to grow much faster than average.

Nature of the Work

Social work is a profession for those with a strong desire to help people, to make things better, and to make a difference. Social workers help people function the best way they can in their environment, deal with their relationships with others, and solve personal and family problems.

Social workers often see clients who face a life-threatening disease or a social problem. These problems may include inadequate housing, unemployment, lack of job skills, financial distress, serious illness or disability, substance abuse, unwanted pregnancy, or antisocial behavior. Social workers also assist families that have serious domestic conflicts, including those involving child or spousal abuse.

Through direct counseling, social workers help clients identify their concerns, consider effective solutions, and find reliable resources. Social workers typically consult and counsel clients and arrange for services that can help them. Often, they refer clients to specialists in services such as debt counseling, childcare or elder care, public assistance, or alcohol or drug rehabilitation. Social workers then follow through with the client to assure that services are helpful and that clients make proper use of the services offered. Social workers may review eligibility requirements, help fill out forms and applications, visit clients on a regular basis, and provide support during crises.

Social workers practice in a variety of settings. In hospitals and psychiatric hospitals, they provide or arrange for a range of support services. In mental health and community centers, social workers provide counseling services on marriage, family, and adoption matters, and they help people through personal or community emergencies, such as dealing with loss or grief or arranging for disaster assistance. In schools, they help children, parents, and teachers cope with problems. In social service agencies, they help people locate basic benefits, such as income assistance, housing, and job training. Social workers also offer counseling to those receiving therapy for addictive or physical disorders in rehabilitation facilities, and to people in nursing homes in need of routine living care. In employment settings, they counsel people with personal, family, professional, or financial problems affecting their work performance. Social workers who work in courts and correction facilities evaluate and counsel individuals in the criminal justice system to cope better in society. In private practice, they provide clinical or diagnostic testing services covering a wide range of personal disorders.

Social workers often provide social services in health-related settings that now are governed by managed care organizations. To contain costs, these organizations are emphasizing short-term intervention, ambulatory and community-based care, and greater decentralization of services.

Most social workers specialize in an area of practice. Although some conduct research or are involved in planning or policy development, most social workers prefer an area of practice in which they interact with clients.

Clinical social workers offer psychotherapy or counseling and a range of diagnostic services in public agencies, clinics, and private practice.

Child welfare or family services social workers may counsel children and youths who have difficulty adjusting socially, advise parents on how to care for disabled children, or arrange for homemaker services during a parent's illness. If children have serious problems in school, child welfare workers may consult with parents, teachers, and counselors to identify underlying causes and develop plans for treatment. Some social workers assist single parents, arrange adoptions, and help find foster homes for neglected, abandoned, or abused children. Child welfare workers also work in residential institutions for children and adolescents.

Child or adult protective services social workers investigate reports of abuse and neglect and intervene if necessary. They may initiate legal action to remove children from homes and place them temporarily in an emergency shelter or with a foster family.

Mental health social workers provide services for persons with mental or emotional problems. Such services include individual and group therapy, outreach, crisis intervention, social rehabilitation, and training in skills of everyday living. They may also help plan for supportive services to ease patients' return to the community.

Health care social workers help patients and their families cope with chronic, acute, or terminal illnesses and handle problems that may stand in the way of recovery or rehabilitation. They may organize support groups for families of patients suffering from cancer, AIDS, Alzheimer's disease, or other illnesses. They also advise family caregivers, counsel patients, and help plan for their needs after discharge by arranging for at-home services—from meals-on-wheels to oxygen equipment. Some work on interdisciplinary teams that evaluate certain kinds of patients—geriatric or organ transplant patients, for example.

School social workers diagnose students' problems and arrange needed services, counsel children in trouble, and help integrate disabled students into the general school population. School social workers deal with problems such as student pregnancy, misbehavior in class, and excessive absences. They also advise teachers on how to cope with problem students.

Criminal justice social workers make recommendations to courts, prepare pre-sentencing assessments, and provide services to prison inmates and their families. Probation and parole officers provide similar services to individuals sentenced by a court to parole or probation.

Occupational social workers usually work in a corporation's personnel department or health unit. Through employee assistance programs, they help workers cope with job-related pressures or personal problems that affect the quality of their work. They often offer direct counseling to employees whose performance is hindered by emotional or family problems or substance abuse. They also develop education programs and refer workers to specialized community programs.

Gerontology social workers specialize in services to the aged. They run support groups for family caregivers or for the adult children of aging parents. Also, they advise elderly people or family members about the choices in such areas as housing, transportation, and long-term care; they also coordinate and monitor services.

Social work administrators perform overall management tasks in a hospital, clinic, or other setting that offers social worker services.

Social work planners and policy-makers develop programs to address such issues as child abuse, homelessness, substance abuse, poverty, and violence. These workers research and analyze policies, programs, and regulations. They identify social problems and suggest legislative and other solutions. They may help raise funds or write grants to support these programs.

Working Conditions

Full-time social workers usually work a standard 40-hour week; however, some occasionally work evenings and weekends to meet with clients, attend community meetings, and handle emergencies. Some, particularly in voluntary nonprofit agencies, work part time. Most social workers work in pleasant, clean offices that are well lit and well ventilated. Social workers usually spend most of their time in an office or residential facility, but also may travel locally to visit clients, to meet with service providers, or to attend meetings. Some may use one of several offices within a local area in which to meet with clients. The work, while satisfying, can be emotionally draining. Understaffing and large caseloads add to the pressure in some agencies.

Employment

Social workers held about 604,000 jobs in 1998. About 4 out of 10 jobs were in State, county, or municipal government agencies, primarily in departments of health and human services, mental health, social services, child welfare, housing, education, and corrections. Most private sector jobs were in social service agencies, hospitals, nursing homes, home health agencies, and other health centers or clinics. Although most social workers are employed in cities or suburbs, some work in rural areas.

Training, Other Qualifications, and Advancement

A bachelor's in social work (BSW) degree is the most common minimum requirement to qualify for a job as a social worker; however, majors in psychology, sociology, and related fields may be sufficient to qualify for some entry-level jobs, especially in small community agencies. Although a bachelor's degree is required for entry into the field, an advanced degree has become the standard for many positions. A master's in social work (MSW) is necessary for positions in health and mental health settings and typically is required for certification for clinical work. Jobs in public agencies also may require an advanced degree, such as a master's in social service policy or administration. Supervisory, administrative, and staff training positions usually require at least an advanced degree. College and university teaching positions and most research appointments normally require a doctorate in social work (DSW or Ph.D).

As of 1999, the Council on Social Work Education accredited over 400 BSW programs and over 125 MSW programs. The Group for Advancement of Doctoral Education in Social Work listed 63 doctoral programs for Ph.D.'s in social work or DSW's (Doctor of Social Work). BSW programs prepare graduates for direct service positions such as case worker or group worker. They include courses in social work practice, social welfare policies, human behavior and the social environment, social research methods, social work values and ethics, dealing with a culturally diverse clientele, promotion of social and economic justice, and populations-at-risk. Accredited BSW programs require at least 400 hours of supervised field experience.

Master's degree programs prepare graduates for work in their chosen field of concentration and continue to develop their skills to perform clinical assessments, to manage large caseloads, and to explore new ways of drawing upon social services to meet the needs of clients. Master's programs last 2 years and include 900 hours of supervised field instruction, or internship. A part-time program may take 4 years. Entry into a master's program does not require a bachelor's in social work, but courses in psychology, biology, sociology, economics, political science, history, social anthropology, urban studies, and social work are recommended. In addition, a second language can be very helpful. Most master's programs offer advanced standing for those with a bachelor's degree from an accredited social work program.

All States and the District of Columbia have licensing, certification, or registration requirements regarding social work practice and the use of professional titles. Although standards for licensing vary by State, a growing number of States are placing greater emphasis on communications skills, professional ethics, and sensitivity for cultural diversity issues. Additionally, the National Association of Social Workers (NASW) offers voluntary credentials. The Academy of Certified Social Workers (ACSW) is granted to all social workers who have met established eligibility criteria. Social workers practicing in school settings may qualify for the School Social Work Specialist (SSWS) credential. Clinical social workers may earn either the Qualified Clinical Social Worker (QCSW) or the advanced credential—Diplomate in Clinical Social Work (DCSW). Social workers holding clinical credentials also may list themselves in the biannual publication of the NASW Register of Clinical Social Workers. Credentials are particularly important for those in private practice; some health insurance providers require them for reimbursement.

Social workers should be emotionally mature, objective, and sensitive to people and their problems. They must be able to handle responsibility, work independently, and maintain good working relationships with clients and coworkers. Volunteer or paid jobs as a social work aide offer ways of testing one's interest in this field.

Advancement to supervisor, program manager, assistant director, or executive director of a social service agency or department is possible, but usually requires an advanced degree and related work experience. Other career options for social workers include teaching, research, and consulting. Some also help formulate government policies by analyzing and advocating policy positions in government agencies, in research institutions, and on legislators' staffs.

Some social workers go into private practice. Most private practitioners are clinical social workers who provide psychotherapy, usually paid through health insurance. Private practitioners usually have at least a master's degree and a period of supervised work experience. A network of contacts for referrals also is essential.

Job Outlook

Employment of social workers is expected to increase much faster than the average for all occupations through 2008. The aged population is increasing rapidly, creating greater demand for health and other social services. Social workers also will be needed to help the sizable baby boom generation deal with depression and mental health concerns stemming from mid-life, career, or other personal and professional difficulties. In addition, continuing concern about crime, juvenile delinquency, and services for the mentally ill, the mentally retarded, AIDS patients, and individuals and families in crisis will spur demand for social workers in several areas of specialization. Many job openings will also stem from the need to replace social workers who leave the occupation.

The number of social workers in hospitals and many larger, long-term care facilities will increase in response to the need to ensure that the necessary medical and social services are in place when individuals leave the facility. However, this service need will be shared across several occupations. In an effort to control costs, these facilities increasingly emphasize discharging patients early, applying an interdisciplinary approach to patient care, and employing a broader mix of occupations—including clinical specialists, registered nurses, and health aides—to tend to patient care or client need.

Social worker employment in home health care services is growing, in part because hospitals are releasing patients earlier than in the past. However, the expanding senior population is an even larger factor. Social workers with backgrounds in gerontology are finding work in the growing numbers of assisted living and senior living communities.

Employment of social workers in private social service agencies will grow, but not as rapidly as demand for their services. Agencies increasingly will restructure services and hire more lower-paid human service workers and assistants instead of social workers. Employment in state and local government may grow somewhat in response to increasing needs for public welfare and family services; however, many of these services will be contracted out to private agencies. Additionally, employment levels may fluctuate depending on need and government funding for various social service programs.

Employment of school social workers is expected to grow, due to expanded efforts to respond to rising rates of teen pregnancy and to the adjustment problems of immigrants and children from single-parent families. Moreover, continued emphasis on integrating disabled children into the general school population will lead to more jobs. However, availability of State and local funding will dictate the actual job growth in schools.

Opportunities for social workers in private practice will expand because of the anticipated availability of funding from health insurance and public-sector contracts. Also, with increasing affluence, people will be better able to pay for professional help to deal with personal problems. The growing popularity of employee assistance programs also is expected to spur demand for private practitioners, some of whom provide social work services to corporations on a contractual basis.

Competition for social worker jobs is stronger in cities where demand for services often is highest, training programs for social workers are prevalent, and interest in available positions is strongest. However, opportunities should be good in rural areas, which often find it difficult to attract and retain qualified staff.

Earnings

Median annual earnings of social workers were $30,590 in 1998. The middle 50 percent earned between $24,160 and $39,240. The lowest 10 percent earned less than $19,250 and the top 10 percent earned more than $49,080. Median annual earnings in the industries employing the largest numbers of medical social workers in 1997 were; Home health care services $35,000, Offices and clinics of medical doctors 33,700, Offices of other health care practitioners 32,900, State government, except education and hospitals 31,800, Hospitals 31,500

Resources for social and human service assistants are combined with social workers, as many resources serve both professions.

SOCIAL WORKERS and
SOCIAL AND HUMAN SERVICE ASSISTANTS

Don't forget! Refer to the general resources listed in Chapter Three.

⚕Association   📖 Book   🗂 Directory   Internet (Web) Site
📋Job Ads   E-mail/Hotline   Job Fairs   Resume Service

⚕   **American Association of State Social Work Board**s - 400 South Ridge Parkway, Suite B, Culpeper, VA 22701. (**http://www.aswb.org**) Contact for licensing requirements and testing procedures for each state.

⚕📖📋 **American Counseling Association (ACA)** - 5999 Stevenson Ave., Alexandria, VA 22304; 800/347-6647, 703/823-9800. The 58,000 members receive *Counseling Today* newspaper free, 12/year, $55 for nonmembers. Five pages of job vacancies are advertised per issue, mostly for counselor educators. (**http://www.counseling.org**, E-mail: lpeele@counseling.org) The placement service is at the annual convention. They publish *Professional Counselors Helping People*, a brochure with basic overviews of careers as school, mental health, career and rehabilitation counselors. The ACA has an e-mail newsletter.

⚕📋 **American Psychological Association** - (**www.apa.org/ads**). Jobs listing from the *APA Monitor*, updated monthly, are listed by country, and by state within the USA. Web site includes list of accredited schools, books, and much more.

♈ 📱📁🎣⚕ **American Public Human Services Association (APWA)** - 810 First St., NE, Washington, DC 20002-4267; 202/682-0100, fax: 202/ 289-6555. (http://www.apwa.org) The APWA publishes an annual *Public Human Services Directory*, $100, or $85 to members, which includes human service agency contacts in all 50 states plus territories. Online job ads do not require membership.

♈ 📱🏷️📝⚕ **American Society on Aging** - 833 Market Street, Suite 511, San Francisco, CA 94103; 415/974-9600. (http://www.asaging.org) Members are nurses, doctors, social workers and anyone providing services to the aging. *Aging Today*, 6 issues/year, $30 for nonmembers, members free, offers display job ads in each issue. Job opportunity file is publicized at annual conferences. Members may list resumes on web site. Job ads online are open to public.

♈ 📁📝⚕ **Child Welfare League of America (CWLA)** - 440 First Street NW, third floor, Washington, DC 20001; 202/638-2952. Association of over 1,100 public and private non-profit agencies that serve and advocate for abused, neglected, and otherwise vulnerable children. *CWLA Directory of Member Agencies* costs $35. The League offers a placement service. Visit their web site at **http://www.cwla.org**. They have an internship program.

♈ 📁📝⚕ **Clinical Social Work Federation (CSWF)** -800/270-9739. The web site, given a Four-Star rating by Mental Health Net, has a State Society Directory page at **http://www.cswf.org/welcome.html**. The federation is made up of 31 state social work societies, some of which have placement services. CSWF publishes a number of brochures.

📱🏷️⚕ **COMMUNITY JOBS: The Employment Newspaper for the Non-Profit Sector** - (http://www.communityjobs.org) ACCESS: Networking in the Public Interest, 1001 Connecticut Ave., NW Suite 838, Washington, DC 20036; 202/785-4233 fax: 202/785-4212. E-mail: commjobs@aol.com. The web site has over 100 job ads, updated daily.

♈ 📁⚕ **Council for Accreditation of Counseling and Related Educational Programs (CACREP)** - 5999 Stevenson Avenue, 4th Floor, Alexandria, Virginia 22304; 800/347-6647 extension 301. E-mail: CACREP@aol.com, **www.counseling.org/cacrep/main.htm**, CACREP accredits counseling programs and publishes the *Directory of CACREP Accredited Programs*, in print and on the web site.

Council on Social Work Education - 1725 Duke St., Suite 500, Alexandria, VA 22314; phone: 703/683-8080, fax: 703/683-8099. (http://www.cswe.org) Publications include; *Summary Information on Master of Social Work Programs* (1999-2000, $13), *Directory of Colleges and Universities with Accredited Social Work Degree Programs* (2000, $11).

Directory of Catholic Charities, Agencies and Institutions in the United States, Puerto Rico - (http://www.catholiccharitiesusa.org) 1731 King Street, #200 Alexandria, Virginia 22314; phone: 703/549-1390, fax: 703/549-1656. This is the largest private network of social service organizations in the United States. Published every other year, the directory lists social service agencies , cost $15.

Employee Assistance Professional Association (EAPA) - 2101 Wilson Boulevard, Suite 500, Arlington, VA 22201; 783/387-1000. (http://www.eap-association.com) The EAPA certifies individuals. Information is online. The web site also has a job bank.

Employee Assistance Society of North America (EASNA) - 230 East Ohio Street, Suite 400, Chicago, IL 60611-3265; 312/644-0828, fax: 312/644-8557. (http://www.haworthpressinc.com/links/EASNA.htm, E-mail: easna@bostrom.com) Members are individuals in the U.S. and Canada working in the employee assistance field, in such specialties as workplace and family wellness, employee benefits, and organizational development. EASNA has a list of accredited programs.

Gerontological Society of America - 1030 15th Street NW, Suite 250, Washington, DC 20005; 202/842-1275. (http://www.geron.org) *Gerontology News,* monthly, $50 for non-members. Features classified ads for social workers. *Directory of Educational Programs in Gerontology and Geriatrics* is on the web site. Employment opportunities on web site.

Good Works: A Guide to Social Change Careers - Essential Information, P.O. Box 19405, Washington, DC 20036. (E-mail: EI@Essential.org, http://www.essential.org/goodworks/about.html) The web site has job ads organized by state. *Good Works* is a national directory of social change organizations, listing over 1000 organizations, with information on contacts, staff openings, internships, etc. ($24.00)

Latino Social Workers Organization (LSWO) Their web site (http://www.lswo.org) provides a job bank, networking and a mentoring program. *LSWO News-letter* has job ads. LSWO sponsors career management workshops. E-mail: LSWO@aol.com.

◫🖉🖰 **Mental Health Net** (http://www.cmhc.com) Sponsored by CMHC Systems. Has chat and discussion forums. Professional resources page at **http://www.mentalhelp.net/joblink**has a position openings page, and you may post your resume.

⚕◫🖉🖰 **National Association of Alcoholism and Drug Abuse Counselors (NAADAC)** - (http://www.naadac.org/index.html, 1911 N. Fort Myer Dr. Suite 900, Arlington, VA 22209; phone: 800/548-0497, fax: 800/377-1136. E-mail: naadac@well.com. NAADAC has a Career Classified program, with job ads posted on the web site. Members can access the listings with the Fax-on-Demand line.

⚕◫📖📁🖉🖰 National Association of Social Workers (NASW) 750 First St. NE, Ste. 700, Washington DC, 20002-4241; 800/638/8799, 202/408-8600, TTD: 202/408-8396. You can search for credentialed social workers on their web site **(http://www.naswdc.org)** or purchase the book or CD, *NASW Register of Clinical Social Workers*, $60.00, at 800/277-3590. Contact information for local chapters on web. NASW JobLink is an Internet national database of social work opportunities.

⚕🖰 **National Board for Certified Counselors (NBCC)** - 3 Terrace Way, Suite D, Greensboro, NC 27403-3660; 336/547-0607, fax: 336/547-0017, **(http://www.nbcc.org)**. The NBCC can refer you to a certified counselor in your area and has information about state licensure

⚕◫🖰 National Organization for Human Service Education (NOHSE) Their purpose is to unite educators, students, practitioners and clients in a conversation about preparation of effective human service workers. Their web site at **(http://www.nohse.com)** has an online discussion group. Each region has a conference in the spring, providing some job matching. E-mail: sweitzer@uhavax.hartford.edu.

📖◫🖰 **New Social Worker**: The Magazine for Social Work Students and Recent Graduates - White Hat Communications, P.O. Box 5390, Dept. WWW, Harrisburg, PA 17110-0390; 717/238-3787, fax: 717/238-2090, **(http://www.socialworker.com**, E-mail: linda.grobman@ paonline.com). The jobs page has 30-35 new position announcements, which are posted on the web also.

⚕📁🖰 **School Social Work Association of America** - P.O. Box 2072, North-lake, IL 60164; 847/288-4527 (voice message system). SSWAA provides information on the 50 state departments of education to inquire about job opportunities, certification requirements and other job related questions. (**http://sswaa.org,** E-mail: sswaa@aol.com)

socialservice.com (**http://socialservice.com/index.htm**) Employment ads for social work or social service jobs. You can subscribe to receive free e-mail updates of new job links posted for your state.

Social Work and Social Services Jobs Online - George Warren Brown School of Social Work, (**http://gwbweb.wustl.edu/jobs**). A resource listing jobs in diverse areas of social work.

SWAN: Social Workers Access Network Technologies Provided by the College of Social Work at the University of South Carolina, this site has information on social work schools, Listservs, organizations. Their mission is to promote technology as an instructional enhancement tool across the social work curriculum. (**http://www.sc.edu/swan**)

World Wide Web Resources for Social Workers - Extensive links to information for social workers provided by Dr. Gary Holden of New York University. (**http://www.nyu.edu/socialwork/wwwrsw**)

Chapter

9

HEALTH DIAGNOSING
OCCUPATIONS & ASSISTANTS

Paul M. Zubritzky, M.D.

Paul M. Zubritzky, M.D. graduated Cum Laude from the University of Pittsburgh in May of 1973. He graduated from Temple University School of Medicine in May of 1977 and he served his residency at Western Pennsylvania Hospital from June 1, 1977 through June 30, 1981. He was certified in 1984 by the American Board of Obstetrics and Gynecology.

Doctor Zubritzky has been in private practice specializing in Obstetrics, Gynecology and Infertility for the past 21 years with offices in the suburbs of Pittsburgh. He is also the Chief of Obstetrics and Gynecology at the Ohio Valley General Hospital and he serves in other staff positions at Western Pennsylvania Hospital.

I asked Dr. Zubritzky why he entered the field, he stated, "I was highly influenced by my father who was a physician. I never contemplated any other career." Kiddingly, he followed up with several exceptions. "At age five I thought about being an auto mechanic. Then at ten a cartoonist and like most 16 year olds I wanted to be a rock star."

Doctor Zubritzky is a member of a number of prestigious professional organizations including the American Medical Association, Pennsylvania Medical Society, American College of Obstetricians and Gynecologists, Diplomat of the American Board of Obstetricians and Gynecologists to name a few. I asked him if he was aware of any unique publications or resources for those seeking career information or placement services. He suggested a number of publications and journals including OB GYN News. This publication offers a number of job classified ads for the field. Many of these resources are listed in this chapter.

The Bureau of Labor Statistics projects that employment of physicians will grow faster than the average for all occupations through the year 2008 due to continued expansion of the health care industries. I asked Dr. Zubritzky what advice he would give to others that want to enter this field. He stated, "It takes lots of work and a total commitment. This is a profession and not a nine to five job. It requires personal integrity, a considerable amount of your time, and you must realize that up front before entering the field." He further stated that, " your personal time and life will be sacrificed, however, there is a balance of both good and bad days." One other point he stressed was that you must have good people skills to be successful and be cognizant of the fact that medicine is in evolution and constantly changing. He said, "you must keep up— more today than when I first started out— with these changes, especially now with the advances that are being made in all fields."

This chapter features occupations that are in the Health Diagnosing and Assistants group. The major occupational groups are:

Chiropractors   Physicians
Dentists   Physician Assistants
Optometrists   Veterinarians

Following each job description are job resource lists: Associations, Books, Directories, Internet Sites, Job Ads, Job Hotlines, Job Fairs, and Placement Services. Job sources are listed alphabetically with the larger sources underlined.

CHIROPRACTORS

Employment of chiropractors is expected to increase rapidly and job prospects should be good.

Nature of the Work

Chiropractors, also known as doctors of chiropractic or chiropractic physicians, diagnose and treat patients whose health problems are associated with the body's muscular, nervous, and skeletal systems, especially the spine. Chiropractors believe interference with these systems impairs normal functions and lowers resistance to disease. They also hold that spinal or vertebral dysfunction alters body functions by affecting the nervous system, and that skeletal imbalance through joint or articular dysfunction, especially in the spine, can cause pain.

The chiropractic approach to health care is holistic, stressing the patient's overall health and wellness. It recognizes that many factors affect health, including exercise, diet, rest, environment, and heredity. Chiropractors use natural, drugless, nonsurgical health treatments, and rely on the body's inherent recuperative abilities. They also recommend lifestyle changes — in eating, exercise, and sleeping habits, for example — to their patients. When appropriate, chiropractors consult with and refer patients to other health practitioners.

Like other health practitioners, chiropractors follow a standard routine to secure the information needed for diagnosis and treatment. They take the patient's medical history, conduct physical, neurological, and orthopedic examinations, and may order laboratory tests. X rays and other diagnostic images are important tools because of the emphasis on the spine and its proper function. Chiropractors also employ a postural and spinal analysis common to chiropractic diagnosis.

In cases in which difficulties can be traced to involvement of musculoskeletal structures, chiropractors manually adjust the spinal column. Many chiropractors use water, light, massage, ultrasound, electric, and heat therapy. They may also apply supports such as straps, tapes, and braces. Chiropractors counsel patients about wellness concepts such as nutrition, exercise, lifestyle changes, and stress management, but do not prescribe drugs or perform surgery.

Some chiropractors specialize in sports injuries, neurology, ortho-pedics, nutrition, internal disorders, or diagnostic imaging.

Working Conditions

Chiropractors work in clean, comfortable offices. The average workweek is about 40 hours, although longer hours are not uncommon. Solo practitioners set their own hours, but may work evenings or weekends to accommodate patients.

Chiropractors, like other health practitioners, are sometimes on their feet for long periods of time. Chiropractors who take x rays employ appropriate precautions against the dangers of repeated exposure to radiation.

Employment

Chiropractors held about 46,000 jobs in 1998. Most chiropractors are in solo practice, although some are in group practice or work for other chiropractors. A small number teach, conduct research at chiropractic institutions, or work in hospitals and clinics. Many chiropractors are located in small communities.

Training, Other Qualifications, and Advancement

All States and the District of Columbia regulate the practice of chiropractic and grant licenses to chiropractors who meet educational and examination requirements established by the State. Chiropractors can only practice in States where they are licensed. Some States have allow chiropractors licensed in one State to obtain a license in another without further examination, provided that educational, examination, and practice credentials meet State specifications.

Most State boards require at least 2 years of undergraduate education, and an increasing number require a 4-year bachelor's degree.

All boards require completion of a 4-year chiropractic college course at an accredited program leading to the Doctor of Chiropractic degree.

For licensure, most State boards recognize either all or part of the four-part test administered by the National Board of Chiropractic Examiners. State examinations may supplement the National Board tests, depending on State requirements.

To maintain licensure, almost all States require completion of a specified number of hours of continuing education each year. Continuing education programs are offered by accredited chiropractic programs and institutions, and chiropractic associations. Special councils within some chiropractic associations also offer programs leading to clinical specialty certification, called "diplomate" certification, in areas such as orthopedics, neurology, sports injuries, occupational and industrial health, nutrition, diagnostic imaging, thermography, and internal disorders.

In 1998, there were 16 chiropractic programs and institutions in the United States accredited by the Council on Chiropractic Education. All required applicants to have at least 60 semester hours of undergraduate study leading toward a bachelor's degree, including courses in English, the social sciences or humanities, organic and inorganic chemistry, biology, physics, and psychology. Many applicants have a bachelor's degree, which may eventually become the minimum entry requirement. Several chiropractic colleges offer prechiropractic study, as well as a bachelor's degree program. Recognition of prechiropractic education offered by chiropractic colleges varies among the State boards.

During the first 2 years, most chiropractic programs emphasize classroom and laboratory work in basic science subjects such as anatomy, physiology, public health, microbiology, pathology, and biochemistry. The last 2 years stress courses in manipulation and spinal adjustments, and provide clinical experience in physical and laboratory diagnosis, neurology, orthopedics, geriatrics, physiotherapy, and nutrition. Chiropractic programs and institutions grant the degree of Doctor of Chiropractic (D.C.).

Chiropractic requires keen observation to detect physical abnormalities. It also takes considerable hand dexterity to perform adjustments, but not unusual strength or endurance. Chiropractors should be able to work independently and handle responsibility. As in other health-related occupations, empathy, understanding, and the desire to help others are good qualities for dealing effectively with patients.

Newly licensed chiropractors can set up a new practice, purchase an established one, or enter into partnership with an established practitioner. They may also take a salaried position with an established chiropractor, a group practice, or a health care facility.

Job Outlook

Job prospects are expected to be good for persons who enter the practice of chiropractic. Employment of chiropractors is expected to grow faster than the average for all occupations through the year 2008 as consumer demand for alternative medicine grows. Chiropractors emphasize the importance of healthy lifestyles and do not prescribe drugs or perform surgery. As a result, chiropractic care is appealing to many health-conscious Americans. Chiropractic treatment of back, neck, extremities, and other joint damage has become more accepted as a result of recent research and changing attitudes about alternative health care practices.

Demand for chiropractic treatment is also related to the ability of patients to pay, either directly or through health insurance. Although more insurance plans now cover chiropractic services, the extent of such coverage varies among plans. Increasingly, chiropractors must educate communities about the benefits of chiropractic care in order to establish a successful practice.

In this occupation, replacement needs arise almost entirely from retirements. Chiropractors usually remain in the occupation until they retire; few transfer to other occupations. Establishing a new practice will be easiest in areas with a low concentration of chiropractors.

Earnings

Median annual earnings of salaried chiropractors were $63,930 in 1998. The middle 50 percent earned between $36,820 and $110,820 a year. Self-employed chiropractors usually earn more than salaried chiropractors. According to the American Chiropractic Association, average income for all chiropractors, including the self-employed, was about $86,500, after expenses, in 1997. In chiropractic, as in other types of independent practice, earnings are relatively low in the beginning, and increase as the practice grows.

CHIROPRACTORS

Don't forget! Refer to the general resources listed in Chapter Three.

American Chiropractic Association (ACA) - 1701 Clarendon Blvd., Arlington, VA 22209; 703/276-8800, fax: 703/ 243-2593. Member Information Center: 800/986-INFO. The ACA has about 20,000 members who are doctors or chiropractic assistants. The Education and Training section of the web site at **http://www.amerchiro.org** is extensive and includes a list of colleges. E-mail: memberinfo@amerchiro.org. Request a free copy of their 20 page career kit.

Canadian Chiropractic Association (1396 Eglinton Avenue West, Toronto, Ontario M6R 2H2, Canada; 416/781-5656, 800/668-2076, fax: 416/781-7344, (**http://ccachiro.org**). Lists colleges, licensing and Canadian Associations. E-mail: ccachiro@inforamp.net.

Chiropractor Finder - **http://www.visiblity.org**   Search for chiropractic doctors throughout the United States and other countries. Search for colleges and organizations.

Chiropractic Neurology Diplomate Web site has extensive chiropractic resources at (**http://home1.gte.net/cpow/chirocll.htm**).

Chiropractic OnLine Today "COTs Classified OnLine" has Practice For Sale / Space For Rent / Associate Wanted areas. Visit their web site at (**http://www.chiro-online.com**).

Council on Chiropractic Education - 8049 North 85th Way, Scottsdale, Arizona 85258-4321, Phone: 480/443-8877, Fax: 480/483-7333. (**http://cce-usa.org**, E-Mail: cce-usa.org) Contact for a list of chiropractic programs and institutions, as well as general information.

Directory of Chiropractic Web Pages in Canada Visit their web site at (**http://www.cdnchiro.com**).

☤ 📱🗁 **Dynamic Chiropractic,** P.O. Box 6100, Huntington, CA 92615. The Internet site (**http://www.chiroweb.com**) has a directory of chiropractors, practices for sale and employment ads.

☤ **Federation of Chiropractic Licensing Boards,** 901 54th Ave., Suite 101, Greeley, CO 80634. Internet: **http://www.fclb.org**. Contact for information on state education and licensure requirements.

☤🖱 **International Chiropractic Pediatric Association** - 5295 Highway 78, Suite #D362, Stone Mountain, GA 30087-3414, Phone: 770/982-9037. Fax: 770-736-1651. The ICPA provides research and training in the field of chiropractic pediatrics. Visit their web site at (**http://www.4icpa.org**).

☤🗁🖱 **International Chiropractic Association (ICA)** - 110 N. Glebe Road, Suite 1000, Arlington, VA 22201; 703/528-5000, 800/423-4690, **http://www.chiropractic.org,** Publishes the *ICA Directory* and "Careers for the Future," free information brochure. They have a sports fitness council, diplomate course for pediatrics and a certification program.

☤🖱 **National Association for Chiropractic Medicine (NACM)** - 15427 Baybrook Drive, Houston, TX 77062; 281/280-8262, fax: 281/280-8262, **http://www.chiromed.org/**, E-mail: **ronlslaughter@hotmail.com**. The NACM offers assistance in finding member practitioners.

📖 **Opportunities in Chiropractic Health-Care Careers** by Louis Sportelli & R. C. Schafer. 1994. Paperback, $10.95, ISBN: 0844241326. Published by VGM Career Horizons, 4255 Touhy Ave., Lincolnwood, IL 60646-1975; 800/323-4900, 847/679-5500, fax: 847/679-2494.

☤🖳🖱 **Student Canadian Chiropractic Association** - 1900 Bayview Avenue, Toronto, ON Canada M4G 3E6; 416/482-2340 ext:186, fax: 416/482-9745, **http://www.scca.ca/**, E-mail: **http:"info@scca.ca**. Members have access to the SCCA Observation and Employment Program ($5.00 service charge). Web site has information about becoming a chiropractor.

DENTISTS

Nature of the Work

Dentists diagnose, prevent, and treat teeth and tissue problems. They remove decay, fill cavities, examine x rays, place protective plastic sealants on children's teeth, straighten teeth, and repair fractured teeth. They also perform corrective surgery on gums and supporting bones to treat gum diseases. Dentists extract teeth and make models and measurements for dentures to replace missing teeth. They provide instruction on diet, brushing, flossing, the use of fluorides, and other aspects of dental care, as well. They also administer anesthetics and write prescriptions for antibiotics and other medications.

Dentists use a variety of equipment, including x-ray machines, drills, and instruments such as mouth mirrors, probes, forceps, brushes, and scalpels. They also wear masks, gloves, and safety glasses to protect themselves and their patients from infectious diseases.

Dentists in private practice oversee a variety of administrative tasks, including bookkeeping, and buying equipment and supplies. They may employ and supervise dental hygienists, dental assistants, dental laboratory technicians, and receptionists. (These occupations are described elsewhere in the Handbook.)

Most dentists are general practitioners, handling a variety of dental needs. Other dentists practice in one of eight specialty areas. Orthodontists, the largest group of specialists, straighten teeth. The next largest group, oral and maxillofacial surgeons, operate on the mouth and jaws. The remainder may specialize as pediatric dentists (dentistry for children); periodontists (treating gums and bone supporting the teeth); prosthodontists (making artificial teeth or dentures); endodontists (root canal therapy); public health dentists; and oral pathologists (studying oral diseases).

Working Conditions

Most dentists work 4 or 5 days a week. Some work evenings and weekends to meet their patients' needs. Most full-time dentists work about 40 hours a week, but others work more. Initially, dentists may work more hours as they establish their practice. Experienced dentists often work fewer hours. A considerable number continue in part-time practice well beyond the usual retirement age.

Most dentists are "solo practitioners," meaning they own their own businesses and work alone or with a small staff. Some dentists have partners, and a few work for other dentists as associate dentists.

Employment

Dentists held about 160,000 jobs in 1998. About 9 out of 10 dentists are in private practice. Others work in private and public hospitals and clinics, the Federal Government, and in dental research.

Training, Other Qualifications, and Advancement

All 50 States and the District of Columbia require dentists to be licensed. In most States, a candidate must graduate from a dental school accredited by the American Dental Association's Commission on Dental Accreditation, and pass written and practical examinations to qualify for a license. Candidates may fulfill the written part of the State licensing by passing the National Board Dental Examinations. Individual States or regional testing agencies give the written or practical examinations.

Currently, about 17 States require dentists to obtain a specialty license before practicing as a specialist. Requirements include 2 to 4 years of postgraduate education and, in some cases, completion of a special State examination. Most State licenses permit dentists to engage in both general and specialized practice. Dentists who want to teach or do research usually spend an additional 2 to 5 years in advanced dental training, in programs operated by dental schools or hospitals.

Dental schools require a minimum of 2 years of college-level predental education. However, most dental students have at least a bachelor's degree. Predental education emphasizes course work in the sciences.

All dental schools require applicants to take the Dental Admissions Test (DAT). When selecting students, schools consider scores earned on the DAT, the applicants' grade point average, and information gathered through recommendations and interviews.

Dental school usually lasts 4 academic years. Studies begin with classroom instruction and laboratory work in basic sciences including anatomy, microbiology, biochemistry, and physiology. Beginning courses in clinical sciences, including laboratory techniques, are also provided at this time. During the last 2 years, students treat patients, usually in dental clinics, under the supervision of licensed dentists.

Most schools award the degree of Doctor of Dental Surgery (D.D.S.). Others award an equivalent degree, Doctor of Dental Medicine (D.M.D.).

Dentistry requires diagnostic ability and manual skills. Dentists should have good visual memory, excellent judgment of space and shape, a high degree of manual dexterity, and scientific ability. Good business sense, self-discipline, and communication skills are helpful for success in private practice. High school and college students who want to become dentists should take courses in biology, chemistry, physics, health, and mathematics.

Some dental school graduates work for established dentists as associates for a year or two in order to gain experience and save money to equip an office of their own. Most dental school graduates, however, purchase an established practice or open a new practice immediately after graduation. Each year about one-fourth to one-third of new graduates enroll in postgraduate training programs to prepare for a dental specialty.

Job Outlook

Employment of dentists is expected to grow slower than the average for all occupations through 2008. Although employment growth will provide some job opportunities, most jobs will result from the need to replace the large number of dentists projected to retire. Job prospects should be good if the number of dental school graduates does not grow significantly, thus keeping the supply of newly qualified dentists near current levels.

Demand for dental care should grow substantially through 2008. As members of the baby-boom generation advance into middle age, a large number will need maintenance on complicated dental work, such as bridges. In addition, elderly people are more likely to retain their teeth than were their predecessors, so they will require much more care than in the past. The younger generation will continue to need preventive check-ups despite treatments such as fluoridation of the water supply, which decreases the incidence of tooth decay.

Dental care will focus more on prevention, including teaching people how to care better for their teeth. Dentists will increasingly provide care that is aimed at preventing tooth loss—rather than just providing treatments, such as fillings. Improvements in dental technology will also allow dentists to provide more effective and less painful treatment to their patients.

However, the employment of dentists is not expected to grow as rapidly as the demand for dental services. As their practices expand, dentists are likely to hire more dental hygienists and dental assistants to handle routine services.

Earnings

Median annual earnings of salaried dentists were $110,160 in 1998. Earnings vary according to number of years in practice, location, hours worked, and specialty.

Self-employed dentists in private practice tend to earn more than salaried dentists. A relatively large proportion of dentists are self-employed. Like other business owners, these dentists must provide their own health insurance, life insurance, and retirement benefits.

DENTISTS

Don't forget! Refer to the general resources listed in Chapter Three.

| ⚕ Association   📖 Book   🗁 Directory   ⌂ Internet (Web) Site |
| 📑 Job Ads   💥 E-mail/Hotline   📁 Job Fairs   📧 Resume Service |

⚕ 🗁 ⌂ **Academy of General Dentistry (AGD)** - 888/AGD-DENT. Their web site at **http://www.agd.org/** has an "Ask an AGD Dentist a Question" area. The members-only area offers a membership directory, bulletin board and chat room.

⚕ 📑 🗁 ⌂ **American Academy of Pediatric Dentistry (AAPD)** - 211 E. Chicago Ave., Suite 700, Chicago, IL 60611-2616; 312/337-2169, (**http://aapd.org**). *Membership Roster*, annual, $200, lists over 4,000 pediatric dentists, retired dentists and student members. Professional Opportunities Program, placement help, is free to members. The award-winning web site has lots of information, classified ads, and links.

⚕ 📑 ⌂ **American Dental Education Association** - 1625 Massachusetts Avenue, NW, Suite 600, Washington, DC 20036-2212; 202/667-9433, fax: 202/667-0642. (**http://www.aads.jhu.edu/**, E-mail: aads@aads.jhu.edu). Most students going into dentistry apply through the AADS. The web site includes a classified section, e-mail lists and student information, including an Opportunities for Minority Students area. The Dental Education Programs area includes Canadian schools.

⚕ 🗁 ⌂ **American Association of Orthodontists** (401 North Lindbergh Boulevard, St., Louis, MO 63141-7816 Phone: 314/993-1700, Fax:

314/997-1745, **http://www.aaortho.org/**, E-mail: info@aaortho.org). Call 1-800-STRAIGHT to ask for orthodontists in your area.

🦷 📁 🖱 **American Association of Public Health Dentistry (AAPHD)** - 3760 SW Lyle Court, Portland, OR 97221, 503/242-0712, fax: 503/242-0721 (**http://www.pitt.edu/~aaphd/**). The web site has one of the best collections of links to Internet sites.

🦷 📄 📁 🖱 **American Dental Association (ADA)** - 211 E. Chicago Ave., Chicago, IL 60611; 312/440-2500, fax: 312/440-2800, **http://www.ada.org/**, E-mail: jperson@adcmail.net. *JADA (Journal of the American Dental Association)*, published monthly, members free, $60/year nonmembers. Advertises around 85 job ads/issue. Classified ads are on the Internet site. It also lists dental organizations and the state dental associations.

🖱 **American Dental Sales** (**http://www.dentalsales.com/**) A network of independent dental practice appraisers and sales consultants. Search using a map of the U.S. Click on the region of interest. This web site is for buying and selling dental practices.

🦷 🖱 **American Society of Dentistry for Children** (875 N. Michigan Ave., Chicago, IL 60611-1901; 312/943-1244). *Journal of Dentistry for Children*, published bimonthly, free to members, $100/year nonmembers. Up to a dozen job ads per issue for faculty dentists. Visit their web site at (**http://cudental.creighton.edu/asdc**).

🦷 📁 🖱 **California Dental Association (CDA)** - 1201 K St. Sacramento, CA 95814; 916/443-0505, **http://www.cda.org**, Web site has classified ads. For the Professional Placement Registry, call Cindy Zazzi at ext. 4250.

🦷 📄 🖱 **Canadian Dental Association** (1815 Alta Vista Drive, Ottawa, Ontario, Canada K1G 3Y6; 800/267-6334, **http://www.cda-adc.ca/public/**). *Canadian Dental Association Journal* has over 30 ads for practices and jobs/issue, and can be read online.

🖱 **The Dental Site** (**http://www.dentalsite.com/**) Provided by Leland Raymond III, DDS. The "For Dentists" area lists links to dental web sites by area of specialty. The "Find a Dentist" area lists over 1200 dental practices , in 44 countries, with web sites.

🦷 📄 **Dental Society of the State of New York** (121 State St., Albany, NY 12207; 518/465-0044, **http://www.dssny.org**). e-mail: **info@nysdental.org**.

📖 **Exploring Careers in Dentistry** by Jessica A. Rickert, D.D.S. Careers Library Div of Rosen Publishing Group, 29 E. 21st St., New York, NY

10010; 800/272-3893. E-mail: rosenpub@tribeca.ios.com. List: $16.95. Discusses education requirements, expenses, and options in dentistry.

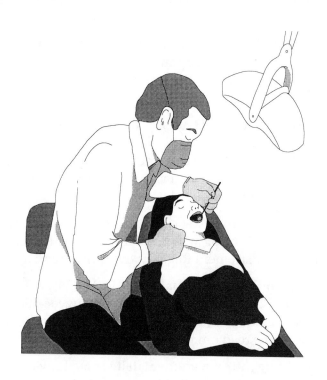 **So you want to be a Dentist?** Provided by Charles H. Cox III and W. Kirk Bond, D.D.S. (**http://www.vvm.com/~bond/home.html**)This informative site is for the individual considering pursuing dentistry as a career. Explains types of dentists and educational requirements.

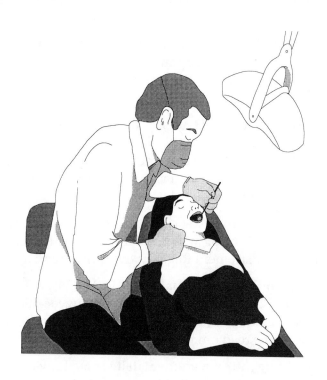 **Virtual Dental Center** This section of Martindale's Health Science Guide has tons of links for dentists and dental researchers. Visit their web site at (**http://www-sci.lib.uci.edu/hse/Dental.html**).

OPTOMETRISTS

Employment growth will be fastest in retail optical stores and outpatient clinics.

Nature of the Work

Over half of the people in the United States wear glasses or contact lenses. Optometrists (doctors of optometry, also known as O.D.'s) provide most primary vision care.

Optometrists examine people's eyes to diagnose vision problems and eye diseases. They use instruments and observation to examine eye health and to test patients' visual acuity, depth and color perception, and their ability to focus and coordinate the eyes. They analyze test results and develop a treatment plan. Optometrists prescribe eyeglasses and contact lenses, and provide vision therapy and low vision rehabilitation. They administer drugs to patients to aid in the diagnosis of eye vision problems and prescribe drugs to treat some eye diseases. Optometrists often provide pre- and post-operative care to cataract, laser vision correction, and other eye surgery patients. They also diagnose conditions due to systemic diseases such as diabetes and high blood pressure, and refer patients to other health practitioners as needed.

Optometrists should not be confused with ophthalmologists or dispensing opticians. Ophthalmologists are physicians who perform eye surgery, and diagnose and treat eye diseases and injuries. Like optometrists, they also examine eyes and prescribe eyeglasses and contact lenses. Dispensing opticians fit and adjust eyeglasses and in some States may fit contact lenses according to prescriptions written by ophthalmologists or optometrists. (See statements on physicians and dispensing opticians elsewhere in the Handbook.)

Most optometrists are in general practice. Some specialize in work with the elderly, children, or partially sighted persons who need specialized visual devices. Others develop and implement ways to protect workers' eyes from on-the-job strain or injury. Some specialize in contact lenses, sports vision, or vision therapy. A few teach optometry, perform research, or consult.

Most optometrists are private practitioners who also handle the business aspects of running an office, such as developing a patient base, hiring employees, keeping records, and ordering equipment and supplies. Optometrists who operate franchise optical stores may also have some of these duties.

Working Conditions

Optometrists work in places—usually their own offices—which are clean, well lighted, and comfortable. Most full-time optometrists work about 40 hours a week. Many work Saturdays and evenings to suit the needs of patients. Emergency calls, once uncommon, have increased with the passage of therapeutic drug laws expanding optometrists' ability to prescribe medications.

Employment

Optometrists held about 38,000 jobs in 1998. The number of jobs is greater than the number of practicing optometrists because some optometrists hold two or more jobs. For example, an optometrist may have a private practice, but also work in another practice, clinic, or vision care center. According to the American Optometric Association, about two-thirds of practicing optometrists are in private practice.

Although many optometrists practice alone, a growing number are in a partnership or group practice. Some optometrists work as salaried employees of other optometrists or of ophthalmologists, hospitals, health maintenance organizations (HMO's), or retail optical stores. A small number of optometrists are consultants for industrial safety programs, insurance companies, manufacturers of ophthalmic products, HMO's, and others.

Training, Other Qualifications, and Advancement

All States and the District of Columbia require that optometrists be licensed. Applicants for a license must have a Doctor of Optometry degree from an accredited optometry school and pass both a written and a clinical State board examination. In many States, applicants can substitute the examinations of the National Board of Examiners in Optometry, usually taken during the student's academic career, for part or all of the written examination. Licenses are renewed every 1 to 3 years and in all States, continuing education credits are needed for renewal.

The Doctor of Optometry degree requires completion of a 4-year program at an accredited optometry school preceded by at least 3 years of preoptometric study at an accredited college or university (most optometry students hold a bachelor's degree or higher). In 1999, 17 U.S. schools and colleges of optometry held an accredited status with the Council on Optometric Education of the American Optometric Association.

Requirements for admission to schools of optometry include courses in English, mathematics, physics, chemistry, and biology. A few schools require or recommend courses in psychology, history, sociology, speech, or business. Applicants must take the Optometry Admissions Test, which measures academic ability and scientific comprehension. Most applicants take the test after their sophomore or junior year. Competition for admission is keen.

Optometry programs include classroom and laboratory study of health and visual sciences, as well as clinical training in the diagnosis and treatment of eye disorders. Included are courses in pharmacology, optics, vision science, biochemistry, and systemic disease.

Business ability, self-discipline, and the ability to deal tactfully with patients are important for success. The work of optometrists requires attention to detail and good manual dexterity.

Optometrists wishing to teach or do research may study for a master's or Ph.D. degree in visual science, physiological optics, neurophysiology, public health, health administration, health information and communication, or health education. One-year postgraduate clinical residency programs are available for optometrists who wish to specialize in any of the following: family practice optometry, pediatric optometry, geriatric optometry, vision therapy, contact lenses, hospital based optometry, primary care optometry, or ocular disease.

Job Outlook

Employment of optometrists is expected to grow about as fast as the average for all occupations through 2008 in response to the vision care needs of a growing and aging population. As baby boomers age, they will be more likely to visit optometrists and ophthalmologists because of the onset of vision problems in middle age, including computer-related vision problems. The demand for optometric services will also increase because of growth in the oldest age group, with their increased likelihood of cataracts, glaucoma, diabetes, and hypertension. Employment of optometrists will also grow due to greater recognition of the importance of vision care, rising personal incomes, and growth in employee vision care plans. Employment growth will be fastest in retail optical stores and outpatient clinics.

Employment of optometrists would grow more rapidly were it not for anticipated productivity gains that will allow each optometrist to see more patients. These gains will result from greater use of optometric assistants and other support personnel, and the introduction of new equipment and procedures. New surgical procedures using lasers are available that can correct some vision problems, but they remain expensive.

In addition to growth, the need to replace optometrists who leave the occupation will create employment opportunities. Relatively few opportunities from this source are expected, however, because most optometrists continue to practice until they retire; few transfer to other occupations.

Earnings

Median annual earnings of salaried optometrists were $68,500 in 1998. The middle 50 percent earned between $43,750 and $93,700 a year. The lowest 10 percent earned less than $24,820 and the highest 10 percent earned more than $123,770 a year. Salaried optometrists tend to earn more initially than do optometrists who set up their own independent practice. In the long run, those in private practice usually earn more.

According to the American Optometric Association, new optometry graduates in their first year of practice earned median net incomes of $55,000 in 1998. Overall, optometrists earned median net incomes of $92,000.

OPTOMETRISTS

Don't forget! Refer to the general resources listed in Chapter Three.

❦ 📁 ⌖ **American Academy of Optometry (AAO)** - 6110 Executive Boulevard, Suite 506, Rockville, MD 20852; 301/984-1441, fax: 301/984-4737, **http://www.aaopt.org/**, E-mail: aaoptom@aol.com. AAO membership directory is on the web site.

❦ 📋📁 🏷️📑⌖ <u>American Optometric Association (AOA)</u> - 243 N. Lindberg Blvd., St. Louis, MO 63141-7881; 314/991-4100, fax: 314/991-4101, **(http://www.aoanet.org/)**. Provides a job fair at the annual AOA Congress. Publishes a journal, news letter, and educational materials. Their National Practice Resource Network Placement Service, matches health care providers with optometrists. The Educational Center of the web site has career guidance with a list of schools and the Meet the AOA area has a listing of AOA state associations.

❦ 📋📁⌖ **Association of Schools and Colleges of Optometry** - 6110 Executive Boulevard, Suite 510, Rockville, MD 20852; 301/231-5944; fax 301/770-1828, **http://home.opted.org/asco/** or **http://www.opted.org**. Web site offers an optometry faculty directory and Job Mart.

❦ ⌖ **The Canadian Association of Optometrists** - 234 Argyle Avenue, Ottawa, Ontario K2P 1B9, Canada; 613/235-7924, fax: 613/235-2025. **(http://www.opto.ca/index.html)** E-mail: dircomm@opto.ca. Information on becoming an optometrist, including costs, and on optometrist assistants.

❦ 📋⌖ **National Optometric Association (NOA)** - Contact Dr. Charles Comer, director, 3723 Main St., or P.O. Box F, East Chicago, IN 46312; 219/398-1832. **(http:/natoptassoc.org,** e-mail: Binfo@natoptassoc.org) The NOA encourages minority group members to enter optometry. Job ads on message board are open to the public.

📖 **Opportunities in Eye Care Careers** by Kathleen Belikoff. 1998. Paperback, $11.95. ISBN: 0844223034. Published by VGM Career Horizons, 4255 Touhy Ave., Lincolnwood, IL 60646-1975; 800/323-4900, 847/679-5500, fax: 847/679-2494.

Lori A. Tharp

Lori Tharp is a Physician Assistant (PA), working for Doctors Moraca, Wharton OB/GYN Association in Sewickley, Pennsylvania. Ms. Tharp majored as a physician assistant at Gannon University and graduated with a BS degree in 1986. When I asked Lori how she came to enter this field, she said, "My mother was hospitalized when I was a junior in high school and her orthopedic surgeon had a PA on staff. I always knew that I wanted to do something in the medical field but I wasn't quite sure what. My mother was an RN and my brother a paramedic and at that time I was fairly certain that I didn't want to enter the nursing field. My mother's physician assistant (PA) made such an impression on me that from that day on I knew that I wanted to enter this field." The PA position is somewhere between nursing and being a physician, Lori indicated, and she explained that you don't have all of the physician's responsibilities yet you can still function independently in many areas.

The PA curriculum requires clinical rotations or preceptorships starting in the junior year. "One rotation is required for each subspecialty of medicine including family, pediatrics, and internal medicine," said Lori, "Every six weeks I moved to a different hospital at locations throughout central and western Pennsylvania. It was a truly rewarding experience. It really helped me grow professionally and personally even though it was a little scary moving to unknown places so frequently."

"To work as a PA you must be board eligible," Lori said, "This means that you successfully graduated from an accredited PA program and that you are scheduled to take the next board exam. If you fail you must wait one full year before retesting. You aren't permitted to continue working as a PA until you pass."

To retain their certification PAs must complete 100 hours of recurrent training every two years and then every six years they must re-register their certificate by taking a recertifying exam through the NCCPA, National Certifying Commission on Physician Assistants.

"I love my job," said Lori, "It's perfect. I see patients in the office, assist in OR, help manage patients in labor, and make rounds in the hospital. There is such a wide variety of interesting responsibilities."

Lori advises, "If you're interested in this field, concentrate on your sciences in high school. A sound science and math background including biology, advanced biology, and chemistry, is essential. Once I settled on my career choice in high school, that in itself motivated me to study harder."

PHYSICIAN ASSISTANTS

Earnings are high and job opportunities should be good.

Nature of the Work

Physician assistants (PAs) provide health care services with supervision by physicians. They should not be confused with medical assistants, who perform routine clinical and clerical tasks. (Medical assistants are discussed elsewhere in the Handbook.) PAs are formally trained to provide diagnostic, therapeutic, and preventive health care services, as delegated by a physician. Working as members of the health care team, they take medical histories, examine patients, order and interpret laboratory tests and x rays, and make diagnoses. They also treat minor injuries by suturing, splinting, and casting. PAs record progress notes, instruct and counsel patients, and order or carry out therapy. In 46 States and the District of Columbia, physician assistants may prescribe medications. PAs may also have managerial duties. Some order medical and laboratory supplies and equipment and may supervise technicians and assistants.

Physician assistants always work with the supervision of a physician. However, PAs may provide care in rural or inner city clinics where a physician is present for only 1 or 2 days each week, conferring with the supervising physician and other medical professionals as needed or required by law. PAs may also make house calls or go to hospitals and nursing homes to check on patients and report back to the physician.

The duties of physician assistants are determined by the supervising physician and by State law. Aspiring PAs should investigate the laws and regulations in the States where they wish to practice.

Many PAs work in primary care areas such as general internal medicine, pediatrics, and family medicine. Others work in specialty areas, such as general and thoracic surgery, emergency medicine, orthopedics, and geriatrics. PAs specializing in surgery provide pre and post operative care and may work as first or second assistants during major surgery.

Working Conditions

Although PAs usually work in a comfortable, well-lighted environment, those in surgery often stand for long periods, and others do considerable walking. Schedules vary according to practice setting and often depend on the hours of the supervising physician. The workweek of PAs in physicians' offices may include weekends, night hours, or early morning hospital rounds to visit patients. They may also be on-call. PAs in clinics usually work a 40-hour week.

Employment

Physician assistants held about 66,000 jobs in 1998. The number of jobs is greater than the number of practicing PAs because some hold two or more jobs. For example, some PAs work with a supervising physician, but also work in another practice, clinic, or hospital. According to the American Academy of Physician Assistants, there were about 34,200 certified PA's in clinical practice, as of January 1999.

Sixty-seven percent of jobs for PA's were in the offices and clinics of physicians, dentists, or other health practitioners. About 21 percent were in hospitals. The rest were mostly in public health clinics, nursing homes, prisons, home health care agencies, and the Department of Veterans Affairs.

According to the American Academy of Physician Assistants, about one-third of all PAs provide health care to communities having fewer than 50,000 residents where physicians may be in limited supply.

Training, Other Qualifications, and Advancement

All States require that new PAs complete an accredited, formal education program. As of July 1999, there were 116 accredited or provisionally accredited educational programs for physician assistants; 64 of these programs offered a bachelor's degree or a degree option. The rest offered either a certificate, an associate degree, or a master's degree. Most PA graduates have at least a bachelor's degree.

Admission requirements vary, but many programs require 2 years of college and some work experience in the health care field. Students should take courses in biology, English, chemistry, math, psychology, and social sciences. More than half of all applicants hold a bachelor's or master's degree. Many applicants are former emergency medical technicians, other allied health professionals, or nurses.

PA programs usually last 2 years. Most programs are in schools of allied health, academic health centers, medical schools, or 4-year colleges; a few are in community colleges, the military, or hospitals. Many accredited PA programs have clinical teaching affiliations with medical schools.

PA education includes classroom instruction in biochemistry, nutrition, human anatomy, physiology, microbiology, clinical pharmacology, clinical medicine, geriatric and home health care, disease prevention, and medical ethics. Students obtain supervised clinical training in several areas, including primary care medicine, inpatient medicine, surgery, obstetrics and gynecology, geriatrics, emergency medicine, psychiatry, and pediatrics. Sometimes, PA students serve one or more of these "rotations" under the supervision of a physician who is seeking to hire a PA. These rotations often lead to permanent employment.

As of 1999, 49 States and the District of Columbia had legislation governing the qualifications or practice of physician assistants; Mississippi did not. All jurisdictions required physician assistants to pass the Physician Assistants National Certifying Examination, administered by the National Commission on Certification of Physician Assistants (NCCPA)—open openly to graduates of accredited PA educational programs. Only those successfully completing the examination may use the credential "Physician Assistant-Certified (PA-C)." In order to remain certified, PAs must complete 100 hours of continuing medical education every 2 years. Every 6 years, they must pass a recertification examination or complete an alternate program combining learning experiences and a take-home examination.

Some PA's pursue additional education in order to practice in a specialty area such as surgery, neonatology, or emergency medicine. PA postgraduate residency training programs are available in areas such as internal medicine, rural primary care, emergency medicine, surgery, pediatrics, neonatology, and occupational medicine. Candidates must be graduates of an accredited program and be certified by the NCCPA.

Physician assistants need leadership skills, self-confidence, and emotional stability. They must be willing to continue studying throughout their career to keep up with medical advances.

As they attain greater clinical knowledge and experience, PAs can advance to added responsibilities and higher earnings. However, by the very nature of the profession, individual PAs are always supervised by physicians.

Job Outlook

Employment opportunities are expected to be good for physician assistants, particularly in areas or settings that have difficulty attracting physicians, such as rural and inner city clinics. Employment of PAs is expected to grow much faster than the average for all occupations through the year 2008 due to anticipated expansion of the health services industry and an emphasis on cost containment.

Physicians and institutions are expected to employ more PAs to provide primary care and assist with medical and surgical procedures because PAs are cost-effective and productive members of the health care team. Physician assistants can relieve physicians of routine duties and procedures. Telemedicine—using technology to facilitate interactive consultations between physicians and physician assistants—will also expand the use of physician assistants.

Besides the traditional office-based setting, PAs should find a growing number of jobs in institutional settings such as hospitals, academic medical centers, public clinics, and prisons. Additional PAs may be needed to augment medical staffing in inpatient teaching hospital settings if the number of physician residents is reduced. In addition, State-imposed legal limitations on the numbers of hours worked by physician residents are increasingly common and encourage hospitals to use PAs to supply some physician resident services. Opportunities will be best in States that allow PAs a wider scope of practice, such as the ability to prescribe medication.

Earnings

Median annual earnings of physician assistants were $47,090 in 1998. The middle 50 percent earned between $25,110 and $71,450 a year. The lowest 10 percent earned less than $18,600 and the highest 10 percent earned more than $86,760 a year. Median annual earnings of physician assistants in 1997 were $41,100 in offices and clinics of medical doctors and $57,100 in hospitals.

According to the American Academy of Physician Assistants, median income for physician assistants in full-time clinical practice in 1998 was about $62,200; median income for first-year graduates was about $54,000. Income varies by specialty, practice setting, geographical location, and years of experience.

PHYSICIAN ASSISTANTS

Don't forget! Refer to the general resources listed in Chapter Three.

🎗️📑📂🏷️✒️🖱️ American Academy of Physician Assistants (AAPA) - 950 North Washington St., Alexandria, VA 22314-1552; 703/836-2272, fax: 703/684-1924, **http://www.aapa.org/**, E-mail: aapa@aapa.org. Offers an extensive array of member services. The *AAPA News* is published bi-monthly for members only and has 30-50 job ads. Web site "Employment Opportunities" section is a part of Medical-AdMart.

🎗️🖱️ American Academy of Physician Assistants in Occupational Medicine (AAPA-OM) - 950 N. Washington St, Alexandria, VA 22314; 800/596-4398, fax: 703/684-1924, **http://www.aapa.org/paom.htm**, E-mail: aapaom@aapa.org. Annual dues: $75, student: $40.

🎗️📑📂🖱️ American Association of Pathologists' Assistants (8030 Old Cedar Avenue South, Bloomington, MN 55425; 800/532-2202, fax: 612/854-1402, **http://meds.queensu.ca/medicine/aapa/aapahome.htm**, E-mail: ZLZS50A@prodigy.com). Web site has a section describing the profession and training and will be adding a jobs area.

🎗️🖱️ Association of Neurosurgical Physician Assistants Web site at **http://www.anpa.org/** or E-mail: jyoodee@aol.com. Dues: $50.

🎗️📂✒️🖱️ Association of Physician Assistants in Cardiovascular Surgery (APACVS) Annual dues: $125; students: $25. Publishes *APACVS Membership Directory*. Offers placement service. Visit their web site at - (**http://www.apacvs.org/**).

🎗️🖱️ Association of Physician Assistant Programs, 950 North Washington St., Alexandria, VA 22314-1552. Internet: **http://www.apap.org** Contact for a list of accredited programs and PA training programs.

✒️🖱️ MED OPTIONS USA (6617 W Boynton Beach Blvd., #202, Boynton Beach, FL 33437; Phone: 800/817-4903, fax: 800/357-8684, (http://www.medoptions.com). Free nurse practitioner and physician assistant job service. They give your profile to prospective employers.

☤ **National Commission of Physician Assistants, Inc.,** - 157 Technology Parkway, Suite 800, Norcross, GA 30092-2913, 770/734-4535. **(www.nccpa.net).** Contact for eligibility requirements and a description of the Physicians Assistant National Certifying Examination.

☤ 📖 ⌐ **PHYSICIAN ASSISTANT** - Springhouse Corp., 1111 Bethlehem Pike, P.O. Box 908, Springhouse, PA 19477-0908; 800/633-2648, **(http://www.springnet.com/).** Contact the AAPA about free subscriptions for physician assistants and students. Free sample issue.

📖 **Physician Assistants in American Medicine** by Roderick S. Hooker & James F. Cawley. 1997. Paperback, 285 pages, $29.95, ISBN: 0443057311. Published by Churchill Livingstone.

☤ 📖 **Physician Assistants in Orthopedic Surgery (PAOS)** - PO Box 389, Bernardsville, NJ 07924; Phone: 800/804-7267, Fax: 206/821-9362. Annual dues: $50. The *Surgical PA* newsletter has job ads.

⌐ **Physician Assistant Web Page** (http://www.halcyon.com/physasst) E-mail: JCS@HALCYON.COM. National resource on the net for and about the physician assistant profession.

☤ ⌐ **Society of Dermatology Physician Assistants** Visit their web site at **(http://www.pacifier.com/~jomonroe/).** Annual dues: fellows and affiliates, $50. E-mail: jomonroe@pacifier.com.

☤ ⌐ **Society of Emergency Medicine Physician Assistants (SEMPA)** - Web site at **http://www.sempa.org/,** E-mail: info@sempa.org. Annual dues: fellows, $50; associates, $75; affiliates, $75; students, residents, $10.

☤ **Association of Physician Assistants in Obstetrics and Gynecology (APAOG)** - PO Box 1109, Madison, WI 53701-1109; 800/545-0636, fax: 608/283-5402. Dues: fellows and affiliates, $25; students, $10.

☤ 📖 **Society of Physician Assistants in Otorhinolaryngology/Head and Neck Surgery** Contact Eugene Larson, PAC, 1000 N. Oak Ave., ENT-4J, Marshfield, WI 54449; 715/387-5245. Annual dues: fellows and affiliates, $25; students, $15. Newsletter has job ads.

PHYSICIANS

Formal education and training requirements are among the longest of any occupation, but earnings are among the highest.

Nature of the Work

Physicians serve a fundamental role in our society and have an effect upon all our lives. They diagnose illnesses and prescribe and administer treatment for people suffering from injury or disease. Physicians examine patients, obtain medical histories, and order, perform, and interpret diagnostic tests. They counsel patients on diet, hygiene, and preventive health care.

There are two types of physicians: The M.D.—Doctor of Medicine—and the D.O.—Doctor of Osteopathic Medicine. M.D.s are also known as allopathic physicians. While both M.D.s and D.O.s may use all accepted methods of treatment, including drugs and surgery, D.O.s place special emphasis on the body's musculoskeletal system, preventive medicine, and holistic patient care.

About a third of M.D.s—and more than half of D.O.s—are primary care physicians. They practice general and family medicine, general internal medicine, or general pediatrics and are usually the first health professionals patients consult. Primary care physicians tend to see the same patients on a regular basis for preventive care and to treat a variety of ailments. General and family practitioners emphasize comprehensive health care for patients of all ages and for the family as a group. Those in general internal medicine provide care mainly for adults who may have problems associated with the body's organs. General pediatricians focus on the whole range of children's health issues. When appropriate, primary care physicians refer patients to specialists, who are experts in medical fields such as obstetrics and gynecology, cardiology, psychiatry, or surgery.

Working Conditions

Many physicians work long, irregular hours. More than one-third of all full-time physicians worked 60 hours or more a week in 1998. They travel frequently between office and hospital to care for their patients. Increasingly, physicians practice in groups or health care organizations that provide back-up coverage and allow for more time off. These physicians often work as part of a team coordinating care for patients; they are less independent than solo practitioners of the past. Physicians who are on-call deal with many patients' concerns over the phone, and may make emergency visits to hospitals or nursing homes.

Employment

Physicians (M.D.s and D.O.s) held about 577,000 jobs in 1998. About 7 out of 10 were in office-based practice, including clinics and Health Maintenance Organizations (HMOs); about 2 out of 10 were employed by hospitals. Others practiced in the Federal Government, most in Department of Veterans Affairs hospitals and clinics or in the Public Health Service of the Department of Health and Human Services.

A growing number of physicians are partners or salaried employees of group practices. Organized as clinics or as groups of physicians, medical groups can afford expensive medical equipment and realize other business advantages. Also, hospitals are integrating physician practices into health care networks that provide a continuum of care both inside and outside the hospital setting.

The New England and Middle Atlantic States have the highest ratio of physicians to population; the South Central States, the lowest. D.O.s are more likely than M.D.s to practice in small cities and towns and in rural areas. M.D.s tend to locate in urban areas, close to hospital and educational centers.

Training, Other Qualifications, and Advancement

It takes many years of education and training to become a physician: 4 years of undergraduate school, 4 years of medical school, and 3 to 8 years of internship and residency, depending on the specialty selected. A few medical schools offer a combined undergraduate and medical school program that lasts 6 years instead of the customary 8 years.

Premedical students must complete undergraduate work in physics, biology, mathematics, English, and inorganic and organic chemistry. Students also take courses in the humanities and the social sciences. Some students also volunteer at local hospitals or clinics to gain practical experience in the health professions.

The minimum educational requirement for entry to a medical or osteopathic school is 3 years of college; most applicants, however, have at least a bachelor's degree, and many have advanced degrees. There are 144 medical schools in the United States—125 teach allopathic medicine and award a Doctor of Medicine (M.D.) degree; 19 teach osteopathic medicine and award the Doctor of Osteopathic Medicine (D.O.) degree. Acceptance to medical school is very competitive. Applicants must submit transcripts, scores from the Medical College Admission Test, and letters of recommendation. Schools also consider character, personality, leadership qualities, and participation in extracurricular activities. Most schools require an interview with members of the admissions committee.

Students spend most of the first 2 years of medical school in laboratories and classrooms taking courses such as anatomy, biochemistry, physiology, pharmacology, psychology, microbiology, pathology, medical ethics, and laws governing medicine. They also learn to take medical histories, examine patients, and diagnose illness. During the last 2 years, students work with patients under the supervision of experienced physicians in hospitals and clinics to learn acute, chronic, preventive, and rehabilitative care. Through rotations in internal medicine, family practice, obstetrics and gynecology, pediatrics, psychiatry, and surgery, they gain experience in the diagnosis and treatment of illness.

Following medical school, almost all M.D.s enter a residency graduate medical education in a specialty that takes the form of paid on-the-job training, usually in a hospital. Most D.O.s serve a 12-month rotating internship after graduation before entering a residency which may last 2 to 6 years. Physicians may benefit from residencies in managed care settings by gaining experience with this increasingly common type of medical practice.

All States, the District of Columbia, and U.S. territories license physicians. To be licensed, physicians must graduate from an accredited medical school, pass a licensing examination, and complete 1 to 7 years of graduate medical education. Although physicians licensed in one State can usually get a license to practice in another without further examination, some States limit reciprocity. Graduates of foreign medical schools can usually qualify for licensure after passing an examination and completing a U.S. residency.

M.D.s and D.O.s seeking board certification in a specialty may spend up to 7 years—depending on the specialty—in residency training. A final examination immediately after residency, or after 1 or 2 years of practice, is also necessary for board certification by the American Board of Medical Specialists (ABMS) or the American Osteopathic Association (AOA). There are 24 specialty boards, ranging from allergy and immunology to urology. For certification in a subspecialty, physicians usually need another 1 to 2 years of residency.

A physician's training is costly, and whereas education costs have increased, student financial assistance has not.

People who wish to become physicians must have a desire to serve patients, be self-motivated, and be able to survive the pressures and long hours of medical education and practice. Physicians must also have a good bedside manner, emotional stability, and the ability to make decisions in emergencies. Prospective physicians must be willing to study throughout their career to keep up with medical advances. They will also need to be flexible to respond to the changing demands of a rapidly evolving health care system.

Job Outlook

Employment of physicians will grow faster than the average for all occupations through the year 2008 due to continued expansion of the health care industries. The growing and aging population will drive overall growth in the demand for physician services. In addition, new technologies permit more intensive care: Physicians can do more tests, and treat conditions previously regarded as untreatable.

Although job prospects may be better for primary care physicians such as general and family practitioners, general pediatricians, and general internists, a substantial number of jobs for specialists will also be created in response to patient demand for access to specialty care.

The number of physicians in training has leveled off and may decrease over the next few years, alleviating any physician oversupply. However, future physicians may be more likely to work less hours, retire earlier, have lower earnings, or have to practice in underserved areas.

Earnings

Physicians have among the highest earnings of any occupation. According to the American Medical Association, median income, after expenses, for allopathic physicians was about $164,000 in 1997. The middle 50 percent earned between $120,000 and $250,000 a year. Self-employed physicians—those who own or are part owners of their medical practice—had higher median incomes than salaried physicians. Earnings vary according to number of years in practice; geographic region; hours worked; and skill, personality, and professional reputation.

Average salaries of medical residents ranged from $34,100 in 1998-99 for those in their first year of residency to about $42,100 for those in their sixth year, according to the Association of American Medical Colleges.

PHYSICIANS

Don't forget! Refer to the general resources listed in Chapter Three.

☤🗐📁🐝✍🗂️🖱 **American Academy of Family Physicians (AAFP)** - 11400 Tomahawk Creek Parkway, Leawood, KS 66211-2672, 913/906-6000. (**http://www.aafp.org**, E-mail: fp@aafp.org). Informations for students considering this career and job ads posted by state. *American Family Physician*, 24/year, $60/year for students, has jobs advertised. AAFP placement service is free for members. Job hotline call 800/237-7027.

☤📁🗐🖱 **American College of Physicians (ACP)** - Independence Mall West, Sixth Street at Race, Philadelphia, PA 19106; 800/523-1546. (**http://www.acponline.org/**, E-mail: interpub@mail.acponline.org) Free membership for medical students, comes with *Meet Internal Medicine*, a booklet about this medical specialty.

☤📖🗐🖱 **American Medical Association (AMA)** - 515 N. State St., Chicago, IL 60610; 800/262-2350 (publications), 800/262-3211 (member services). Web site at (**http://www.ama-assn.org**). Read the Journal online, including classifieds.

📖 **Becoming a Physician: A Practical and Creative Guide to Planning a Career in Medicine** by Jennifer Danek & Marita Danek. 1997. Paperback, $14.95, 217 pages. Published by John Wiley & Sons.

☤🗐 **Canadian Medical Association** (1867 Alta Vista Drive, Ottawa, Ontario K1G 3YR Canada; 613/731-9331, 800/267-9703, fax: 613/523-0937, (**http://www.cma.ca/**). Publishes several journals. Online classifieds.

📖 **How to Get into the Right Medical School** by Carla S. Rogers. 1996. Paperback, $11.95, ISBN: 084424161. Published by VGM Career Horizons.

☤🗐✍🖱 **National Medical Association (NMA)** - 1012 10th St. NW, Washington DC 20001; 202/347-1895, **http://www.natmed.org**, E-mail: nma@natmed.org. The NMA focuses primarily on health issues related to African Americans and medically under-served populations.

New England Journal of Medicine - 10 Shattuck Street, Boston, MA 02115-6094, Phone: 617/734-9800, Fax: 617/734-4457 (http://www.nejm.org/, E-mail: comments@massmed.org). Published weekly, $65/year for students, the journal has up to 500 job ads.

Further information on the numerous specialties for physicians can be found through medical associations listed below. We have also placed these links on http://healthcarejobs.org. This site lists and provides direct links to many resources that will help including a list of 24 of the key medical associations.

Aerospace Medical Association (http://www.asma.org)

American Academy of Dermatology (http://www.aad.org)

American Academy of Neurology (http://www.aan.com)

American Academy of Pediatrics (http://www.aap.org)

American Association of Immunologists (http://www.aai.org)

American College of Occupational and Environmental Medicine (http://www.acoem.org)

American Academy of Ophthalmology (http://www.eyenet.org)

American College of Sports Medicine (http://www.acsm.org)

American Gastroenterological Association (http://www.gastro.org)

American Medical Women's Association (http://www.amwa-doc.org)

American Osteopathic Association (http://www.am-osteo-assn.org)

American Podiatric Medical Association (http://www.apma.org)

American Psychiatric Association (http://www.appi.org/news)

American Psychological Society (http://www.psychorg)

American Roentgen Ray Society (http://www.arrs.org)

American Society of Anesthesiologists (http://www.asahq.org)

American Society of Clinical Pathologists (http://www.ascp.org)

American Society of Handicapped Physicians (Contact Will Lambert, Director, 3424 S. Culepper, Springfield, MO 65804; 417/881-1570.)

Canadian Medical Placement Service (http://www.cmps.ca)

The Endocrine Society (http://www.endo-society.org)

National Medical Network (http://www.natmednet.org)

Radiological Society of North America (http://www.rsna.org)

Society of Nuclear Medicine (SNM) (http://www.snm.org)

Society of Critical Care Medicine (http://www.sccm.org)

VETERINARIANS

RELATED OCCUPATIONS

Animal trainers, animal breeders, and veterinary technicians work extensively with animals. Like veterinarians, they must have patience and feel comfortable with animals. However, the level of training required for these occupations is substantially less than that needed by veterinarians.

Nature of the Work

Veterinarians play a major role in the health care of pets, livestock, and zoo, sporting, and laboratory animals. Some veterinarians use their skills to protect humans against diseases carried by animals and conduct clinical research on human and animal health problems. Others work in basic research, broadening the scope of fundamental theoretical knowledge, and in applied research, developing new ways to use knowledge.

Most veterinarians perform clinical work in private practices. More than one-half of these veterinarians predominately, or exclusively, treat small animals. Small animal practitioners usually care for companion animals, such as dogs and cats, but also treat birds, reptiles, rabbits, and other animals that can be kept as pets. Some veterinarians work in mixed animal practices where they see pigs, goats, sheep, and some nondomestic animals, in addition to companion animals. Veterinarians in clinical practice diagnose animal health problems; vaccinate against diseases, such as distemper and rabies; medicate animals suffering from infections or illnesses; treat and dress wounds; set fractures; perform surgery; and advise owners about animal feeding, behavior, and breeding.

A small number of private practice veterinarians work exclusively with large animals, focusing mostly on horses or cows but may also care for various kinds of food animals. These veterinarians usually drive to farms or ranches to provide veterinary services for herds or individual animals. Much of this work involves preventive care to maintain the health of the food animals. These veterinarians test for and vaccinate against diseases and consult with farm or ranch owners and managers on animal production, feeding, and housing issues. They also treat and dress wounds, set fractures, and perform surgery—including cesarean sections on birthing animals. Veterinarians also euthanize animals when necessary. Other veterinarians care for zoo, aquarium, or laboratory animals.

Veterinarians who treat animals use medical equipment, such as stethoscopes; surgical instruments; and diagnostic equipment, such as radiographic and ultra-sound equipment. Veterinarians working in research use a full range of sophisticated laboratory equipment.

Veterinarians can contribute to human as well as animal health. A number of veterinarians work with physicians and scientists as they research ways to prevent and treat human health problems, such as cancer, AIDS, and alcohol or drug abuse. Some determine the effects of drug therapies, antibiotics, or new surgical techniques by testing them on animals.

Some veterinarians are involved in food safety at various levels. Veterinarians who are livestock inspectors check animals for transmissible diseases, advise owners on treatment, and may quarantine animals. Veterinarians who are meat, poultry, or egg product inspectors examine slaughtering and processing plants, check live animals and carcasses for disease, and enforce government regulations regarding food purity and sanitation.

Working Conditions

Veterinarians often work long hours, with one-third of full-time workers spending 50 or more hours on the job. Those in group practices may take turns being on call for evening, night, or weekend work; and solo practitioners can work extended and weekend hours, responding to emergencies or squeezing in unexpected appointments.

Veterinarians in large animal practice also spend time driving between their office and farms or ranches. They work outdoors in all kinds of weather, and have to treat animals or perform surgery under less-than-sanitary conditions. When working with animals that are frightened or in pain, veterinarians risk being bitten, kicked, or scratched.

Veterinarians working in non-clinical areas, such as public health and research, have working conditions similar to those of other professionals in those lines of work. In these cases, veterinarians enjoy clean, well-lit offices or laboratories and spend much of their time dealing with people rather than animals.

Employment

Veterinarians held about 57,000 jobs in 1998. About 30 percent were self-employed in solo or group practices. Most others were employees of another veterinary practice. The Federal Government employed about 1,900 civilian veterinarians, chiefly in the U.S. Department of Agriculture, and about 400 military veterinarians in the U.S. Army and U.S. Air Force. Other employers of veterinarians are State and local governments, colleges of veterinary medicine, medical schools, research laboratories, animal food companies, and pharmaceutical companies. A few veterinarians work for zoos; but most veterinarians caring for zoo animals are private practitioners who contract with zoos to provide services, usually on a part-time basis.

Training, Other Qualifications, and Advancement

Prospective veterinarians must graduate from a 4-year program at an accredited college of veterinary medicine with a Doctor of Veterinary Medicine (D.V.M. or V.M.D.) degree and obtain a license to practice. There are 27 colleges in 26 States that meet accreditation standards set by the Council on Education of the American Veterinary Medical Association. The prerequisites for admission vary by veterinary medical college. Many of these colleges do not require a bachelor's degree for entrance; but all require a significant number of credit hours—ranging from 45 to 90 semester hours—at the undergraduate level. However, most of the students admitted have completed an undergraduate program.

Preveterinary courses emphasize the sciences; and veterinary medical colleges typically require classes in organic and inorganic chemistry, physics, biochemistry, general biology, animal biology, animal nutrition, genetics, vertebrate embryology, cellular biology, microbiology, zoology, and systemic physiology. Some programs require calculus; some require only statistics, college algebra and trigonometry, or precalculus; and others require no math at all. Most veterinary medical colleges also require core courses, including some in English or literature, the social sciences, and the humanities.

Most veterinary medical colleges will only consider applicants who have a minimum grade point average (GPA). The required GPA varies by school, from a low of 2.5 to a high of 3.2, based on a maximum GPA of 4.0. However, the average GPA of candidates at most schools is higher than these minimums. Those who receive offers of admission usually have a GPA of 3.0 or better.

In addition to satisfying preveterinary course requirements, applicants must also submit test scores from the Graduate Record Examination (GRE), the Veterinary College Admission Test (VCAT), or the Medical College Admission Test (MCAT), depending on the preference of each college.

Additionally, in the admissions process, veterinary medical colleges weigh heavily a candidate's veterinary and animal experience. Formal experience, such as work with veterinarians or scientists in clinics, agribusiness, research, or in some area of health science, is particularly advantageous. Less formal experience, such as working with animals on a farm or ranch or at a stable or animal shelter, is also helpful. Students must demonstrate ambition and an eagerness to work with animals.

Competition for admission to veterinary school is keen. The number of accredited veterinary colleges has remained at 27 since 1983, whereas the number of applicants has risen. About 1 in 3 applicants was accepted in 1998. Most veterinary medical colleges are public, State-supported institutions and reserve the majority of their openings for in-state residents. Twenty-one States that do not have a veterinary medical college agree to pay a fee or subsidy to help cover the cost of veterinary education for a limited number of their residents at one or more out-of-state colleges. Nonresident students who are admitted under such a contract may have to pay out-of-state tuition, or they may have to repay their State of residency all, or part, of the subsidy provided to the contracting college. Residents of the remaining 3 States (Connecticut, Maine, and Vermont) and the District of Columbia may apply to any of the 27 veterinary medical colleges as an at-large applicant. The number of positions available to at-large applicants is very limited at most schools, making admission difficult.

While in veterinary medical college, students receive additional academic instruction in the basic sciences for the first 2 years. Later in the program, students are exposed to clinical procedures, such as diagnosing and treating animal diseases and performing surgery. They also do laboratory work in anatomy, biochemistry, medicine, and other scientific subjects. At most veterinary medical colleges, students who plan a career in research can earn both a D.V.M. degree and a Doctor of Philosophy (Ph.D.) degree at the same time.

Veterinary graduates who plan to work with specific types of animals or specialize in a clinical area, such as pathology, surgery, radiology, or laboratory animal medicine, usually complete a 1-year internship. Interns receive a small salary but usually find that their internship experience leads to a higher beginning salary, relative to other starting veterinarians. Veterinarians who seek board certification in a specialty must also complete a 2- to 3-year residency program that provides intensive training in specialties, such as internal medicine, oncology, radiology, surgery, dermatology, anesthesiology, neurology, cardiology, ophthalmology, and exotic small animal medicine.

All States and the District of Columbia require that veterinarians be licensed before they can practice. The only exemptions are for veterinarians working for some Federal agencies and some State governments. Licensing is controlled by the States and is not strictly uniform, although all States require successful completion of the D.V.M. degree—or equivalent education—and passage of a national board examination. The Educational Commission for Foreign Veterinary Graduates (ECFVG) grants certification to individuals trained outside the U.S. who demonstrate that they meet specified requirements for the English language and clinical proficiency. ECFVG certification fulfills the educational requirement for licensure in all States except Nebraska. Applicants for licensure satisfy the examination requirement by passing the North American Veterinary Licensing Exam (NAVLE), which replaces the National Board Examination (NBE) and the Clinical Competency Test (CCT) as of April 2000. The new NAVLE, administered on computer, takes one day to complete and consists of 360 multiple-choice questions, covering all aspects of veterinary medicine. The NAVLE also includes visual materials designed to test diagnostic skills.

The majority of States also require candidates to pass a State jurisprudence examination covering State laws and regulations. Some States also do additional testing on clinical competency. There are few reciprocal agreements between States, making it difficult for a veterinarian to practice in a different State without first taking another State examination.

Thirty-nine States have continuing education requirements for licensed veterinarians. Requirements differ by State and may involve attending a class or otherwise demonstrating knowledge of recent medical and veterinary advances.

Most veterinarians begin as employees or partners in established practices. Despite the substantial financial investment in equipment, office space, and staff, many veterinarians with experience set up their own practice or purchase an established one.

Newly trained veterinarians can become U.S. Government meat and poultry inspectors, disease-control workers, epidemiologists, research assistants, or commissioned officers in the U.S. Public Health Service, U.S. Army, or U.S. Air Force. A State license may be required.

Prospective veterinarians must have good manual dexterity. They should have an affinity for animals and the ability to get along with animal owners. Additionally, they should be able to quickly make decisions in emergencies.

Job Outlook

Employment of veterinarians is expected to grow faster than the average for all occupations through the year 2008. Job openings stemming from the need to replace veterinarians who retire or otherwise leave the labor force will be almost as numerous as new jobs resulting from employment growth over the 1998-2008 period.

Most veterinarians practice in animal hospitals or clinics and care primarily for companion animals. The number of pets is expected to increase more slowly during the projection period than in the previous decade and may moderate growth in the demand for veterinarians who specialize in small animals. One reason for this is that the large baby-boom generation is aging and will probably acquire fewer dogs and cats than earlier. However, as non-necessity income generally increases with age, those who own pets may be more inclined to seek veterinary services. In addition, pet owners are becoming more aware of the availability of advanced care and may increasingly take advantage of nontraditional veterinary services, such as preventive dental care, and may more willingly pay for intensive care than in the past. Finally, new technologies and medical advancements should permit veterinarians to offer better care to animals. Veterinarians who enter small animal practice will probably face competition. Large numbers of new graduates continue to be attracted to small animal medicine because they prefer to deal with pets and to live and work near highly populated areas. However, an oversupply does not necessarily limit the ability of veterinarians to find employment or to set up and maintain a practice in a particular area. Such an oversupply could result in veterinarians taking positions requiring much evening or weekend work to accommodate the extended hours of operation that many practices are offering. Others could take salaried positions in retail stores offering limited veterinary services. Most self-employed veterinarians will probably have to work hard and long to build a sufficient clientele.

The number of jobs for large animal veterinarians is expected to grow slowly, because productivity gains in the agricultural production industry mean demand for fewer veterinarians than before to treat food animals. Nevertheless, job prospects may be better for veterinarians who specialize in farm animals than for small animal practitioners, because most veterinary medical college graduates do not have the desire to work in rural or isolated areas.

Continued support for public health and food safety, disease control programs, and biomedical research on human health problems will contribute to the demand for veterinarians, although such positions are few in number. Also, anticipated budget tightening in the Federal Government may lead to low funding levels for some programs, limiting job growth. Veterinarians with training in public health and epidemiology should have the best opportunities for a career in the Federal Government.

Earnings

Median annual earnings of veterinarians were $50,950 in 1998. The middle 50 percent earned between $39,580 and $78,670. The lowest 10 percent earned less than $31,320 and the highest 10 percent earned more than $106,370.

VETERINARIANS

Association   Book   Directory   Internet (Web) Site
Job Ads   E-mail/Hotline   Job Fairs   Resume Service

American College of Veterinary Surgeons - 4340 East West Highway, Suite 401, Bethesda, MD 20814; 301/718-6504. *ACVS Directory of Diplomates*, online job ads, and information on becoming a veterinary surgeon. Internet site is lolcated at **http://www.acus.org**.

American Humane Association - 63 Inverness Drive East, Englewood, CO 80112-5117; Phone: 303/792-9900. *Directory of Animal Care and Control Agencies*. Web site is located at **http://www.amerhumane.org**. State editions are available for a small fee. Web site has Animal Protection Job Opportunities section for managers, veterinarians and technicians.

American Veterinary Medical Association (AVMA) - 1931 N. Meacham Rd., Suite 100, Schaumburg, IL 60173; 800/248-2862, 847/925-8070, (**http://www.avma.org** or **http://www.avma.org/netvet**). *Journal of the American Veterinary Medical Association* features about 30-35 classified job ads per issue. AVMA Job Placement Service, free to DVM members, while technicians need not be members. The award-winning Web site called "NetVet" & "Electronic Zoo" has links to thousands of veterinary medical and animal-related online resources.

Association of American Veterinary Medical Colleges - 1101 Vermont Avenue NW, Suite 710, Washington, DC 20005; 202/371-9195, fax: 202/842-0773, E-mail: Ljohnston@aavmc.org, **www.aavmc.org**.

Careers in Animal Care and Veterinary Science - by Deborah A. Marinelli. 2000. $25.25. Rosen Publishing Group, Inc., 29 E. 21st St., New York, NY 10010.

California Veterinarian Medical Association (CMV) - 5231 Madison Ave., Sacramento, CA 95841; 916/344-4985, fax: 916/344-6147, (**http:www.scva.org**) E-mail: cmva@aol.com. *California Veterinarian* is $35 for nonmembers and has lots of job ads and practices for sale.

DVMSearch - (**http://www.dvmsearch.com**) Web site for jobs and job seekers, practice buyers and practice sellers. Post your resume. You can search by state.

Chapter

10

HOME HEALTH CARE & MEDICAL INFORMATION MANAGEMENT

Lily Chan, RN

Lily Chan, a registered nurse with Children's Home Care in Los Angeles, was born in Hong Kong May 23, 1953. She completed a three year nursing program and worked four years as a staff nurse there before moving to England. She took additional courses in pediatric and cardiothoracic nursing before coming to the United States.

When asked why she chose nursing, Lily said she felt "the need to take care of someone as a basic personality trait." In addition, she enjoyed studying biology and anatomy, and felt nursing could provide her with a good income. She also thought that "the education and experience in nursing would help me take care of my own health." Lily feels that the most satisfying aspect of a nursing career is "providing a quality environment for the patient. Even the more menial tasks become satisfying if you look at it that way."

A recruiting agency arranged for Lily to come to the United States in 1983 and take the NCLEX licensing exam for RNs. They also found employment for her at Methodist Hospital in Lubbock, Texas, as an interim permittee while waiting for her RN license. In April of 1984, she began working at Childrens Hospital Los Angeles. In 1995, Children's Home Care was formed as an affiliate of CHLA.

Lily pointed out the advantages to working in home health care. "In home health, you have time to deal with just one patient and family at a time. In the hospital you can get pulled in five directions at once when it gets busy." You also have a more flexible time schedule.

Lily was asked why she specifically likes pediatric home health care. "With pediatrics, you are interacting with the whole family." Once she was taking care of a child and complimented the mother on how good the chicken she was cooking smelled. When she finished with the patient, the table was set with dinner for her.

Lily advised that anyone considering home health as a career evaluate their capabilities. "For home care you have to have a very broad knowledge base and be creative and flexible. You have to improvise a lot." She also warned, "The fear of many who transfer to home health care is that in a hospital, if there is any problem, you can just yell and get assistance, while with home care that security is lost. On the other hand, home care patients may not be as ill as those in the hospital and there is emergency help available, such as calling 911."

When asked for advice in finding employment, Lily responded, "It is hard for a new graduate to get into, as they need a few years in acute care in a hospital to develop the assessment skills." *NurseWeek* and the local newspaper are good sources for job ads. Check with hospitals, too. Some have their own home health care department.

I asked how to evaluate a home health care agency as a potential employer. "Look for leadership quality. The whole mission and philosophy of the agency has to support staff providing quality care. This affects how good you feel about yourself. The agency has to balance the quality with cost."

If you really enjoy working with people and have confidence in your skills, you will probably derive great satisfaction from caring for your patients in their homes.

This chapter features an overview of the home health field (one of fastest growing areas of medical care), and career descriptions with resources for

Homemaker-Home Health Aides   Computer Careers
Medical Information Technicians   Billing and Coding Specialists

Also presented are resources for the many professionals involved in caring for patients in the home. These include, but are not limited to:

Physicians   Dieticians
Nurses   Pharmacists
Physical Therapists   Social Workers
Occupational Therapists   Speech-language Pathologists

HOME HEALTH CARE OVERVIEW

Home health care has a long tradition, with the first home care agencies established more than a century ago. The National Association for Home Care (NAHC) counted 20,215 home care organizations in the United States and its territories, including home health agencies, home care aide organizations, and hospices.[1] The explosive growth in the home care sector is linked to the increase in size of the health care field overall.

Health care services will increase 26 percent and account for 2.8 million new jobs, the largest numerical increase of any industry from 1998-2008. Patients will increasingly be shifted out of hospitals and into outpatient facilities, nursing homes, and home health care in an attempt to contain costs. Opportunities for registered nurses and other health-related specialists have surged in response to the rapid growth in demand for health services. Personal and home care aides, and home health aides, will be in great demand to provide personal care for an increasing number of elderly people and for persons who are recovering from surgery and other serious health conditions. This is occurring, as hospitals and insurance companies require shorter stays for recovery to reduce costs.[2]

Home health care can often dramatically lower costs. For example, home care for a low-birthweight infant can save over $25,000 per month. Chemotherapy costs can be cut by almost $14,000 per month. For many patients, the availability of home health care services can reduce the length of hospital stays, thus lowering costs.[3]

> # Personal and home care aides, and home health aides, will be in great demand.

Not all patients needing home care are elderly. Disabled people of any age may need some degree of home care. Patients recuperating from acute illness or injury may need temporary home care. Children and adults with chronic illnesses may need medical treatment that can be provided at home by a home health professional, or may need training in specific medical therapies such as parenteral nutrition (intravenous infusion of nutrient solutions prepared by a pharmacy).

Home Health Care Defined

Home health care means providing health services and equipment to patients in their home. Depending upon the needs of the individual patient, services may be delivered 24 hours per day. Sometimes the purpose of home care is restoration of health and/or function, while other times it is to maintain comfort, as in hospice care. Home health care may provide for both the medical and the personal needs of patients and their family members. Professionals involved include physicians, nurses, physical therapists, occupational therapists, dieticians, pharmacists, social workers, speech-language pathologists, homemakers and home care aides.

Many, but not all, patients are referred to home health care agencies after a period of hospitalization. Patients should have a thorough evaluation, including not just medical needs, but also assessment of the mental state of the patient. In addition to evaluating the patient's ability to comply with treatment such as dietary recommendations and/or drug schedules, the family and social environment needs to be considered. Various health care professionals may be involved in the evaluation.

Numerous factors may influence the decision to provide care for the patient in the home rather than in a hospital, nursing home or other facility. Among these are studies that have shown patients tend to recuperate sooner from an accident or illness in familiar surroundings with caring family members. Another consideration is the availability of competent assistance from family or friends. The physical layout of the home must also be evaluated for adaptability to the patient's needs. For example, a patient in a wheelchair will need appropriate access to shower and toilet facilities.

Once the decision has been made that home health care is appropriate for a patient, service is usually provided by a home health agency, hospice or homemaker/home care aide agency. Staffing and private-duty agencies can provide nurses, homemakers, home health aides or companions, but are not always required to be licensed. Pharmaceutical and infusion therapy companies employ pharmacists and nurses to assist patients requiring intravenous infusions. Medical equipment suppliers and manufacturers may provide installation of medical equipment and instruct patients on use. Some provide respiratory therapy services. Registries connect home health nurses and aides with individual patients, who employ them directly. Many home health care professionals are independent of agencies and are employed directly by the patient or self-employed, often having several clients at once.

How Home Health Agencies Work

The National Council on the Aging defines a home health agency as "a company that provides many professional health care services, in the home, under the direction of a physician. These comprehensive services include skilled nursing, personal care assistance, physical, occupational and speech therapy, and medical social work. Medical equipment, supplies and infusion therapies may also be available. Home care agencies have an administrator or a director who is responsible for the business and managerial operations. This person is often a doctor, nurse, or social worker who has education or experience in administration."[4]

Certified agencies must meet the licensing requirements of their state. In addition, some are accredited by the Joint Commission on Accreditation of Healthcare Organizations, **(www.jcajo.org,** 603/792-5000). Other accrediting agencies include Accreditation Commission for Health Care, Inc. (919/872-8609, **http://www.achc.org**), Community Health Accreditation Program (212/363-5555, **http://www.chapinc.org**), and the National Committee for Quality Assurance (888/ 275-7585, **http://www.ncqa.org**). Those participating in Medicare must also meet federal requirements.

Do You Have What it Takes?

A recent article by Lazelle Benefield, PhD, RN, in the American Journal of Nursing explored the personal qualifications required for nurses to be happy in their choice of home health nursing.[5] The considerations cited apply to many other professions. One advantage to home care nursing is the ability to follow your patient's progress consistently.

One issue in caring for patients in their home is the freedom of making independent decisions versus the responsibility of making clinical decisions on one's own. Some people relish the independence, while others may feel comfortable with more structure and more interaction with peers and supervisors. Dr. Benefield emphasizes being proactive. Ask for advice from others in the field, subscribe to home health journals and focus your continuing education units.

A problem in home health is sorting out the variety of restrictions placed on patient services by all the different HMOs, PPOs and insurance companies. The home health nurse is responsible for documenting patient progress and justifying continuing care based on patient capabilities or safety.

In an accompanying article, Janet Dyer is very specific about the personality traits needed for success in the home health care field.[6] She writes, "Nurses who flourish in home health tend to be self-starters, independent and creative thinkers...they also need to be well-versed in the latest technology...home health tends to reward flexibility and well-rounded skills..."

BIBLIOGRAPHY

[1] "Basic Statistics About Home Care," Online, Available: http://www.nahc.org/Consumer/hcstats.html, Updated Mar., 2001.

[2] Michael H. Pilot, "Tomorrow's Jobs," *Bureau of Labor Statistics*, Online, Available: http://stats.bls.gov/oco2003.htm, Jan. 21, 1998.

3 Janet Dyer, "Home Health Care: Where the Jobs Are", *American Journal of Nursing*, Jan., 1998, p. 18.

[4] "Family Care Resource - Home Health Care," The National Council on the Aging, Online, Available: http://www.ncoa.org, Dec. 22, 1997.

[5] Lazelle E. Benefield, PhD, RN, "Are You Really for Home Health Nursing?" *American Journal of Nursing*, Jan., 1998, pp 17-18.

[6] Janet Dyer, 1998.

HOMEMAKER-HOME HEALTH AIDES

While many of the health professions featured in *Health Care Job Explosion* are utilized in home health care, Homemaker - Home Health Aides are specific to the field.

Numerous job openings will result due to very fast employment growth and very high turnover.

Nature of the Work

Home health and personal care aides help elderly, disabled, and ill persons live in their own homes instead of in a health facility. Most work with elderly or disabled clients who need more extensive care than family or friends can provide. Some home health and personal care aides work with families in which a parent is incapacitated and small children need care. Others help discharged hospital patients who have relatively short-term needs.

In general, home health aides provide health-related services, such as administering oral medications under physicians' orders or direction of a nurse. In contrast, personal care and home care aides provide mainly housekeeping and routine personal care services. However, there can be substantial variation in job titles and overlap of duties.

Most home health and personal care aides provide some housekeeping services, as well as personal care to their clients. They clean clients' houses, do laundry, and change bed linens. Some aides plan meals (including special diets), shop for food, and cook. Home health and personal care aides may also help clients move from bed, bathe, dress, and groom. Some accompany clients outside the home, serving as guide, companion, and aide.

Home health and personal care aides also provide instruction and psychological support. For example, they may assist in toilet training a severely mentally handicapped child, or just listen to clients talk about their problems.

Home health aides may check pulse, temperature, and respiration; help with simple prescribed exercises; and assist with medication routines. Occasionally, they change nonsterile dressings, use special equipment such as a hydraulic lift, give massages and alcohol rubs, or assist with braces and artificial limbs.

In home care agencies, it is usually a registered nurse, a physical therapist, or a social worker who assigns specific duties and supervises home health and personal care aides. Aides keep records of services performed and of clients' condition and progress. They report changes in the client's condition to the supervisor or case manager. Home health and personal care aides also participate in case reviews, consulting with the team caring for the client—registered nurses, therapists, and other health professionals.

Working Conditions

The home health and personal care aide's daily routine may vary. Aides may go to the same home every day for months or even years. However, most aides work with a number of different clients, each job lasting a few hours, days, or weeks. Aides often visit four or five clients on the same day.

Surroundings differ from case to case. Some homes are neat and pleasant, while others are untidy or depressing. Some clients are angry, abusive, depressed, or otherwise difficult; others are pleasant and cooperative.

Home health and personal care aides generally work on their own, with periodic visits by their supervisor. They receive detailed instructions explaining when to visit clients and what services to perform. Many aides work part time, and weekend hours are common.

Aides are individually responsible for getting to the client's home. They may spend a good portion of the working day traveling from one client to another; motor vehicle accidents are always a danger. They are particularly susceptible to injuries resulting from all types of overexertion when assisting patients, and falls inside and outside their homes. Mechanical lifting devices that are available in institutional settings are seldom available in patients' homes.

Employment

Home health and personal care aides held about 746,000 jobs in 1998. Most aides are employed by home health and personal care agencies, visiting nurse associations, residential care facilities with home health departments, hospitals, public health and welfare departments, community volunteer agencies, nursing and personal care facilities, and temporary help firms. Self-employed aides have no agency affiliation or supervision, and accept clients, set fees, and arrange work schedules on their own.

Training, Other Qualifications, and Advancement

In some States, this occupation is open to individuals with no formal training. On-the-job training is generally provided. Other States may require formal training, depending on Federal or State law.

The Federal Government has enacted guidelines for home health aides whose employers receive reimbursement from Medicare. Federal law requires home health aides to pass a competency test covering 12 areas: Communication skills; observation, reporting, and documentation of patient status and the care or services furnished; reading and recording vital signs; basic infection control procedures; basic elements of body function and changes; maintenance of a clean, safe, and healthy environment; recognition of, and procedures for, emergencies; the physical, emotional, and developmental characteristics of the patients served; personal hygiene and grooming; safe transfer techniques; normal range of motion and positioning; and basic nutrition.

A home health aide may take training before taking the competency test. Federal law suggests at least 75 hours of classroom and practical training supervised by a registered nurse. Training and testing programs may be offered by the employing agency, but must meet the standards of the Health Care Financing Administration. Training programs vary depending upon State regulations.

The National Association for Home Care offers national certification for home health and personal care aides. The certification is a voluntary demonstration that the individual has met industry standards.

Successful home health and personal care aides like to help people and do not mind hard work. They should be responsible, compassionate, emotionally stable, and cheerful. Aides should also be tactful, honest, and discreet because they work in private homes.

Home health and personal care aides must be in good health. A physical examination including State regulated tests such as those for tuberculosis may be required.

Advancement is limited. In some agencies, workers start out performing homemaker duties, such as cleaning. With experience and training, they may take on personal care duties. The most experienced home health aides assist with medical equipment such as ventilators, which help patients breathe.

Job Outlook

A large number of job openings are expected for home health and personal care aides, due to substantial growth and very high turnover.

Home health and personal care aides is expected to be one of the fastest growing occupations through the year 2008.

The number of people in their seventies and older is projected to rise substantially. This age group is characterized by mounting health problems requiring some assistance. Also, there will be an increasing reliance on home care for patients of all ages. This trend reflects several developments: Efforts to contain costs by moving patients out of hospitals and nursing facilities as quickly as possible, the realization that treatment can be more effective in familiar surroundings rather than clinical surroundings, and the development and improvement of medical technologies for in-home treatment.

In addition to jobs created by the increase in demand for these workers, replacement needs are expected to produce numerous openings. Turnover is high, a reflection of the relatively low skill requirements, low pay, and high emotional demands of the work. For these same reasons, many people are unwilling to perform this kind of work. Therefore, persons who are interested in this work and suited for it should have excellent job opportunities, particularly those with experience or training as home health, personal care, or nursing aides.

Earnings

Median hourly earnings of home health and personal care aides were $7.58 in 1998. The middle 50 percent earned between $6.41 and $8.81 an hour. The lowest 10 percent earned less than $5.73 and the highest 10 percent earned more than $10.51 an hour.

Most employers give slight pay increases with experience and added responsibility. Aides are usually paid only for the time worked in the home. They normally are not paid for travel time between jobs. Most employers hire only "on-call" hourly workers and provide no benefits.

HOME HEALTH RESOURCES

Don't forget! Refer to the general resources listed in Chapter Three and in the chapter on your specific profession. One of the many resources you should check in chapter 3 is the **National Association of Health Career Schools.**

| ☤ Association | 📖 Book | 🗀 Directory | ⏺ Internet (Web) Site |
| 🗐 Job Ads | 💥 E-mail/Hotline | ↩ Job Fairs | ✍ Resume Service |

⏺ **CARE GUIDE Online (http://www.thecareguide.com)** This Internet resource, provided by Care Planning Partners Inc., helps Canadian seniors, their families, and advisors search for home health care services, retirement homes and long term care homes.

🗀⏺ **extended care .com (http://www.elderconnect.com)** This database contains information on over 80,000 rehabilitation providers, retirement communities, and providers of long-term nursing care as well as home health agencies. Check the "For Everyone" section.

🗀⏺ **Google.com (www.google.com)** has directories of hospices, extended care facilities and home health agencies.

💥✍⏺ **(http://www.homehealthcarejobs.com) Health Care Job Store, Inc.** Post your resume, view employer profiles, get help writing a resume, have e-mail job notices sent to you and find health care recruiters.

✍⏺ **(http://www.homehealthaidefinders.com) Home Health Aide Finders - (888/396-6331)** Home health aides can list their resume and families pay to access the database of available job seekers. Free for job seekers as of date of publication.

🗐✍⏺ **home health provider.com** This site has job searches, news, employer profiles, a recruiter center, salary surveys and you can post your resume. Check the links for **long term care provides.com** and other resources. **(http://www.homehealthprovider.com/content/homepage/default.asp)**

Jobscience.com (http://www.jobhomehealth.org/, 510/208-jobs) The Web site has Live Counseling, a feature that offers contact with experts. Post your resume.

National Association for Home Care (NAHC) - 228 Seventh Street SE, Washington, DC 20003, 202/547-7424, fax: 202/547-3540, (http://www.nahc.org/home.html). Members are agencies providing home care. The Web site provides a Home Care & Hospice Agency Locator with information on more than 22,000 providers and NAHC's International Job Exchange. Contact information is available for NAHC member home care and hospice state associations.

National Association of Area Agencies on Aging (NAAAA) - 927 15th St. NW, 6th floor, Washington, DC 20005; 202/296-8130, fax: 202/296-8134, (http://www.n4a.org/). The NAAAA represents a majority of the more than 660 area agencies on aging. The **Eldercare Locator** us a toll-free number for information on more than 4800 service providers, such as adult day care and respite services, nursing home ombudsman assistance, consumer fraud, in-home care complaints, etc. The Eldercare Locator, 800/677-1116, is available weekdays, 9:00 am to 8:00 pm (ET). A few jobs are posted on the Web site.

National Association of Psychiatric Health Systems (325 Seventh Street NW, Suite 625, Washington, DC 20004; 202/393-6700, (http://www.haphs.org). Institutions offering mental health and substance abuse treatment. Membership Directory costs $32.10, but many members have links on the Web site.

Nursing Home INFO (http://www.nursinghomeinfo.com/) Search for a facility by state, city county or type of service.

Opportunities in Gerontology and Aging Services Careers by Ellen Williams, 1995. Hardcover, $14.95. ISBN: 0844244368. Published by VGM Career Horizons, 4255 Touhy Ave., Lincolnwood, IL 60646-1975; 800/323-4900, 847/679-5500, fax: 847/679-2494.

Senior Living Alternatives (http://www.senioralternatives.com) Search by state for retirement communities, state licensed nursing homes, residential care facilities (assisted living), or home health care agencies or call 800/350-0770.

State departments of health or insurance may be helpful in locating a Medicare Survey Report on home health care providers in your area. Use any search engine with the keywords "health department" and the name of your state or use the state government listings in your telephone book to contact them.

COMPUTERS IN YOUR HEALTH CARE CAREER

Most people working in the health care field will need to use computers. Some will be using programs written specifically for certain tasks, such as tracking patient specimens and reporting laboratory results, while others will use standard office suites, graphics or statistical programs. Medical researchers may even have to write their own database programs. A solid understanding of computers will at least lower your stress level and will probably make you a more valuable employee. The office computer guru can often save co-workers time and increase productivity.

Most community colleges and night schools offer basic courses in computer skills. Tutorials are available on CD, but do not offer the convenience of having an instructor to answer your questions. There are also courses available on the Internet, offered by computer publishers such as ZDNet (**http://www.zdnet.com**). Make sure your browser will view the virtual classrooms correctly before you sign up.

COMPUTER INDUSTRY CAREERS

The BLS Industry employment projections state that the fastest growing industry in the entire economy in terms of employment, and the third-fastest growing in terms of out-put, is the computer and data processing services industry.

Computer and data processing services will add over 1.8 million jobs from 1998-2008. Computer programmers write, test, and maintain programs (also called software or applications) that handle specific jobs within an organization, such as a program used in scheduling patient appointments. The job calls for patience, persistence, and the ability to work on exacting analytical work, especially under pressure. Programmers are expected to work in teams and may interact directly with users of their software.

Software engineers or software developers also may create custom software applications for clients. They are more concerned with analyzing and solving programming problems than with simply writing the code for the programs. Systems analysts may design entirely new systems, including both hardware and software, or add a single new software application to harness more of the computer's power. Many systems analysts are involved with "networking" or connecting all the computers in an individual office, department, or establishment. In some organizations a single worker called a programmer-analyst is responsible for both systems analysis and programming.

Other computer professionals include database administrators and computer support specialists. Database administrators work with database management systems software, coordinating changes to, testing, and implementing computer databases. Computer support specialists provide assistance and advice to users. They interpret problems and provide technical support for hardware, software, and systems.

A growing number of computer professionals are employed on a temporary or contract basis—many of whom are self-employed.

At least 17 million people have searched the Internet for information about health and pharmeceuticals. The growth in medical Web sites providing information to the public is expected to increase phenomenally, according to E. Loren Buhle Jr. in an article for *The Scientist* (June, 1999). He expects consumers to use "smart agents," software that searches the Web for customized information. Programmers who understand the health care field will be needed to design the sophisticated software required by agents that learn from experience with individual consumers habits.

Education and training

Bachelor's degrees are now commonly required. Graduate degrees in related fields may be required for more complex jobs. Students also can greatly improve their employment prospects by taking courses in fields for which they wish to write software. Many people develop advanced computer skills in other occupations in which they work extensively with computers, and then transfer into computer occupations.

Earnings

Median annual earnings of computer programmers were $47,550 in 1998. The middle 50 percent earned between $36,020 and $70,610 a year. The lowest 10 percent earned less than $27,670; the highest 10 percent earned more than $88,730. According to the National Association of Colleges and Employers, starting salary offers for graduates with a bachelor's degree in computer programming averaged about $40,800 a year in 1999.

According to Robert Half International, average annual starting salaries in 1999 ranged from $38,000 to $50,500 for applications development programmers and from $49,000 to $63,000 for systems programmers. Average starting salaries for Internet programmers ranged from $48,800 to $68,300.

Median annual earnings of computer systems analysts were $52,180 in 1998. The middle 50 percent earned between $40,570 and $74,180 a year. The lowest 10 percent earned less than $32,470 and the highest 10 percent earned more than $87,810.

Median annual earnings of computer engineers were $61,910 in 1998. The middle 50 percent earned between $46,240 and $80,500. The lowest 10 percent earned less than $37,150 and the highest 10 percent earned more than $92,850.

Median annual earnings of computer support specialists were $37,120 in 1998. The middle 50 percent earned between $28,880 and $48,810. The lowest 10 percent earned less than $22,930 and the highest 10 percent earned more than $73,790.

Median annual earnings of database administrators were $47,980 in 1998. The middle 50 percent earned between $36,440 and $69,920. The lowest 10 percent earned less than $28,320 and the highest 10 percent earned more than $86,200.

Starting offers for graduates with a bachelor's degree in computer science averaged about $44,600; in computer programming, about $40,800; in information sciences, about $38,900; and in management information systems, $41,800 in 1999.

COMPUTER CAREER RESOURCES

Those interested in pursuing a career in computers and health care may want to read the August 1997 issue of *Communications of the ACM* located at (**http://www.acm.org/**) and published by the Association for Computing Machinery. This article focuses on computer technology for health care. The ACM also has a special interest group on biomedical computing for computer scientists and professionals in the health and biological sciences. Other organizations that may provide information are the American Medical Informatics Association (http://www.amia.org/), the National Association of Health Data Organizations Web site at (**http://www.nahdo.org**), the Healthcare Information and Management Systems Society (**http://www.himss.org**), and the Medical Records Institute (**http://www.medrecinst.com**).

Computer professionals who want to work in health care will probably prefer to do their own surfing. A great place to start is the **Google.com** directory "Information Technology." Sites specific for computer jobs include **http://geekfinder.com, http://www.computer jobsbank.com,** and **http://www.computerjobs.com.** Check ZDNet's Yahoo! Internet Life Web site for the latest ratings of career sites for information and computer technology. **http://www.guru.com** is rated as the best site for freelancers.

Computer magazines often rate career Web sites and at least one has started their own career site for technology professionals. ZDNet has a career site with advice and job ads: **http://www.techies.com**. The Internet is exploding with job sites, over 2500 and counting, so it helps to have a site like the Riley Guide to sort them out for you. Find this at **http://www.dbm.com/jobguide.**

Chapter 3 has many good general job sites that can help you locate employment listings. Use the directories there or in the appendix to locate companies in your area. Contact their employment or human resources offices for specific job openings. The associations listed in this book may employ network administrators or other specialists. The appendix lists many directories of companies you could investigate as job sources.

HEALTH INFORMATION TECHNICIANS

Health information technicians are projected to be one of the 20 fastest growing occupations.

Nature of the Work

Every time health care personnel treat a patient, they record what they observed, and how the patient was treated medically. This record includes information the patient provides concerning their symptoms and medical history, the results of examinations, reports of x-rays and laboratory tests, diagnoses, and treatment plans. Health information technicians organize and evaluate these records for completeness and accuracy.

Health information technicians, who may also be called medical record technicians, begin to assemble patients' health information by first making sure their initial medical charts are complete. They ensure all forms are completed and properly identified and signed, and all necessary information is in the computer. Sometimes, they talk to physicians or others to clarify diagnoses or get additional information.

Technicians assign a code to each diagnosis and procedure. They consult classification manuals and rely, also, on their knowledge of disease processes. Technicians then use a software program to assign the patient to one of several hundred "diagnosis-related groups," or DRG's. The DRG determines the amount the hospital will be reimbursed if the patient is covered by Medicare or other insurance programs using the DRG system. Technicians who specialize in coding are called health information coders, medical record coders, coder/abstractors, or coding specialists. In addition to the DRG system, coders use other coding systems, such as those geared towards ambulatory settings.

Technicians also use computer programs to tabulate and analyze data to help improve patient care or control costs, for use in legal actions, or in response to surveys. Tumor registrars compile and maintain records of patients who have cancer to provide information to physicians and for research studies.

Health information technicians' duties vary with the size of the facility. In large to medium facilities, technicians may specialize in one aspect of health information, or supervise health information clerks and transcribers while a health information administrator manages the department (see the statement on health services managers elsewhere in the Handbook). In small facilities, an accredited health information technician sometimes manages the department.

Working Conditions

Health information technicians usually work a 40-hour week. Some overtime may be required. In hospitals where health information departments are open 18-24 hours a day, 7 days a week, they may work day, evening, and night shifts.

Health information technicians work in pleasant and comfortable offices. This is one of the few health occupations in which there is little or no physical contact with patients. Because accuracy is essential, technicians must pay close attention to detail. Health information technicians who work at computer monitors for prolonged periods must guard against eyestrain and muscle pain.

Employment

Health information technicians held about 92,000 jobs in 1998. About 2 out of 5 jobs were in hospitals. The rest were mostly in nursing homes, medical group practices, clinics, and home health agencies. Insurance firms that deal in health matters employ a small number of health information technicians to tabulate and analyze health information. Public health departments also hire technicians to supervise data collection from health care institutions and to assist in research.

Training, Other Qualifications, and Advancement

Health information technicians entering the field usually have an associate degree from a community or junior college. In addition to general education, course-work includes medical terminology, anatomy and physiology, legal aspects of health information, coding and abstraction of data, statistics, database management, quality improvement methods, and computer training. Applicants can improve their chances of admission into a program by taking biology, chemistry, health, and computer courses in high school.

Hospitals sometimes advance promising health information clerks to jobs as health information technicians, although this practice may be less common in the future. Advancement usually requires 2-4 years of job experience and completion of a hospital in-house training program.

Most employers prefer to hire Accredited Record Technicians (ART), who must pass a written examination offered by AHIMA. To take the examination, a person must graduate from a 2-year associate degree program accredited by the Commission on Accreditation of Allied Health Education Programs (CAAHEP) of the American Medical Association. Technicians trained in non-CAAHEP accredited programs, or on the job, are not eligible to take the examination. In 1998, CAAHEP accredited 168 programs for health information technicians. Technicians who specialize in coding may also obtain voluntary certification.

Experienced health information technicians usually advance in one of two ways—by specializing or managing. Many senior health information technicians specialize in coding.

In large health information departments, experienced technicians may advance to section supervisor, overseeing the work of the coding, correspondence, or discharge sections, for example. Senior technicians with ART credentials may become director or assistant director of a health information department in a small facility. However, in larger institutions, the director is a health information administrator, with a bachelor's degree in health information administration.

Job Outlook

Job prospects for formally trained technicians should be very good. Employment of health information technicians is expected to grow much faster than the average for all occupations through 2008, due to rapid growth in the number of medical tests, treatments, and procedures scrutinized by third-party payers, regulators, courts, and consumers.

Hospitals will continue to employ a large percentage of health information technicians. Increasing demand for detailed records in offices and clinics of physicians should result in fast employment growth, especially in large group practices. Rapid growth is also expected in nursing homes and home health agencies.

Earnings

Median annual earnings of health information technicians were $20,590 in 1998. The middle 50 percent earned between $16,670 and $25,440 a year. The lowest 10 percent earned less than $14,150 and the highest 10 percent earned more than $31,570 a year. The median annual salary for accredited health information technicians was $30,500.

Resources for health information technicians are combined with medical billing, claims examining and patient accounting below.

MEDICAL BILLING, CLAIMS EXAMINING and PATIENT ACCOUNTING
Article contributed by Suzan Hvizdash

Suzan Hvizdash presents a comprehensive review of the medical billing field including nature of work, working conditions, job outlook and employment, training and other qualifications and advancement, and earnings. Ms. Hvizdash started in the medical billing business working as a Claims Analyst at Nationwide Insurance, the Medicare carrier for West Virginia and Ohio. She moved to the Pittsburgh area where she became a billing coordinator for two doctors, and was asked to sit on the Physician Relations Board at Mercy Hospital. Hvizdash was the Medicare Supervisor in Patient Services at Stadtlanders Pharmacy and then the Medicare Specialist at HMI Pharmacy (now part of Stadtlanders). She has had the opportunities to speak at several conventions and corporate meetings which included a regional sales meeting for Sandoz Drug Company (now Navardis) and The Michigan Nurses Conference. Ms. Hvizdash is currently the Medial Billing/Health Claims Examining Instructor at North Hills School of Health Occupations, and in that capacity visits providers throughout the Pittsburgh area to stay current with the latest rules, regulations, and technologies. She is a member of AHIMA (American Health Information and Management Association) and AAMB (American Association of Medical Billers).

OCCUPATIONAL TITLES

Billing Specialist   Coding Specialist
Patient Account Representative   Medical Collector
Claims Analyst   Claims Processor
Electronic Claims Processor   Claims Reviewer
Reimbursement Specialist   Billing Coordinator
Claims Assistant Professional

Nature of the Work

A successful biller/examiner will know medical terminology, anatomy, proper form completion, and required coding. This person will also need to know basic computer information and have a typing speed of at least 35 words-per-minute. We work with patients, other offices' staff, medical personnel and other office personnel. Customer Service is very important, as the people we contact are either colleagues of ours or the practice, or they are patients that could be at stressful points in their lives.

Working Conditions

Medical billers usually work in an office setting. Sometimes we're not working near where the patients are being seen. There are billing offices and services in large corporate buildings, in small suburban offices, and in the doctor's office itself. Our hours are usually daylight, Monday through Friday, 40-hour work weeks. Overtime is often available, and sometimes mandatory. Positions at insurance companies are more likely to have a few overnight or late hour shifts available.

Job Outlook and Employment

Medical Billing and its related occupations are one of the fastest growing opportunities in health care. Insurance companies and the government are spending more time and money researching and controlling claims' fraud, abusive practices, and medical necessity issues. Because of this, insurance companies are hiring more, and doctors, hospitals, pharmacies, and other providers are also hiring more.

Most companies and practices are looking for experience and or schooling, again because of the legal ramifications of incorrect billing practices.

Medical billers are also able to work independently out of their homes. They can set up electronic billing through their home computers. Also available is the ability to be an insurance specialist. This would be a position of self-employment to help patients understand their insurance bills and what they should be paying.

Positions are available in doctors' offices, hospitals, pharmacies, nursing homes, rehabilitation centers, insurance companies, and consulting firms.

Training, Other Qualifications and Advancement

At present, there is no set standard for educational requirements in these fields. However, more employers are looking for some formal training at an accredited vocational or career training school. These schools range in training time from nine months to two years. Anything shorter is not advised.

Certification in these fields is also not required, but recommended. There are several organizations sponsoring these types of examinations.

American Association of Medical Billers (AAMB) offers Certified Medical Biller (CMB) and Certified Medical Billing Specialist (CMBS) examinations. The National Association of Claims Assistant Professionals (NACAP) offer Certified Claims Assistance Professional (CCAP) and Certified Electronic Claims Professional (CECP). The examinations for Certified Procedural Coder (CPC), Certified Coding Specialist (CPS), Accredited Record Technician (ART), and Registered Record Administrator (RRA), are administered through the American Health Information Management Association (AHIMA).

There are other certifications available for different specialization's. These certifications are all fairly new, and it is advised to research each to find the best one suited.

It's also important to know that the advancement opportunities are unlimited including office managers, supervisors, managers, and directors of billing or examining departments.

Earnings

These fields have a wage range between $8-$10 an hour to start and up to $30-$40 an hour for years of experience and responsibility.

MEDICAL BILLING, CLAIMS EXAMINING
PATIENT ACCOUNTING
HEALTH INFORMATION TECHNICIANS

The organizations for Medical Billing Specialists, Claims Assistance Professionals, Coders, and the like are listed below. It is recommended that you join at least one, but research them beforehand, to find the appropriate one for your career goals. Keep in mind that these organizations may have a local chapter as well, so check your local Telephone Directory for local groups.

Don't forget! Refer to the general resources listed in Chapter Three (such as **HEALTHeCAREERS.com**).

| ⚕ Association | 📖 Book | 📁 Directory | 🖱 Internet (Web) Site |
| 📱 Job Ads | 📧 E-mail/Hotline | 🏷 Job Fairs | 📄 Resume Service |

📱🖱 <u>ADVANCE</u> **Newsmagazines** (**http://www.advanceforhim.com**) *ADVANCE for Health Information Professionals,* and *ADVANCE for Health Information Executives.* Call 800/355-1088 for additional information. Free to qualified professionals, these publications have extensive classified ads and meeting lists online.

⚕📱 <u>American Academy of Professional Coders</u> **(AAPC)** - 309 West 700 South, Salt Lake City, UT 84101, 800/626-CODE **(http://www.aap cnatl.org/)** Certification and extensive information for Coders, Office Managers, Claims Examiners, Hospital Outpatient Coders, Experienced Reimbursement Specialists and Coding Educators.

⚕📱🖱 <u>American Association of Medical Billers</u> **(AAMB)** - 1840 E. 17th Street, Suite 140, Santa Ana, California 92701, 1-888-BILLERS **(http://www.billers.com)** The Web site has a video about the career. It also has sample test questions to prepare for t certification examinations. By joining this organization you can sit for the Certified Medical Biller (CBM) exam, or the Certified Medical Billing Specialist (CMBS) exam.

☤▯✍▭◔ **American Association for Medical Transcription (AAMT)** - 3460 Oakdale Road, Suite M, Modesto, CA 95355-9690; 209/551-0883, fax: 209/551-9317. Their Web site at **http://www.aamt.org** has career information, employment opportunities, and lists state and regional associations. They will post your resume online for $25 for members, $50 for nonmembers.

☤◔ **American College of Medical Practice Executives (ACMPE)** - (**http://www.mgma.com/acmpe/**)Affiliated with the MGMA (below, same address) this group has separate branches for different specialties such as Endocrinology, Cardiovascular, etc.

☤ **American Guild of Patient Account Management (AGPAM)** - National Certification Examination Program, 1101 Connecticut Ave, NW Suite 700, Washington, DC 20036, 202/857-1179. This association is for patient account managers, personnel managers in the Health Care industry, hospital management, and physician office management.

☤▯◔ **American Health Information Management Association (AHIMA)** - 233 N. Michigan Ave., Suite 2150, Chicago, IL 60611-5800; 312/233-1100, fax: 312/233-1090. (**http://www.ahima.org**, E-mail: info@ahima.org) AHIMA has brochures for those considering entering the health information management (HIM) profession. Web site has information on careers, financial aid, certification, schools, independent study and state associations. AHIMA

☤◔ **Computer-based Patient Record Institute** - 1000 E. Woodfield Rd., Suite 102, Schaumburg, IL 60173-4742; 847/706-6746, fax: 847/706-6747. (**http://www.cpri.org**). Provides information about computer-based patient records. Members are large organizations or companies.

☤◔ **Health Professions Institute (HPI)** - PO Box 801, Modesto, CA 95355-0801, 209/551-2112, fax 209/551-0404; (**http://www.hpisum.com/**) Publishes many books, periodicals and conducts seminars. Contact them via E-mail: **hpi@hpisum.com**. They also have a Student Network in medical transcription courses across the country. *Perspectives*

☤▯▭✍◔ **Healthcare Information and Management Systems Society** - 230 East Ohio, Suite 500, Chicago, IL 60611-3269; 312/664-HIMSS, fax: 312/664-6143 (E-mail: himss@himss.org). Their Web site at **http://www.himss.org** has a membership directory for members only and the Career Match Resume Database Matching Service.

📖**Medical Transcription Career Handbook, The,** by Keith A. Drake, Paperback, 149 pages, $21.95. Published by Prentice Hall, 1999.

⚕ **International Billing Associations, Inc.** - 7315 Wisconsin Ave., Suite 424 East, Bethesda, MD 20814, 301/961-8680.

⚕📱📠 **Medical Group Management Association (MGMA)** - 104 Inverness Terrace East, Englewood, CO 80012, 303/799-1111, Fax 303-643-4427. **(www.mgma.com)** This organization is designed for the manager or supervisor of a medical office setting. You can obtain a Certified Medical Office Manager (CMOM) designation. The Web site has job ads, networking, career planning and a placement service.

⚕🖱 **Medical Records Institute** - 567 Walnut Street, P.O. Box 600770, Newton, MA 02460; 617/964-3923, fax: 617/964-3926. (E-mail: cust_service@medrecinst.com, **http://www.medrecinst.com**) This organization supports the electronic health records industry and developers. You can sign up for *Medical Record News* to be e-mailed to you.

📠🖱 **Medical Transcription Education Center, Inc. (M-TEC)** Their Web site at **http://www.mtecinc.com** has information on home-study courses offered by M-TEC, including a message board and student/teacher chat (CyberClassroom) for anyone interested in the MT profession. Online tests to see if this is the career for you. Placement

⚕📁🖱 **Medical Transcription Industry Alliance (MTIA)** - 800/543-MTIA, (**http://mtia.com**, 711 Broadway East, #7, Seattle, WA 98102 1-800-543-MTIA). MTIA is an association for medical transcription services. MTIA keeps members informed about the technology of computer-based patient records.

📱📠🖱 **MT Daily for Medical Transcriptionists** *MT Daily* provides medical transcription networking information and resources including jobs. URL (**http://www.mtdaily.com/**). Has free weekly e-mail newsletter. They post over 100 jobs a month, and will post your resume.

🖱 **MT Monthly (http://www.mtmonthly.com)** - 809 Regency Drive, Kearney, MO 64060; 800/951-5559, 816/628-3013, fax: 816/628-3661. *MT Monthly* is a national newsletter for medical transcriptionists. The Web site has a sample copy, terminology lists, article reprints, computer help, links, a bulletin board, chat rooms, and home-study information.

⚕ **National Association of Claims Assistance Professionals, Inc. (NACAP)** - 5329 S. Main St., Suite 102, Downers Grove, IL 60515-4845,

708/963-3500. This organization provides the Certified Claims Assistance Professional (CCAP) and the Certified Electronic Claims Professional (CECP) examinations.

☥ 📰✍ **Professional Association of Health Care Office Managers (PAHCOM)** - 461 East Ten Mile Road, Pensacola, Florida 32534-9714, 800/451-9311. **(http://www.pahcom.com/)** You can acquire a Certified Patient Account Technician (CPAT), Certified Clinic Account Technician (CCAT), Certified Patient Account Manager (CPAM), or Certified Clinic Account Manager (CCAM) designation through this organization. Members may post resumes online for $35.

Appendix

A

HEALTH CARE CORPORATIONS!

Thousands of companies manufacture products or provide services for the medical profession. The major manufacturers have large research and development budgets and many operate health care facilities. The production of medical instrument, equipment and supplies is projected to generate 48,000 new jobs before the year 2008. It is one of only four industries expected to produce faster then average growth. (Bureau of Labor Statistics, Monthly Labor Review, Nov., 1999)

Positions include sales representatives, computer experts and consultants. Research facilities must be staffed by medical professionals: technicians, physicians, bio-statisticians and PhD scientists. Many fields in health care have their own magazines focusing on sales. *Proofs: The Magazine of Dental Sales* is one such publication.

Corporate contacts offer abundant employment opportunities for health care workers. Large corporations like Merck, Medtronic, Bergen Brunswig, and Baxter International realize billions in sales yearly. Baxter International's 1999 sales increased by 12 percent and sales for the first three quarters of the year 2000 alone reached $4,600,000,000. They employ approximately 42,000 people in 100 countries, market thousands of health care products, and operate outpatient health care centers.

Directories of health care service providers, medical supply companies, and manufacturers are available at many public or college libraries and are listed below. These directories provide names and contact information for thousands of companies in the health care field. The American Chemical Company publishes a directory of scientific corporations listed by product or service. Many medical companies are highly diversified and are not restricted to a single product or service. Check out the "Yellow Pages" entry near the end of this appendix.

Refer to the Thomas Register at your local library to start your search for companies that manufacture specific products. The Thomas Register provides a cross reference between product and company. To locate manufacturers of X-ray equipment you would look up X-ray equipment in the index and it will direct you to the appropriate manufacturers. The company name, address and phone number is provided along with other valuable data.

Publicly traded companies will generally be listed in either the *Value Line Investment Survey* (1700 listings), Standard and Poor's (over 4300 listings), or the *Moody's Manual* (12,000 public companies). These references are generally available at larger libraries and provide company information including product lines, gross sales, number of employees, etc.

You can also find information on thousands of companies by searching the Internet. More and more corporations are posting job openings on their Web sites. Stock brokers' Internet sites may have company profiles. Many medical or scientific web sites have company profiles or links to corporate web sites.

Don't forget! Refer to the general resources listed in Chapter Three, especially the ones with directory icons, or any other chapter discussing a profession that interests you. The search engines/directories can be especially helpful in finding corporate web sites.

Achoo Healthcare Online (http://www.achoo.com) Achoo is a search engine with an extensive category structure. One of the directory options is "Business of Health," with companies, products and services.

Allbusiness.com (http://www.allbusiness.comfind.com)   Search for companies by category or name. There are 29 categories containing the term "medical."

American Chemical Company (P.O. Box 3337, Columbus, OH 43201; 614/447-3776, 800/333-95111, **http://pubs.acs.org**). Use the web site to search for products, companies or services. It provides detailed information for companies.

BioMedNetJobs (http://jobs,bmn.com) This web site serves the biological and medical community. It posts many jobs available in academia and with commercial firms. There is also facility to post your resume online.

BizWeb (http://www.bizweb.com) There are nearly 700 companies listed in the Medical category alone.

Buyers Index (http://www.buyersindex.com) This site is for finding mail order companies, many of which manufacture and sell home health care products such as wheelchairs. Search or browse by category.

Companies online (http://www.companiesonline.com) Provided by Lycos and Dun and Bradstreet, this site allows you to search for company web sites. Medical Services is one category to search, with 10,000 entries.

Dental-X-Change (http://dentalxchange.odont.com) This site has a companies section which includes laboratories. You can look at job ads or post your resume.

Dentistinfo.com (853 Sanders Road, Suite 252, Northbrook, IL 60062; 847/564-5329, fax: 847/564-5328, **http://www.dentistinfo.com**, E-mail: info@dentistinfo.com). Web site has Find a Dentist section and a Job Search section for dentists, hygienists, assistants and sales reps.

Emergency Medical Services Magazine Buyers Guide Issue (Summer Communications, Inc., 7626 Densmore Ave., Van Nuys, CA 91406-2042; 800/224-4EMS, 818/ 786-4EMS). Subscription to journal is $19.95/year. Buyers Guide has 175 pages of companies that make equipment for emergency medicine.

Emory University (http://www.cc.emory.edu) Click on MedWeb Bio-medical Internet Resources to find an impressive list of medical sites. Extensive links to companies on this site.

Healthcare Careers Online (http://www.healthcareers-online.com) Search the jobs database or search for a company.

Health Care Purchasing and Management Information Center (URL: http://online-info.com/health-care/?) The "?" is part of the URL. Products, Services, Supplies & Equipment Sources page lists over 30,000 products, services, and vendors with complete contact information. The Trade Shows section has complete contact information.

Hoover's Online (http://www.hoovers.com) This site profiles thousands of companies.

Hospital Web (http://neuro-www.mgh.harvard.edu/hospitalweb.nclk) Created by the Department of Neurology at Massachusetts General Hospital, this site's goal is to list all of the Hospitals on the Web. There are also links to medical companies.

jobscience.com (http://www.jobmedical.net) This well-organized site has jobs and advice, with a detailed directory structure.

Laboratory Internet Directory (International Scientific Communications, Inc., P.O. Box 870, Shelton, Connecticut 06484-0870; **http://iscpubs.com**, 203/926-9300). Lists 1300 manufacturers with URLs.

LocalEyes (http://www1.localeyes.com) This search engine is designed to return information about businesses, products and services in the US and other countries. They have a proprietary mapping system to narrow your search to almost 34,000 areas in the US.

Magellan (http://www.mckinley.com) This site can be searched using an excellent hierarchy of subjects including "Business" (Companies, Jobs). The Companies category has health care as an option. It has reviews of many web sites with links.

MedCatalog.com (http://www.medcatalog.com) Extensively indexed site with businesses listed by product. The Web site includes an employment page.

MedSearch Health Care Careers (http://www.medsearch.com) Search extensive list of companies, hospitals, medical facilities by keyword or by discipline or click on major employers listed. You can post a resume free.

<u>NetPartners Internet solutions Inc.</u> Resource Center contains the Company Site Locator. Use **http://www.netpart.com/search/html** to search for companies' Web sites by complete company name, partial company name, or a specific domain name.

Worldwide Directory of Electronic Addresses This site located at URL: http://worldwide-directory.com provides company profiles.

Opportunities in Medical Sales Careers (VGM Opportunities Series) by Chad Wayne Ellis, 1997. Paperback, 160 pages, $11.95. Published by VGM Career Horizons.

Pharmaceutical Online Employment Opportunities allows you to view ads or post your resume at (**http://www.pharmaceuticalonline.com**) through their searchable database of companies.

<u>PharmInfoNet</u> (**http://pharminfo.com**) Pharmaceutical Information Network has a list of pharmaceutical companies on the net.

<u>PharmWeb</u> (**http://www.pharmweb.net**) The PharmWeb Yellow Pages includes companies, pharmacies, and hospitals.

Proofs: The Magazine of Dental Sales (PennWell Publishing, P.O. Box 1260, Tulsa, OK 74101; 800/331-4436). Published 10 times/year, members $15/year. Features sales and manufacturers' representative positions under "Want Ads".

Quicken.com (**http://www.quicken.com/investments**) Click on the Company Info category to access the most comprehensive directories of companies on the Internet. This site also has detailed reviews of companies.

<u>The Riley Guide</u> (**http://www.dbm.com/jobguide/employer. html**) This web site has links to sites that help you find companies.

Science Online (**http://www.sciencemag.org**) A publication of American Association of Science, this web site has an Electronic Marketplace and Product Link, which provide information on biomedical companies.

Search engines and web directories - Several search engines have excellent directories of health care information and companies. Two of the best are **Yahoo!** (http://www.yahoo.com) and **Google** (http://www.google.com). Yahoo! has a Finance section with profiles of companies. Google has a directory called Medical Equipment > Manufacturers which has very short descriptions and links to the companies' Web sites. More search engines and directories can be found in chapter three.

SLACK (http://www.slackinc.com) This web site provides extensive links to companies.

TradingDay.com (http://www.tradingday.com) It is designed for investors, so you will only find companies on the major stock exchanges, but the links will probably take you to the information you want.

Thomas Register of American Manufacturers This comprehensive directory can be found in many library reference desks or http://www2.thomasregister.com/index.cgi?balancing,

Yellow Pages Most large libraries have Yellow Pages for major cities all over the country. Business-to-Business Yellow Pages often have the best information. Look up "Medical Equipment & Supplies" among other categories. There are several "yellow page" services on the Internet.

ZDNet Company Finder (http://www.companyfinder.com) - This site is for computer and Internet industries.

Zip2 Yellow Pages (http://www.zip2.com) Millions of US businesses are listed.

Appendix

B

SCHOLARSHIPS / TUITION HELP

Wouldn't it be great to get an education and have someone else pay for it? In some health care fields, competent workers are in such short supply that employers are willing to pay part or all of a student's tuition and sometimes the companies also offer monthly payments of $1000 or more for living expenses.

Several programs offer tuition, tuition and living expenses or loan repayment for those who are willing to commit to working in rural or inner city health care. The Rural Recruitment and Retention Network (see chapter 3) and the Rural Information Center Health Service (800-633-7701) can be contacted for specific information and guidance. Visit **http://www.nal.usda.gov/ric/richs** to find out more about these programs.

One of the most informative Web sites for financial aid for various careers is RuralNet (**http://ruralnet.marshall.edu**) provided by the Marshall University School of Medicine. Review their Rural Health Resources section for excellent annotated links. For physicians, Rural Family Medicine has a considerable amount of information online at **http://www.ruralfamilymedicine.org**.

There are at least 82 state-sponsored programs for scholarships or loan forgiveness for physicians, nurse practitioners, nurse midwives, and physician assistants. Contact your state government. The National Health

Service Corps (**http://www.bphc.hrsa.gov/nhsc**) offers loan repayment and scholarship programs for certain health professionals who commit to serve in specific areas.

Assistance is available to minority students through programs offered by institutions such as the Indian Health Service. Visit their web site at (**http://www.ihs.gov**). Contact the financial aid office of your school or of the nearest medical school.

The United States Army offers abundant educational opportunities. If you enlist for 5-6 years they will train you for many health care technician and technologist or computer-related careers. If you have one or more years of college when you enlist, they will repay one third of your student loans per year. Registered nurses who enlist, in addition to loan repayment, may work towards a degree as a nurse practitioner or physician assistant. Students who have their pre-med degree can arrange to have their medical or dental school paid for. Calling your local Army recruiter is the best way to get details on education programs or visit their web site at **http://www.goarmy.com**. The other armed forces have similar programs.

There are many programs available for those who take the time to seek them out. Contact local hospitals that are short staffed and other medical providers to ask about tuition assistance programs. Many employers offer tuition assistance to current employees who show initiative and maintain good grades. It is amazing just how many programs are available especially when unemployment is low and competition for workers is fierce between recruiters and medical facilities in general.

There are also magnet school in some cities like Los Angeles, that specialize in health care training. The Los Angeles Unified School District has three magnet high schools for students who are interested in the medical field. In addition to math and science classes, the students earn credit for time spent working with doctors and nurses in hospitals.

Locate programs that you find attractive through the use of the resources listed in this chapter and in all of the other resource sections located throughout this book. Don't forget to contact occupational associations to find out what information they may have concerning scholarships and tuition assistance programs. The more contacts you make the more programs you will uncover in your research.

Index

B

C

D

E

F

G

HEALTH CARE JOB EXPLOSION!: *High Growth Health Care Careers and Job LOCATOR*, 3rd ed, by Dennis V. Damp. **$17.95, 288 pages**, ISBN: 0-943641-20-9

Explore high growth health occupations and use this book's 1,000 + resources to find job vacancies and networking contacts. This title presents detailed information for all major occupations.

THE BOOK OF U.S. GOVERNMENT JOBS: *Where They Are, What's Available, and How to Get One*, 7th edition, by Dennis Damp. $18.95, **256 pages**, paperback, ISBN: 943641-18-7.

Damp provides a detailed view of the federal employment system which has more employees than the top 16 Fortune 500 companies combined. Discover what jobs are available, where they are, and how to get one. Plus 1000 resources to get you started.

This book covers job applications, resumes, electronic job information sources, new testing criteria, professional/entry-level jobs, handicapped employment, veterans preference, student hiring, overseas jobs, Postal jobs, and interviewing techniques.

POST OFFICE JOBS: How To Get A Job With The U.S. Postal Service 2nd edition, by Dennis V. Damp, **$17.95, 224 pages**, paperback, ISBN: 0-943641-15-5.

A one-stop resource for those interested in working for the Postal Service. Presenting what jobs are available, where they are, and how to get one. This book dispels the myth that everyone in the postal service is a mail carrier or clerk. About a third of the 850,000 Postal Service workers are employed in hundreds of occupations—from janitors and truck drivers to accountants, personnel specialists, electronics technicians, and engineers. Many professional & other jobs do not require written exams.

PRESENTS Eight steps to successfully landing a job:

❶ Identify job openings.
❷ Match your skills to hundreds of jobs.
❸ Exam scheduling.
❹ Score between 90% - 100% on tests.
❺ Complete job applications.
❻ Prepare for the job interview.
❼ Apply for jobs without written tests.
❽ Pass the drug screening test.

ORDERING INFORMATION

Use this order form to purchase the following titles. Include shipping charges and sales tax, if appropriate, in accordance with the instructions on this page and enclose your check or money order. Individuals must prepay before we can ship your order. Purchase orders are accepted only from bookstores, libraries, universities, and government offices. Also available with credit card toll free at 1-800-782-7424.

ORDER FORM

QTY.	TITLE	TOTAL
__	$17.95 Health Care Job Explosion (3rd Ed)	_____
__	$19.95 Book of U.S. Gov't Jobs (7th Ed.)	_____
__	$17.95 Post Office Jobs (2nd Ed)	_____

	SUBTOTAL	$ ___.___
☞	Shipping/handling: ($5.25 for first book)	$ 5.25
☞	Additional Books, __ x $1.25	$ ___.___
☞	Pennsylvania residents add 7% sales tax	$ ___.___
☞	TOTAL	$ ___.___

SHIP TO: (PLEASE PRINT)

First Name_____ Last Name_____

Address _____ Apt #_____City _____

State _____ Zip _____ Phone # _____ Ext _____

Orders from individuals or private businesses must be prepaid. Purchase orders are accepted only from libraries, universities, bookstores, and government offices.

❑ Enclosed is a check/money order (to Bookhaven Press) for $ _____
❑ Charge to credit card: ___VISA ___ MC ___ Discover Card
Card Number _____ Expiration Date: _____

(Send to Bookhaven Press LLC, P.O. Box 1243, Dept 01, Moon Township, PA 15108)

For faster service call our **TOLL FREE (orders only)** number

CALL 1-800-782-7424

WE ACCEPT ALL MAJOR CREDIT CARDS